Zac Copeland - Greene

MGS

2018

CW01481239

MODERNISING THE CLASSICS
A Study in Curriculum Development

MODERNISING THE CLASSICS

A Study in Curriculum Development

by

MARTIN FORREST

UNIVERSITY
of
EXETER
PRESS

First published in 1996 by
University of Exeter Press
Reed Hall, Streatham Drive
Exeter, Devon EX4 4QR
UK

British Library Cataloguing in Publication Data
A catalogue record of this book is available
from the British Library

ISBN 0 85989 486 X

Typeset in Monotype Plantin
by Exe Valley Dataset Ltd., Exeter

Printed and bound in Great Britain
by Antony Rowe Ltd, Chippenham

Contents

List of Illustrations

Preface

The Cambridge School Classics Project is widely recognised as having been one of the more successful of the British curriculum developments of the 1960s and 1970s. Its impact on the teaching of Latin in schools has been remarkable and its development of courses in Greek and Roman civilisation have helped to lay the foundations for classical elements in the National Curriculum programmes of study for History. From early in its existence, the Project's work stimulated interest in Europe and North America and, since 1982, an American edition of the Cambridge Latin Course has been published and widely adopted in the United States and Canada.

This historical study of the Cambridge Project concentrates upon the origins and early history of the Project. It has been written by a former teacher of Classics and History in schools who was himself a full-time member of the Project team and who has continued since that time to be closely associated with the Project. The main focus is upon the establishment and operation of the Project during its full-time existence (1966–70). No attempt has been made to tell in detail the history of the Project since 1970, including the revision of the Cambridge Latin Course and important developments that have taken place in other countries, particularly in America. However, the early dissemination of the Project's thinking and its materials, the evaluation study of 1976 and the extension to the Classical Civilisation developments based in Bristol (1973–8) are all featured in the book.

Towards the end, there is a brief overview of the present position of school Classics, especially in England and Wales following the passage through the British Parliament of the 1988 Education Reform Act. Reference is also made to developments in North America. Few retrospective accounts have, as yet, been published of curriculum development projects sponsored by the Nuffield Foundation and the Schools Council. This history of the Cambridge School Classics Project has been written using abundant archival material and drawing upon the first-hand experience of the author as a participant in the Project's work throughout most of its lifetime. The study, which deals in considerable detail with the micro-politics of curriculum development, is presented against a backdrop of political change at a national level in the United Kingdom, in particular the moves towards abolishing selective secondary education and the creation of comprehensive schools. A recurrent theme is the catalytic effect of comprehensive reorganisation in concentrating the minds of Classics teachers and in assisting the transformation of a subject traditionally reserved for a privileged few into a subject appropriate for the many.

The history of the Cambridge School Classics Project offers many insights into the working of a full-time curriculum development project of the 1960s. During the full-time life of the Project, as well as in its wake, two major tensions emerge. Firstly, there is the problem of balancing the urgent need to reform Latin teaching against the pressure to develop broadly based courses in Classical Civilisation. Secondly, and with specific regard to the trialling of a new language course, there is the constant need to reconcile the conflicting demands of time-consuming linguistic research with the pressures exerted by trial schools for new material.

Readers will recognise, in the way that the Cambridge Project was originally set up, the form of curriculum project which the American R.G. Havelock has characterised as the 'Research, Development and Diffusion' model, a style of curriculum development which has been much criticised for its 'top down' and often unsatisfactory approach to curriculum change. In the final chapter, an attempt is made to show ways in which the Cambridge School Classics Project departed from the classic R D and D model and to suggest reasons why this project has been particularly successful in disseminating its thinking to a large clientele around the world.

During the thirty years which have elapsed since the Project's first beginnings, there have been many individuals who have made their contribution to the development of its work and whose names do not appear in the text and whose contribution is not explicitly acknowledged here. Quite apart from the enormous number of school pupils and their teachers who used the Project's materials at various stages of their development, there have been many individuals employed by the Project, including a sizeable number of secretaries, research and administrative assistants: some have worked in a full-time, others in a part-time capacity. All have made an important contribution to the Project's developments. There have been others too, both at the Cambridge University Press and at the Former Schools Council, who have played their part in producing the Project's many publications.

The research which forms the basis of this book began in the mid-1980s when the author was working for his doctorate at the University of Exeter. The thesis entitled 'Classics teachers, comprehensive reorganisation and curriculum change' explores the changes which have taken place in the teaching of school Classics since the Second World War and was presented in 1989. The accumulated archive of the Cambridge School Classics Project provided much of the documentary evidence for the full-time workings of the Project and for subsequent developments. This documentation included several files of material relating to the early period of the Project's history which came to light after the PhD thesis was complete. The author was also fortunate enough to come across a number of files dating to the early history of the Joint Association of Classical Teachers (JACT) which were conserved in the JACT office and which provided crucial evidence for the setting up of the Cambridge School Classics Project. The author is greatly endebted to Miss E.P. Story, current Director of the Cambridge School Classics Project, and to Mrs M.M. Collins, the Project's Secretary, for their help. The author also wishes to record his thanks to his colleagues at the University of the West of England Faculty of Education who have supported both the initial research and the preparation of this book.

Thanks are due to Dr M. Golby and Professor T.P. Wiseman of the University of Exeter, who supervised the research undertaken during the 1980s, and to many others, including Mr J.V. Muir, King's College London, who have keenly supported the publication of this book. Help with reading draft sections of the text has come from many quarters. The author would especially like to thank Mr R.M. Griffin, Mr J.V. Muir, Miss E.P. Story and Professor T.P. Wiseman, all of whom have read through much of the draft material at various stages of development. Professor R.A. Becher, Professor J.C. Dancy, Professor E. Phinney, Mr R.W. Morris, Mr J.E. Sharwood Smith, Dr C.A. Stray, Mr W.B. Thompson, Dr J.B. Wilkins and the late Mr K.G. Todd have all read and commented on selected parts of the text. Responsibility for the text in it's final form however, rests with the author alone.

Thanks are also due to those organisations which have made their archival collections available for study and have agreed to the inclusion of material therefrom and from their publications in this book. Collections belonging to the following organisations have been consulted for the purposes of this book: the Nuffield Foundation, the Joint Association of Classical Teachers, and the Classical Association. In addition, many individuals have provided documentary material from their personal collections, further details of which are recorded in the bibliography: Mr B.A. Knott, Mr D.J. Morton, Mrs N. Silver, Mr J.E. Sharwood Smith, Mr W.B. Thompson and the late Canon Rev F.C. Vyvyan Jones. A number of those named above kindly agreed to be interviewed by the author.

Acknowledgement should also be made to the School Curriculum and Assessment Authority (SCAA), who now hold the copyright of materials published by the former Schools Council, for permission to reproduce material from the Project's publications and for permission to refer to publications of the Schools Council's Impact and Take-up Project's survey of Classics teachers. Brief quotations have been included from the *Times Educational Supplement*, *Latin Teaching* and from *Greece and Rome* by permission of Times Newspapers, the Association for the Reform of Latin Teaching, and Oxford University Press respectively. Figure 2 has been produced with kind permission of Angela Coombes. Thanks are also due to the Committee of the Cambridge School Classics Project for a grant of £500 towards the cost of publication. Acknowledgement is also made to Cambridge University Press for their cooperation and interest.

The author is greatly indebted to a number of individuals who have helped in the preparation of this book and without whom publication would not have been possible. He would like to thank in particular colleagues Gaye Denley and Lyn Cooke at the University of the West of England, who have both worked on the preparation of the text, Barbara Fortune for her help in compiling the index, and Simon Baker, Genevieve Davey and Richard Willis at the University of Exeter Press and the copy-editor Jane Raistrick. He wishes to thank his wife, Pat Forrest, for her constant support and assistance not only at the time the book was being written, but over the many years of their close association with the Cambridge School Classics Project.

Finally, it seems appropriate in a history of the Cambridge School Classics Project to pay tribute to Clary Greig, a talented writer and much-loved member of the Project team, whose critical scholarship, fine sense of humour and entertaining company were very much part of the Project during the early years of its existence. His untimely death in 1978 was a great loss to the whole world of Classics teaching.

Martin Forrest, Bristol 1995

CHAPTER ONE

Classics Teaching Unreformed

The Victorian legacy

For many people in late-twentieth-century Britain it may be hard to imagine a time, not all that long ago, when most, if not all, pupils who embarked on a grammar school education were expected, at least to begin with, to study compulsory Latin. There was the same expectation also in the case of those pupils who attended independent schools, whether at the preparatory or senior stage of their education. Yet this was the situation which still obtained throughout the 1950s. The immediate post-war period was also a time when the British system of schooling in the maintained sector was rigidly segregated. It was possible to study Classics only in grammar schools. The vast majority of pupils who attended the secondary modern schools (successors to the elementary schools) had no contact with specialist Classics teachers and had no opportunity either to learn a classical language or even to study the classical world.

In order to understand the situation in mid-twentieth-century Britain, it is first necessary to refer to the classical curriculum of earlier times. M.L. Clarke, in his detailed historical account of classical education from the Renaissance period up to the close of the nineteenth century, describes the changes which had taken place over three hundred years. The nineteenth-century attitude to the Classics was very different from that of the Renaissance. Whereas the earlier emphasis had been upon the complete mastery of oral as well as written Latin, by the mid-nineteenth century new arguments were being adduced to justify a classical education.

A classical education in the schools of Victorian Britain differs in two principal respects. Firstly, as Clarke has expressed it:

> the old rhetoric gave place in the nineteenth-century to the
> new linguistic discipline that resulted from careful and accurate

translation from and into the ancient languages. A classical education was now valued as a training in accuracy and precision, excellent qualities, but different from that copiousness and elegance of style which had been the aim of the older type of teaching.[1]

The chief concern of classical teaching both at school and university was now the writing of the ancient languages in prose and verse along with the reading and translating of ancient texts. Secondly, the study of classical antiquity provided what we today would refer to as 'good role models', examples of individual greatness to counteract the mediocrity of contemporary society. Examples of patriotism and service to the state served to counteract its selfishness. Whereas the Renaissance had used classical learning as a springboard for new achievement, to Victorian classicists their classical learning worked in a more restricted way and their experience of the ancient world provided a framework for the adoption of new concepts:

> A nineteenth century Englishman could ignore the differences produced in time and could interpret his society in Roman terms. He could look for Cicero's virtues in his legislators and see the faults of Spartacus in Feargus O'Connor. He could regard India as a province, the North-West Frontier as Hadrian's Wall and hope that the subjugation of the Zulus would be followed by the civilizing effort that justified the defeat of Boadicea.[2]

In the nineteenth century, Greek as well as Latin prose composition was introduced and Greek verse composition came to be more generally practised. Translation of English into Greek and translation of English passages into Greek and Latin prose and verse gradually became established.

Among the innovators responsible were Samuel Butler and Benjamin Hall Kennedy at Shrewsbury School and Thomas Arnold at Rugby. At this period classical teaching in the grammar schools was said to be frequently poor and sometimes non-existent. Samuel Butler introduced regular examinations for his pupils, setting them unseen translation from Latin and Greek and translation into Latin and Greek. Such a preparation equipped his pupils extremely well for undertaking scholarship examinations at Cambridge University. Butler's methods were widely admired and came to be adopted by other schools.[3] The basis of the traditional classical education to be found in the mid-twentieth-century English public and grammar schools may thus be recognised a hundred years previously at Shrewsbury. The emphasis was upon the acquisition of linguistic skills of translation (in both directions) in their written form. Students of Classics were taught in this way in the expectation that they would proceed in due course to university. All the textbooks that appeared in the nineteenth century and which in some cases continued in widespread use into the mid-twentieth century were geared to the production of classical scholars whose ultimate aim was university entrance which acted as a gateway to the professions. Since Samuel Butler's day, there had been generations of Classics teachers at public and grammar schools grounding their pupils in a thorough linguistic training which would equip them, assuming that they got that far, for more advanced study at university.

To the great German classical scholar Wilamowitz, the purpose of studying the classical languages was to bring the past of the ancient Greeks and Romans to life so that students through their *Altertumswissenschaft* might recreate 'the poet's song, the thought of the philosopher and the law giver, the sanctity of the temple and the feelings of believers and unbelievers, the bustling life of market and port, the physical appearance of land and sea, mankind at work and play'.[4] But what of the majority who never got far beyond the lower levels of study in elementary Latin and Greek? They as likely as not rarely progressed beyond the translating of freestanding English sentences into Latin and learning of some of the necessary accidence and syntax to help them in their task.

The continuance of this nineteenth-century tradition of teaching classical languages could be witnessed in all the more prestigious public and grammar schools during the mid-twentieth century. In these schools preparation for the annual scholarship examinations at Oxford and Cambridge was seen as of central importance in every classical sixth form. In these same schools the teaching of Classics below sixth-form level was closely geared to the purpose of generating future Classics specialists. There were many grammar schools, however, where Classics was to be equated only with the learning of Latin. For in many of the newer grammar schools of the twentieth century, Greek was non-existent. Nonetheless, in all maintained grammar and independent schools all pupils had the opportunity to take Latin and the subject was normally compulsory, at least to begin with. In all schools where Latin was taught in the mid-twentieth century the central purpose was seen as primarily linguistic. Pupils during their early years of studying Latin would be concentrating on the systematic acquisition of language skills which would enable them in due course to translate from English into Latin and also translate Latin texts (both verse and prose) into English.

The Spens Report, published just before the Second World War in 1938, posed something of a potential threat to the universal provision of Latin in the grammar school in recommending what was, in effect, a common core curriculum for all pupils during the first two years of a grammar school education.[5] Latin was not one of the subjects identified for inclusion in the core. There were, however, said to be strong arguments for choosing an ancient language, especially in the case of pupils going on to do sixth-form work.[6] In a detailed section of the report dealing with the content of the curriculum, concern about the nature of Latin as traditionally taught is expressed: 'In no other subject has the end been placed at so great a distance and the realisation of its value emerged so late'.[7] The Committee went on to recommend that Latin should be taught in such a way that something definite should be gained long before the university stage. Proposals to reform the Classics curriculum focused on two areas. These were: Latin and 'the Roman inheritance'.

In the first two years of study, the Committee argued, the reading of Latin should occupy the chief place, using 'made-up' Latin and moving on as soon as possible to simplified passages from Latin authors chosen primarily to illustrate Roman life and customs. The minimum of grammar should be taught at first. Matters of syntax should be taken as they occur without being first formalised into an ordered system.[8] Translation from English into Latin should not be attempted too soon.[9] In the following two years there should be a wider selection of Latin authors with works chosen for their value in illustrating Roman life, thought, method and achievement.

The Spens Committee also made an important recommendation which related to the legacy of the classical world. Long before they began Latin, the Committee argued, and even if they were never going to learn it, pupils should be given experience of some of the ways in which Rome and its language have affected their environment. A study of the Roman inheritance would include legends of early Rome (and Greece), the stories of many of its heroes, which are part of our national cultural tradition, and early familiarity with the Latin element in English.[10]

The Spens Report had a mixed reception at the Annual General Meeting of the Classical Association (CA) in 1939.[11] One of His Majesty's Inspectors who was present thought that the recommendations on Latin teaching were suitable for modern conditions. Something had to be done when such a small proportion who started Latin reached the 'credit' standard in School Certificate. Others, however, expressed their misapprehensions. The President of the Association for the Reform of Latin Teaching (ARLT), Miss A. Woodward of Royal Holloway College, London, was concerned at what she considered to be the 'sacrifice of the academic pupils to the non-academic', in the Spens Report. Another member felt that the Committee had been largely inspired by the course book *Latin for Today*.[12]

Consolidation of tradition

Two major factors militated against reform in the immediate wake of the Spens Committee's Report. Firstly, there were the existing requirements

4

of examination boards, and secondly, there was the intervention of the Second World War. The temporary replacement during the 1939–45 war of many younger able-bodied classicists by an older generation of teachers is likely to have reinforced old-style methods and attitudes rather than the reverse.

When the Norwood Report was published in 1943, with its opening paragraph written in defence of tradition, it was seen as 'a rainbow in the sky'.[13] Furthermore, some of the more vocal Classics teachers saw the 1944 Act and the implementation of a tripartite system as ensuring that grammar schools would remain citadels of academic study, with pupils selected for their ability and able to profit by an academic education.

In the anticipated reform of the curriculum which would follow the new Education Act, Classics teachers should know their ground and be prepared to defend it to the 'very fifth declension'.[14] T.W. Melluish, Head of Classics at the Bec School, Tooting, published a 'Charter for Latin' in which he argued for a compulsory Latin course of five years duration in all grammar schools. No less than five periods of study a week of not less than forty-five minutes duration should be allotted. All grammar school pupils would take Latin for two years and in the last three years a great majority would continue studying the subject.[15] Those who argued for the inclusion of a cultural element as background to their linguistic study were seen by D.G. Bentliff, Head of Classics at a Liverpool grammar school and a close associate of Melluish, as 'specious' and 'dangerous'.[16] A course based on the life, society and history of Rome, Melluish asserted, might be offered to those who abandoned Latin after two years of study but was conceded as a 'very poor second best'.

By 1944 the CA had established an Education Sub-committee which was to devote itself to school matters, giving advice on textbooks, syllabuses and methods of teaching.[17]

The Sub-committee, with Melluish and Bentliff at its helm, was essentially a conservative force dedicated to reinforcing and preserving grammar school Classics in its traditional forms. As the Second World War drew to a close, Melluish expressed his disappointment that his own vigorous defence of tradition was not echoed in higher places:

> While the ancient universities for the most part slumber like the perpetual mountains, and professors, scholars and men of letters hibernate on their cocoons, those chalky units, the master and the mistress, are within the classroom engaged on a campaign in which the total war effort, the tactics, strategy, ammunition, supplies, and propaganda become the responsibility of ordinary privates. The barbarians murmur against the Classics, . . . the very Brains Trust of the BBC seditiously encourages young rebels to mutiny against

their grammar. We look in vain for an answering roar from our classical big guns.[18]

Another classical organisation which supported Classics teachers in the post-war period was the Orbilian Society, founded after the war in 1946. The eponymous Orbilius was the schoolteacher of Horace, described by the poet as 'the flogger'.[19] The Society was not open to a general membership. Instead individuals were invited to become honorary members. All adult subscribers to the Latin newspaper *Acta Diurna*, which was published three times a year were regarded as associate members and they received a regular newsletter.[20] The Editor of *Acta Diurna* for many years was the Senior Classics Master at Blackpool Grammar School, G.M. Lyne. Other individuals associated with the Society in its early days were Messrs T.W. Melluish, A.H. Nash-Williams and R.D. Wormald. In addition to the newspaper, the Society also published through an associated company, Centaur Books, an increasing range of material to supplement and enrich the teaching of Latin in schools. One publication greatly valued by Classics teachers in the 1950s and 1960s was the Orbilian Society's catalogue of visual (later audio-visual) aids.[21]

It seems clear that the activities of the Orbilian society were entirely geared to the needs and interests of those who were studying the Latin language in grammar schools. *Acta Diurna* provided additional reading material through which middle school Latinists might be stimulated to extend and enrich their knowledge of the Latin language and its cultural context largely in their own time. For those schools which did not have a generous allocation of timetabled hours for Latin or where Latin was begun later, the materials generated by the Orbilian Society were an invaluable resource.

Although Orbilian Society activists were people of energy and dedication, and although many of the resulting products were ingenious, the Orbilian Society was directed towards preserving the *status quo*, a device for enriching and securing the place of Latin for the selected minority who were in grammar and public schools, rather than for laying the foundations for new course structures aimed at a wider school population, within the education system as a whole.

The third organisation concerned with the teaching of Classics in schools was the Association for the Reform of Latin Teaching (ARLT). The Association had originally been formed to investigate, by discussion and experiment, ways of realising in different types of school, the aims of Latin teaching. Throughout its history, the ARLT had been specially though not exclusively concerned with the direct method of teaching Latin and Greek pioneered earlier in the century by Dr W.H.D. Rouse at the Perse School, Cambridge.[22]

Where the direct or 'oral' method was taught in schools, language

6

acquisition was built up through imitation, repetition, association and induction. Grammar was taught inductively with the learning of paradigms only coming after oral practice of the language. The first two years of study were devoted to teaching the mechanics of Latin, and in the third year a transition was made to real Latin. Direct method included English into Latin translation, but this was preceded by oral language work.[23]

The movement survived two world wars and continued to be fostered in the post-war period by activists of the ARLT, through its regular publication *Latin Teaching* and its annual promotion of a summer school and a weekend refresher course; the latter was supported also by the Classical Association. The movement to adopt the direct method spread widely in Britain and the approach was enthusiastically taken up by teachers some grammar and in some independent schools.

An authoritative guide to the teaching of Classics in schools, one of a series aimed at teachers in the post-1944 secondary schools, was published in 1953 by the Incorporated Association of Assistant Masters (IAAM). This publication, which was updated at regular intervals, generally speaking may be seen as a restatement of traditional values in Classics teaching. Bentliff and Melluish were both members of the Committee which compiled it and Melluish was Secretary to the Committee. The principal concern of this group was with the teaching of Latin, although some space was also devoted to considering other elements in the full Classics course.

New directions for school Classics?

The possibility that the classical world might play some small part in the education of pupils in the newly designated secondary modern schools (attended by the majority of pupils in the maintained sector) was given some consideration by the IAAM Committee. In fact, the Committee members prided themselves on having devoted a chapter to demonstrating how widely the Classics might be used as 'an educative factor among those children who have not the time to learn Latin or Greek as languages'.[24] Confidence was expressed that there was much in the Classics for such children irrespective of the type of secondary school they attended. In 1949 Mr F. Kinchin Smith, who was at that time responsible for the training of Classics teachers at the University of London Institute of Education, had organised a conference attended by more than thirty training college representatives entitled 'Classical background in emergency training colleges and modern schools'. This conference had passed a resolution supporting courses on the 'growth of civilisation and culture and Classics in translation'. He had subsequently attempted to interest the Classical Association in this issue.[25] The person responsible for the IAAM Handbook chapter entitled 'Classics in the secondary modern school' was Mrs Dora Pym of Bristol University, another lecturer responsible for training Classics teachers. During the mid-1950s Mrs Pym organised in her own university two conferences for classicists at which the whole place and purpose of Classics in the school curriculum was challenged in a fundamental way. Mrs Pym's intentions are revealed in a memorandum to her professor before the first conference:

> The teaching of Classics in all but a few schools is hampered, not, as appears on the surface, *only* by a shortage of time, unsuitable examination requirements and deep controversy about 'methods', but also by unexamined assumptions as to the place and contribution of the Classics in contemporary schools.[26]

Members of the first conference held in October 1954 were said to have generally agreed that the teacher of Classics had a responsibility to the whole secondary school population.[27] The second conference held the following year included in its discussions a course of study for children in secondary modern schools and for 'less linguistic children' in grammar schools, and also the nature and purpose of the 'O' level Latin course.[28]

During the 1950s, there is clear evidence that some members of the ARLT had begun to look beyond the narrow horizons of grammar school language teaching and at ways in which the Classics teacher might make a wider contribution to secondary education. C.W.E. (Cyril) Peckett, as Editor of *Latin Teaching*, declared himself 'privileged to print' an account of the first Bristol conference held in October 1954.[29] The report of Mrs Pym's conference on the place of the Classics in English education today, concluded by posing the key conference questions to members of the Association.[30] The report suggested that this conference could only be the beginning but there were two lines of thought that needed following up. Firstly, there was a need to engage in debate with others in the educational world before being able to prove to others the value of the heritage they were seeking to preserve. Secondly, there was a great need to think more about bringing Classics to the secondary modern school.

The very next issue of *Latin Teaching* carried an account of one course, already in operation for at least five years, which demonstrated the way in which Classics could make a full contribution to the teaching of lower school Humanities through the medium of English in a local authority grammar school.[31] The course had been constructed in the belief that great stories are the basis of our civilisation. The great myths and significant historical events, and works of art produced as the result of their impact on the minds of men, were used to make an impact in turn on the minds of pupils.[32] This was one school's attempt at a course aimed at all the pupils in the grammar school irrespective of whether or not they went on to study Latin. This description would appear to be that of the Priory School, Shrewsbury, where a 'Humanities' course for all had been introduced by Peckett. The course was later published as *The Heritage of the West* by Peckett and his colleague Dr H. Loehry, and provided a model which other schools might follow.[33]

Here was an attempt to reappraise the role of Classics in the post-war grammar school. Classics teachers were looking at ways in which they might best make their contribution to the curriculum along with their colleagues who taught English and History. This represented a positive attempt by classicists in a grammar school to teach the common Western European tradition, derived mainly from the Graeco-Roman civilisation as it was transformed by Christianity.[34] There is little evidence, however, that this form of course was ever widely adopted in its fully developed form.

During the later years of the decade *Latin Teaching* provided a platform upon which the arguments for extending Classics to all pupils through the medium of English might be rehearsed. This time the initiatives came from classicists who were involved in teacher training. In the November issue of *Latin Teaching* 1958, W.S. Fowler, a lecturer in the University of Sheffield Department of Education, contributed an article entitled 'Common core Classics'. Signalling the advent of comprehensive and bilateral schools, he argued for a re-think of basic syllabus requirements in the first two years of secondary school Classics teaching. Fowler referred to early comprehensive experiments, including the Leicestershire Plan, where a common school was envisaged for at least the first two years for all pupils. This article went right to the very heart of Classics as traditionally conceived and taught in the post-war period under a consolidated selective system.[35] Fowler sought in his article to develop further the attempt at a scheme of Classical Studies for the secondary modern school which had been published in the IAAM Handbook. Such a course of general common core Classics or Humanities would, Fowler argued, be of value to all streams of a comprehensive or grammar school and could be adapted for the secondary modern school. In the case of comprehensive schools it would also give the potential student of Latin something to begin with before the more formal middle school Latin course began.

In the same issue of *Latin Teaching* was a report of a provocative talk given to Classics teachers by Professor A.D.C. Peterson, Principal of the Department of Education at the University of Oxford and a classicist. Peterson was highly critical of the existing 'O' level syllabus which he described as 'ill-designed as a final examination in Latin for the majority' and not worth the protection afforded to it by the entrance requirements of the older universities.[36] Peterson went on to propose an exam in what he referred to as 'General Classics'. This would consist of History, Philosophy, Sociology and translation from Latin with the aid of a dictionary, but there would be no translation from English into Latin and no formal grammar. A course leading to an examination of this kind, Peterson argued, would be better educationally and would afford a more fitting conclusion to their study of Classics for the vast majority of pupils.

In 1959, under the *aegis* of the weekend refresher course, Mr W.B. (William) Thompson, Lecturer in Classical Method at the University of Leeds, was invited to introduce a discussion of the theme of 'The role of Classics in modern education' on the first evening of the conference. His central concern was the role of Classics in the education of a much wider group of the population than one would expect to find in the grammar school. Thompson stressed the essential need to preserve our own heritage of English literature. He argued that the Classics were an essential part of the education of a substantial proportion of the population.[37]

Thompson's main concern was that there should be some classical provision in secondary modern schools (or in comprehensive schools where they existed). He was not concerned whether pupils pass the 'O' level examination in Latin. He wanted a substantial part of the population to have 'entered the Classics far enough' for them not, for example, to feel 'awkward and unhappy' about meeting words in Latin. He was arguing not for an academic study of classical Latin and Greek but a distillation of the Graeco-Roman part of our heritage through the teacher.[38]

Those who argued the case for widening the scope of Classics in schools inevitably attracted criticism. A vigorous reaction to the views of Fowler and Peterson was published in *Latin Teaching*.[39] An anonymous letter from a Classics teacher assailed the suggestion that the title Latin should be dropped in favour of something 'culled variously from 'Humanities', antiquities, History and what not'. The correspondent went on to assert the linguistic nature of Latin studies and called for renaming the Association 'The Association for the survival of Latin teaching'.

Progressive and traditionalist values: the dominance of the linguistic tradition

In educational terms, generally, the years 1945–59, are not noted as a period of radical change. No attempt was was made by ministers of the Labour governments 1945–51 to change the 1944 Butler Education Act, and in the local authorities there was little challenge to the tripartite system. For although changes had taken place in Labour Party thinking in the years after the war and comprehensive education became policy at Party level, this was not to become a significant factor until the 1960s.

In the largely traditional educational environment of post-war tripartism, examples of what one might characterise as 'progressive' thinking in Classics are easily identified. Those who publicly advocated such views were relatively few in number, and their advocacy of change was sometimes thrown into sharp relief by the traditionalist reaction which greeted it. Their progressive thinking may be summarised as follows.

Firstly, the Classics had something to offer most if not all pupils irrespective of whether or not they proceed to linguistic study. Classics is concerned with our common Western European inheritance. Secondly, the study of Latin was generally of the traditional kind, narrowly geared to the needs of the able few who aim for university, at the expense of the many who fall by the wayside. Thirdly, the traditional Latin course should be reformed: more Latin literature should be read in the original and less time should be devoted to English into Latin composition and formal grammatical analysis. Fourthly, translations should be used to facilitate a wider study of Latin and Greek literature. There should be more opportunity for studying the cultural aspects.

Initiatives such as those launched early in the 1950s by Kinchin Smith, Dora Pym and Peckett, and later in the decade by Thompson and others, represented the very first steps in the direction of reform. By contrast, the Education Sub-committee of the CA was less concerned with extending the frontiers of Classics within the education system than with reinforcing the existing place of Classics within the grammar school and with defending the traditional role of Latin in the curriculum.

At the end of the 1950s, the 'O' level examination in Latin meant for most candidates: formal grammar questions, English into Latin translation and translation from Latin into English (either from unprepared passages of prose and verse or from set books). Questions on the 'background' to Latin were few and carried a small weighting in terms of marks; understanding of the literature read was mainly tested by requiring candidates to translate pieces of text into English.

In the late 1950s, moves to change the nature of classical teaching in schools continued to cause dissension. A spate of correspondence, some of it from Classics teachers, provoked a forthright editorial in the *Times Educational Supplement*. The authorship of the article is unknown, but it neatly exemplifies the traditionalist position regarding the nature of school Classics:

> It seems that there is a desperate venture afoot to prove that Latin can be fun . . . What is to be done? For a start we should sweep away the insidious suggestions that the hard linguistic course should be leavened with literature in translation. There may be a case, even a strong case, for giving pupils a wide acquaintance with the writings of the ancients in an English version. But it is is not the case for Latin. Latin is a language. Its claim to a place in the school

11

curriculum must rest on the mental discipline it offers to the pupils in grappling with an inflected tongue. In short it is not SENECA but the subjunctive that makes Latin the subject for the school. The pity is that so few teachers realize this. Even if they do realize it, they too often look on the linguistics as a necessary evil . . . Latin will not survive like that. It needs teachers who believe in the ablative absolute. It needs men and women who have convictions about the gerund.[40]

CHAPTER TWO

Crisis and Response

The first serious crisis for school Classics

The year 1960 must be seen as a watershed. It was to herald the first of
two major crises which the teaching of school Classics underwent in the
1960s. What will be referred to as Crisis One began for Classics teachers
as the climax of a protracted debate regarding moves to abolish the
compulsory entry requirement of an 'O' level pass in GCE in a classical
language at the Universities of Oxford and Cambridge. On 17 May, at
Oxford, a new statute was approved giving effect to the abolition of Latin
(or Greek) as a compulsory entry requirement to the University for
scientists, complementing the decision reached four days earlier by the
banks of the River Cam, that an 'O' level pass in Latin was no longer
necessary for admission to the University of Cambridge.[1]

Beneath the shadow cast by the final stages of these moves, the Annual
Meeting of the CA took place in Southampton. During one session an
important debate was initiated by Professor C.O. Brink, Kennedy
Professor of Latin at the University of Cambridge. Brink's theme was the
reform of 'O' level Latin.[2] Brink's introduction was followed by
discussion and the passing of a resolution (carried by 200 votes to 1)
calling for a general reconsideration of the aims and syllabus of the 'O'
level Latin examination with special reference to the requirements of non-
specialists.[3] Although Brink was himself involved in the rearguard action
in his own university opposing the abolition of Latin as an entrance
requirement, at the same time he publicly urged reform of the existing
Latin 'O' level examination. He appears to have been stung by charges
that he and his Cambridge colleagues were defending 'archaic and
restrictive ideas'.[4] Brink's initiative triggered off widespread initial
support for a review from teachers of Classics, who had plenty of
criticisms to make about the existing examination. Her Majesty's Staff
Inspector for Classics, C.W. (Charles) Baty, joined forces with Brink.

Both men were pragmatists who in the changing circumstances took up the cause which progressives had been urging for some time. Shortly after this, however, surveys of grass-root teacher opinion carried out by the CA were said to show no overwhelming desire for change. Whilst teachers might recognise that in future they would have no guarantee of clients to study their subject, and their future would depend on renewing both content and method, inclination towards change was very cautious. Retention of English into Latin was almost universally supported, although there was some support for a shift in emphasis. Teachers in schools were also reluctant to see their subject as other than linguistic. Apart from one isolated proposal, there was no suggestion that Classics should be for all pupils and there was a reluctance to treat 'classical civilisation' issues separately from the study of Latin texts.[5]

In a CA statement sent to the examination boards, progressive views about reform were squeezed out. Having democratically consulted their member organisations on a wide scale, the CA felt duty-bound to reflect the thinking of their members in their official submission, and chose to emphasise the linguistic nature of Latin study, high standards of accuracy and the retention of English into Latin translation. They noted the concern about the pass rate but were at pains to point out their opposition to lowering standards. There was, however, a proposal that maximum flexibility should be allowed for choice and freedom to innovate.[6]

Reappraisal

It was too early for the impact of abolition to be fully realised; even in 1962 Baty, writing in a specially produced supplement to *Greece and Rome* entitled *Reappraisal* and edited by T.W. Melluish, referring to the numbers coming forward to study Latin, suggested: 'There is, in fact, every sign that the change in those requirements is having little or no effect in schools'.[7] As long as they were still getting their numbers for Latin either through compulsion or through option choice, teachers in schools would not feel under any great pressure to change.

In *Reappraisal*, Brink was given the opportunity to reiterate his Southampton plea. He argued that 'O' level lacked a clearly defined purpose: too little Latin was read and too much time spent 'slogging away at English into Latin sentences'. He continued:

> But whether it is English into Latin, or Latin into English, I suggest that it should be *chiefly* a one-way road. The sophisticated dual carriage-way of the classical tradition asks too much of the small Latinist, and offers him too little.[8]

Baty, together with Brink, spelt out the negative side of Latin as it was at that date: large wastage through drop-outs, inappropriateness of 'O' level Latin for the majority of pupils following outdated textbooks and an unsuitable examination rubric. There was a need to switch the emphasis to reading Latin literature. The supporting articles in *Reappraisal* advocated between them use of dictionaries with harder unseens, an improved Latin course to facilitate enhanced reading and comprehension skills, a new approach to Latin teaching to 'O' level, and a new approach for the two-year Latinist; there was also a case made out for oral Latin.

The most notable absentee from this publication is any reference to courses in Classical Civilisation, whether aimed at the sixth former or at the broad ability range. Despite the pioneering work of Cyril Peckett and the advocacy of such an approach by progressive-minded classicists such as Thompson and Peckett, this was not seen to be sufficiently important an item for inclusion in the supplement. It is apparent from Committee papers, however, that something on sixth-form Classical Civilisation was originally planned.

With hindsight, *Reappraisal* may be seen as a useful contribution to the debate which widened the discussion about the negative aspects of the syllabus and examination related to 'O' level Latin, in particular its inappropriateness for the vast majority of pupils and the high rate of wastage. Progressive views were taken up by Brink and Baty, but only in so far as reform of the existing 'O' level was concerned; they must have realised that in the longer term, Latin would not be able to survive for long, despite the rosy picture painted by Baty in *Reappraisal* which was intended for public consumption. Baty expressed his concern about quality but it was not to be long before Her Majesty's Inspectors (HMI) were also agonising over a steady decline in the number of candidates entered for public examinations in Greek and Latin.[9] At this date the need to reform 'O' level Latin for pupils in the grammar (and also public) schools was clearly seen as the priority. Comprehensive reorganisation was not yet an issue to be reckoned with. Progressive values were adopted which were relevant to the task of reforming Latin within the existing tripartite tradition for the existing clientele.

Proposals for change were dependent upon forces which lay beyond the reach of classroom teachers: speedier methods of teaching pupils to read Latin literature in the original and reform of external examinations needed to be tackled centrally. *Reappraisal*, at best, could only provide a forum for new ideas; it did not provide a basis for practical action in the classroom.

Reappraisal also indicated that the possibility of comprehensive education was not yet a serious concern of classicists, by the complete absence of any reference to schools other than grammar schools and those in the independent sector. The decision to appoint Melluish as

Editor of this publication ensured in practice that business was conducted within the parameters with which he felt at home, and that the content was restricted to Classics in its more traditional forms.

A Joint Association of Classical Teachers

The initiative for a new organisation which would bring together all Classics teachers under a single umbrella was largely due to the energy, persistence and skill of J.E. (John) Sharwood Smith who had succeeded Kinchin Smith at the London Institute of Education. A relative newcomer to a university department of Education (UDE), Sharwood Smith was impressed by the urgent need for concerted action following the events of 1960 at Oxford and Cambridge. Like Brink and Baty, he was a pragmatist who could foresee the bleak prospects for Latin in its unreformed state in grammar and public schools.

There was an urgent need for research into the teaching of Latin and for applying new technology to Classics teaching; there was, moreover, a need to network information to teachers in school in order to provide them with the necessary support. Working in London, where some of the earlier comprehensive schools were already in existence, Sharwood Smith was aware that this could in future be an additional compelling reason for setting up a new association of classical teachers, although there is little evidence that the comprehensive issue was a major factor in the minds of those who were responsible for setting up the Joint Association of Classical Teachers (JACT). Sharwood Smith came to the realisation that working through the existing organisations simply would not work; there were too many vested interests and entrenched attitudes among certain leading members of those organisations.

Thompson and Sharwood Smith in their separate ways attempted to make the existing organisations into more effective instruments of change. Thompson had tried to persuade the CA to increase its subscription which had remained unchanged from five shillings since the Association's foundation and to transform itself into an organisation that would support teachers of school Classics.[10] Sharwood Smith had been involved in moves to expand the functions and to change the name of the ARLT.

When it became clear that these efforts had met with insurmountable resistance, Sharwood Smith began by making overtures to a number of carefully selected individuals in the first instance with a view to creating an alternative organisation.[11] An alliance was forged with the progressives in the ARLT who had long been anxious for reform on a broader front (Classical Civilisation courses for all, increased opportunities for reading Latin literature and a reduction in prose composition). Subsequently, Sharwood Smith began building up support inside the Classical

16

Association and the Orbilian Society. He was given strong support from certain of his more progressive-minded UDE colleagues. There were others who were schoolteachers, including headteachers on whom he could rely. There was not a great deal of help forthcoming at this stage from university Classics teachers, but Professor T.B.L. Webster of the Institute of Classical Studies in London University, together with Brink, and at a later stage Professor D.M. (David) Balme of Queen Mary College, London, provided solid support for his enterprise.[12]

Whereas there were those on whom Sharwood Smith could rely for support, there was within each of the three organisations also a core of active members with a more traditionalist frame of mind with whom he had also to reckon, including Melluish, who as a leading member of the CA, ARLT and Orbilian Society (as well as being Honorary Secretary to the IAAM Handbook Committee) effectively acted as a gatekeeper, guarding the road to radical reform. Opposition from the more traditionally minded individuals in the existing societies focused on four main arguments: the proliferation of societies, the cost of an additional subscription, doubts about support from independent schools, and the indifference of teachers generally.

Much of the hostility to the new organisation can be shown to have been of a personal nature. The decision to establish JACT as an umbrella organisation which would support all Classics teachers during a period of change, was not made by rank and file Classics teachers but by a small number of activists in the world of classical teaching who recognised the urgency. It had been suggested by some that consultation with grass-roots Classics teachers in schools would show little enthusiasm for a new organisation. An appeal to the minority of classical teachers who were already members of one or other organisation might well have met with such a reaction, but some UDE lecturers had polled their own students and had obtained a more encouraging response, which showed promise for the future.[13] Although dissent and scepticism continued in some quarters, the establishing of JACT provided a potential vehicle for initiating change that was to be crucial in the years ahead.

A second serious crisis for school Classics

The second crisis for school Classics teaching in the 1960s, henceforth referred to as Crisis Two, was the widespread emergence of comprehensive schools. It has been noted above that the prospect of comprehensive reorganisation was not a major factor in the development of the Joint Association of Classical Teachers, or for that matter in the initiatives that were taken to reform the teaching of Classics in the very early 1960s. Although there were in existence by 1962 as many as 235 schools in England and Wales which could be described as 'broadly comprehensive in character', many of these schools had been purpose-built and had not in any case involved the merging of existing grammar schools.[14] During the 1950s and in the early 1960s, the actions of Conservative government ministers were likely to have given some reassurance to Classics teachers working in grammar schools in the few places where reorganisation was in progress that the character of their schools would be maintained.

By 1964, however, change on a much larger scale was well on the way and for the country as a whole the prospect of comprehensive reorganisation was just round the corner. By January 1964, a number of local education authorities (LEAs), having recently undergone a change of political control, were planning schemes of reorganisation and in October a Labour government was elected that was pledged to abolish selection at 11+ for the first time and to introduce comprehensive education nationwide.

One feature of early moves to establish comprehensive schools in England and Wales was that the change had often been made with relatively little controversy.

Since the mid-1950s, the ministers had made it clear that they would be prepared to agree to comprehensive schools in rural areas and on new housing estates, but that they would not permit their development in cases where the abolition of an existing efficient grammar school was involved.[15]

In Leicestershire, where, from the late 1950s, a new kind of school system of junior and senior high schools was being introduced, the Education Committee took care to adopt a phased approach. They first ensured that they had the right building and staff resources. They also undertook the necessary preparatory work and negotiated with governors, parents and teachers' associations before introducing each stage.[16]

The evidence from Leicestershire, Bristol and other areas which introduced comprehensive reorganisation at an early date, suggests that schools were willing to keep Latin going in its traditional form.[17] The Latin specialist was seen as fulfilling the needs of a relatively small minority of pupils who might one day need Latin for university entrance or as an ancillary to other Arts subjects. If senior management saw their comprehensive school as providing an extension of grammar school education for all, then Latin would continue to play a small, but diminished and increasingly insignificant role in the curriculum. In schools where the curriculum was completely reshaped, particularly in the light of its comprehensive intake, in the years following the arrival of Crisis One, the Latin specialist was likely to be placed under considerable pressure. Although some individual examples of innovative enterprise are known, it was not until after the formation of JACT that progressive thinking could be channelled through a central source to Classics teachers in grammar schools who were facing reorganisation. The first published reference to comprehensive reorganisation in JACT publications appears in the fourth *JACT Bulletin*, for February 1964. The membership, now amounting to some 1,400 out of an estimated 4,000 teachers in England and Wales engaged primarily in teaching Classics or Latin in schools, was advised as to JACT's policy regarding reorganisation and invited to consult the Association.

> JACT is not inclined to campaign for more Latin among weaker pupils; but its policy is to insist that a proper Latin course contributes an important element to general education and does not merely aim at overcoming ever lowered examination hurdles by means of rushed courses . . . If courses are to take a new form (and there is a great deal to be said for jolting some of them out of their old ways!) we can help to secure that the planning of these is at least on workable and educational lines.[18]

The issue of reorganisation appears to have been first raised at the Committee's fourth meeting in October 1963 by Cyril Peckett, but the first major discussion did not take place until the next meeting. By this time the JACT office at Gordon Square had received a number of letters from Classics teachers concerned about the effect that local reorganisation schemes might have upon their subject. An internal memo drafted at the JACT office in March by Sharwood Smith after discussions with Baty, sets out the basis of a policy in which the Association might take a positive view of comprehensive reorganisation:

> However sound the arguments may be against the Leicestershire Plan, it would be a mistake for JACT to campaign against it. To do so would be to reinforce the popular identification of classics with reaction and to consolidate progressive opinion in favour of the Plan; we have not enough influence seriously to affect the issue and we could only damage any attempt to get Latin and Greek taught in Leicestershire-type schools. . . .
> JACT should oppose Latin in the middle school, except in very favourable circumstances (ie a carefully thought-out scheme to be carried out by keen and capable teachers with the backing of their Headmaster). On the other hand, JACT should press for general classics of some sort (eg., Literature in Translation, ancient history, art etc.) and JACT might well try to mobilize its resources in dons and schoolmasters to run courses for middle school teachers and that sort of thing. It is important that there should be an opportunity for kindling an interest in Greco-Roman civilisation at

this stage, so that a pupil may opt for Latin as soon as he reaches the Upper School.[19]

The memorandum then went on to outline needs in the upper school for pupils who would start Latin at 14 and Greek at 15 or 16. It was felt there was a need also for a new syllabus, new textbooks and new examinations. An 'O' level examination with no grammar questions, no composition and a number of general classical questions might be part of the answer, although another possibility would be for the pupils to go straight on for a four-year course to 'A' level. The memorandum continued: 'If Classics teachers could face the Leicestershire-type Upper School as an interesting challenge, and be equipped with interesting new syllabuses, the spread of the Plan could be invigorating to the classics instead of catastrophic'.[20]

An action plan

At their fifth meeting held in April 1964, the Committee of JACT heard a report from W.B. Thompson on comprehensive reorganisation schemes and their effect on the Classics. Thompson referred to confusion, apathy and resentment among some Classics teachers who were lamenting the situation but doing nothing about it.[21] It was for their newly formed Association to provide the means whereby teachers of Classics might help one another to meet such challenges of changing circumstances in all sorts of schools. He did not restrict what he had to say to grammar schools, but referred, as on previous occasions, to the opportunities in modern schools. They should not regard reorganisation of secondary education as being of itself a bad thing or of itself a good thing. Teachers might have their own views, but the Association should not. Reorganisation presented a most exciting challenge and it was the Association's function to help teachers meet that challenge. Thompson completed his contribution as follows:

> As always back to the usual question. Why are we teaching Latin? Far too many Classics teachers still don't know. I don't in some ways regret this challenge—the outcome could be good. I like challenges; they are exciting. I'm sure this one is.[22]

It seems unlikely that Thompson's proposed solutions would have found universal favour with all members of the JACT Committee. It was, however, closely in tune with the memorandum already prepared by Sharwood Smith in consultation with Baty as a basis for executive action. It appears that three, at least, of the classical method lecturers in UDEs were all beginning to think along similar lines. In addition to Thompson and Sharwood Smith, D.J. (David) Morton, who trained Classics teachers at Nottingham University, was also advocating this strategy.[23] The minutes of the meeting record that a lengthy discussion then took place during which 'a good deal of alarm was felt and some despondency'.[24] The minutes record that it was finally agreed to ask Mr Sharwood Smith to organise a conference and to publish a pamphlet along the lines of one which had already been produced.[25]

The conference was convened at Hughes Hall, Cambridge to consider the 'Leicestershire Plan' and its effect on classical teaching in schools. The conference which took place on 27–8 June 1964 stimulated a mixed response. The response of the two teachers from Leicestershire who attended was felt by some to be particularly disappointing. For their response to proposals along the lines of those already formulated to meet the Leicestershire situation was seen as very negative.[26] A more positive outcome was that the conference paved the way for the publication of what was to prove a seminal pamphlet on Classics teaching and comprehensive reorganisation. This publication was to provide a blueprint for the continuance of Classics in the curriculum of comprehensive schools of different types in the years ahead.[27] A central figure at this conference was Charles Baty, who had already spent eighteen months as Secretary General of JACT, having retired from HMI in 1962. The person chosen to edit the pamphlet was David Morton. Contributions were submitted by a number of individuals who had attended the conference and Baty kept in very close touch with Morton throughout the production period.

At the same time that these initiatives were taking place under the *aegis* of JACT, another even more important development was unfolding behind the scenes. Soon after the Leicestershire conference, the first of a series of meetings took place which was to lead to the setting up of the Cambridge School Classics Project (CSCP). The consultations and discussion involving Baty and his successor as HM Staff Inspector for Classics, Kenneth Todd, took place during the second half of 1964. Only four individuals took part in the early private meetings. Even at a fairly advanced stage, there were few, including some JACT Committee members who were at all aware of what was taking shape. As JACT activists of the time recall, there was an air of conspiracy about the whole affair.

Melluish, meanwhile, who had not been party to any of these developments, chose to take his own initiative in defence of Classics. Although a member of the JACT Committee, he did not take part in the 'Leicestershire Plan Conference' and appears to have been unaware of any initiatives since the last JACT Committee meeting in April. In his role as one of the joint secretaries of the CA, Melluish proposed to adopt a more confrontational approach. He proposed a resolution which was unanimously adopted by the meeting of CA Council held on 4 July 1964 which read as follows: 'That the Classical Association is gravely concerned at the prospect that new schemes for the reorganisation of secondary education may make it extremely difficult, or even impossible, for pupils to take Greek and Latin'.[28] It was further agreed that a letter embodying the resolution be sent under the signature of the Association's President, Sir Basil Blackwell, to the main newspapers and to the then Secretary of State for Education and Science, Mr Quintin Hogg. Although Melluish had received unanimous support for his resolution at the CA Council, his action was subsequently viewed by some individuals as, at the very least, unhelpful. At worst, the Association was appearing to align itself with the forces of reaction and this was bound to be damaging to the cause of Classics.[29]

CHAPTER THREE

The Origins of the Cambridge School Classics Project

It was against the background of the two crises outlined in the preceding chapter that the first moves towards establishing a curriculum development project in Classics were made. Latin was no longer a general entry requirement for Oxford and Cambridge, and there was now the imminent prospect of grammar schools being abolished and replaced by schools for pupils of all abilities. Both developments prompted widespread questioning of the future place of Classics in the school curriculum and, at the very least, seemed likely to cause a reduction in allocated teaching hours.

The effect was to galvanise into action those individuals who recognised the need for change and who were in a position to do something about it. There was a recognition that little could be done without first carrying out a programme of research and experimentation relevant to the needs of Classics teachers in schools. The inauguration of the Joint Association of Classical Teachers, resulting from the tireless and skilful actions of John Sharwood Smith, was a crucial step towards initiating change.

Documents prepared for the first conference leading to the formation of JACT had cited the need for an organisation which could conduct systematic research and experiment in relation to examination syllabuses.[1] Rule 15 of the new organisation advocated the establishment of a standing sub-committee which would 'plan, co-ordinate and, if necessary, finance investigations, studies and researches into topics connected with the teaching of Classics in Schools'.

By the early 1960s, the impact of the curriculum revolution in the United States was beginning to make itself felt across this side of the Atlantic. The 1960s and 1970s in Britain are associated with attempts to bring about curriculum change in schools on a previously unprecedented scale, particularly through centrally funded projects. The many curriculum projects established and resourced firstly by the Nuffield

Foundation and later by a government-funded agency known as the Schools Council, followed a tidal wave of curriculum reform initiatives in the United States. These initiatives were aimed at improving the curriculum of schools in the United States following the launch of the first Soviet Sputnik in 1957.

An enormous volume of literature associated with curriculum development in America came to influence British educational thinking during the 1960s. Subject-based curriculum development projects, centrally funded and based upon rational curriculum planning with a view to securing curriculum change in schools, in due course, provided inspiration for the first Nuffield and Schools Council developments in Britain.

A Classics project: first beginnings

At their fourth meeting on 5 October 1963, members of the JACT Committee noted that they were bound by their constitution to establish a sub-committee concerned with research, but agreed to postpone a decision until their next meeting in April 1964, despite the fact that some names had already been put forward.[2] In fact, correspondence had been continuing for a substantial part of 1963, up to the eve of the fourth meeting of the JACT Committee, between the Honorary Secretary General, Charles Baty, and other individuals regarding the possibility of their joining a research committee.[3] However, by the late spring there were good reasons why Baty might have wished to avoid establishing a research sub-committee as such. The earliest correspondence relating to the proposal for a curriculum development project in Classics is dated May 1964, and it is likely that informal discussion about the possibility of a link with the Nuffield Foundation may have taken place during the preceding weeks. In this case, Baty may have felt that he would have a freer hand in negotiation if he were not committed to certain principles laid down in advance by a sub-committee of the Association.

The key person in bringing JACT into contact with Nuffield was R.W. (Robert) Morris, a senior member of Her Majesty's Inspectorate of schools based in the Ministry of Education at Curzon Street, who had been seconded to work for the Curriculum Study Group established by the Education Minister, Sir David Eccles, and who was to become one of the joint secretaries of the emergent Schools Council.[4] The Nuffield Foundation was already investing sizeable sums of money in curriculum development. The possibility of a grant to facilitate new developments in Classics was seen as a sequel to Nuffield sponsorship of Science, Mathematics and Modern Languages. Morris, although himself a mathematician, was a keen advocate of Classics benefiting from a share of the funding which Nuffield was now making available to education, and was the originator of the proposal that Classics should be a beneficiary.

During regular informal conversations (over lunch), R.A. (Tony) Becher of the Nuffield Foundation and Morris were accustomed to work together to identify areas for curriculum reform and to promote projects which might benefit from Nuffield money. Having already established projects in a number of major curriculum areas, the time came to consider what might be tackled next. Morris, in suggesting that Classics might be the next subject to benefit, advanced the case for Latin and Greek as being fundamental to Western scholarship. If you want a good tree, Morris recalls arguing at the time, then take care of its roots.[5]

It was not long before Baty, in his capacity as Secretary General of JACT, was informally approached through Kenneth Todd and the two were invited to meet with Morris and Becher.[6] Writing in 1965, Baty explains how his approach came about and in effect confirms the view that the invitation came from Becher and Morris who then approached Baty through HM Staff Inspector for Classics, Kenneth Todd: 'Nuffield, in informal contact with Curzon Street, was led into asking our advice and suggestions in a matter which seemed just up our street, and it is only now that it has become a possible course of action'.[7] The first formal meeting about a Classics project involving Baty, Todd, Morris and Becher took place on 17 July 1964. A draft document setting out the case for an enquiry was prepared for the Nuffield Foundation by Baty in consultation with Todd and Sharwood Smith. This document was intended to form the basis of discussions and several versions were prepared. Morris was shown the document and proposed that it also be sent to Becher before their first encounter on 17 July. Morris clearly wanted the preliminary proposals to go further than an expression of value judgements and argue for a 'team of go-ahead Classicists' who would produce the teaching materials that classroom teachers could use to 'put the new ideas into practice'.[8] The document was also passed to Mr B.M.W. (now Sir Brian) Young, who was about to leave his post as Headmaster of the independent school Charterhouse in order to become Director of the Nuffield Foundation. Young, who was at this time still teaching Classics, gave his support to the proposal, although he was not in a position to take part in the preliminary discussion.[9]

The first meeting between Baty, Todd, Morris and Becher, held at Nuffield Lodge near Regent's Park in London on 17 July, went well.[10] From this point on, discussions between the several interested parties appear to have developed fruitfully. A further revision of the document was sent to Becher and reference to the Leicestershire Plan was now inserted. The Hughes Hall conference had taken place since the original paper had been drafted. The revised discussion document identified the specific need to establish a 'small expert sub-committee of only four or five persons' which would tackle the following issues:

> In schools where Latin is (or Greek and Latin are) taught, how can the teaching (especially of Latin) be improved and made more appropriate, in content and method, to the ages and interests of the pupils of today? And that without loss of what is genuine in the traditional values of a Latin course? Could, for example, some of the newer modern-language teaching techniques, or any analogous methods, be applied with success to the teaching of Latin? It would be assumed that the aim was to bring, by stress on reading and understanding, a worthwhile standard of attainment within the short time now generally given to Latin in the schools. Is there a common basis of attainment in Latin appropriate both to those who will give it up at the age of 16 and for those who will proceed farther? And is there an allowance of time below which the study of Latin is unprofitable and therefore inexpedient? . . .
>
> In schools in which the Latin and Greek languages are not taught, what can effectively be done to communicate some knowledge of, and interest in, Greece and Rome, and to arouse an informed curiosity about the contribution of the ancient world to civilisation?[11]

Becher, in response to Baty suggested that even the revised paper, whilst clearing up some initial misunderstandings, did not go far enough in establishing the nature and objectives of a 'new look' course in Classics.[12] He offered to produce an amended version during the summer which said more about the 'shape and pattern' of the proposed course and outlined procedures for establishing a committee to make progress. Baty politely confessed to being needlessly cautious and agreed that Becher should make the next move.[13] Morris, too, who had left the Nuffield meeting early, was keen to maintain momentum and felt that they were already working towards a conference which might lead to 'consideration of several kinds of new courses for schools'.[14]

Becher's redrafted document entitled 'New possibilities in the teaching of Classics' was sent to Charles Baty in early September, with an invitation to Baty and Todd to submit their critical comments and agree a date for the next round of discussions.[15] The document concludes with the hope that an acceptable scheme for action would be put into effect as the result of future discussions.[16] The four parties to the earlier meeting, Becher, Baty, Morris and Todd, met again at Nuffield Lodge on 13 October 1964 to consider the next moves.[17]

Becher's redrafted document attempted to take into account as much as possible of the discussion which had taken place at the earlier meeting.[18] Developments proposed include:

1 An eighteen month intensive audio-lingual course plus life of classical Rome plus selected literature in translation.

2 Up to the age of 16, carefully graded reading programmes plus literature in translation plus life, history, social structure, values etc plus Greek literature and legacy of the Classical period.

3 Sixth-form specialists: if thought necessary, Latin translation and composition, grammatical studies of Latin literature.

The document continues by identifying problems that would arise in implementing such reforms within the existing system, including the need for examination reform. The document goes on to explain what had been done for other areas of the curriculum:

> The introduction of new courses has attempted in these other subjects (Science, Mathematics and Modern Languages) by collecting together teams of experienced practising teachers who, with the help and guidance of university scholars, have been given time to prepare comprehensive and interrelated sets of teaching materials: teachers' guides, students' texts and visual and other aids. These materials are tested extensively under classroom conditions, revised in the light of the experience so gained before being made generally available. They are intended to provide a basis for future development, rather than to constitute a new orthodoxy: and teachers are of course free to adapt them or not as they see fit.[19]

The document then proceeds to link new course developments with the need for in-service (referred to as 're-training') programmes for teachers and refers to the need for examination boards to offer alternative examinations with different types of questions calling for insights and understanding rather than factual knowledge and technical skill. In a further section, the document proposes 'courses with no linguistic content':

> if it is agreed that such pupils [less able pupils who are contrasted with their abler peers in grammar and public schools] should also be acquainted with Greek and Roman civilisations, without being required to undergo any formal linguistic training, a possible pattern of teaching might follow . . . items in Section D which omit all reference to language: namely, a wide reading of literature in translation and an introduction to the history, social structures and values of ancient Greece and Rome and a study of the influence of their culture on our own.[20]

27

The document stressed that the presentation would need to differ from that thought suitable for the upper reaches of the intellectual scale: the literature (even in translation) might need to be simplified and the other studies would need to be approached 'in a less academic way.'[21] In short, Becher's document envisages two main thrusts:

1   A move to reform the teaching of Latin (and possibly Greek too) to 'O' level and beyond.
2   An attempt to offer some study of the ancient world to all pupils through the medium of English (non-linguistic courses, as they were described).

The Nuffield Lodge conferences

The second meeting at Nuffield Lodge on 13 October 1964 resulted in agreement to continue the discussion and to involve a wider group. A short-list of names was drawn up by Charles Baty (no doubt assisted by Todd) with a view to calling two conferences towards the end of the year, to consider the draft document. The Trustees of the Nuffield Foundation had agreed to inform themselves fully of the present state of opinion about new ways of teaching pupils to read Latin and about non-linguistic courses that might give pupils some insight into classical literature and civilisation and would receive a report on the conference in due course.[22] Those invited to attend were informed that these conferences were to be of a 'purely exploratory and informal nature'.[23]

Baty, as the JACT representative, was eager that they should go ahead and seek support from the Nuffield Trustees for an enquiry followed by a 'large amount of practical work'.[24] Equally Todd, representing the Classics HMI, appears to have warmly welcomed the potential marriage between Nuffield resources and the long-standing needs of secondary school Classics. Morris, for his part, was pleased that his initiative had successfully put the Foundation and Baty 'in touch with one another'.[25] He was shortly due to move to the newly created Schools Council. He promised 'to watch from the wings' and await further developments.[26]

The document contained a set of proposals which were in essence those which had long been advocated by progressive Classics teachers. The two-pronged attack on Classics teaching would seek not only to reform the teaching of Latin but also to offer a more appropriate study for the non-specialist, to provide some study of the ancient world to a broad range of ability.

The Nuffield Trustees, a number of whom had no doubt learned their Latin the hard way, had previously expressed their willingness to help in a reappraisal of the objectives and content of Classics teaching.[27] The framework for a curriculum project along the lines of those already in operation for Science, Mathematics and Modern Languages was established in the minds of Becher, Morris, Baty and Todd, but support from the Trustees was essential if grant funding were to be forthcoming. A positive recommendation would need to be presented to the Trustees by Becher.

The concerns of the Trustees to inform themselves about new ways of teaching Latin and about non-linguistic courses would best be met by sounding out those who had first-hand experience of new developments in language teaching and of teaching pupils of school age about the ancient world through the medium of English. Their first objective, however, must have been to secure the support of 'respectable' academic opinion among those teaching in university Classics departments. Any attempt to reform Classics teaching at school level would surely have foundered without such support. The strategy adopted for the conference, therefore, appears to have been to invite the university representatives first in the hope that they would provide their clear and unequivocal support for the enterprise. Consultation would then follow with practising teachers from schools who might have some suggestions as to how the curriculum project team should set about their task.

A handwritten list prepared by Baty identifies a number of names of possible conference members under separate headings and likely names are marked with asterisks.[28] The intention of the consultative conferences was evidently to bring together a number of carefully selected individuals from five distinct constituencies. These were: classical scholars of university standing, university departments of Education, public schools, grammar schools and HMI. A distinction was drawn between 'pundits' and 'practitioners'.[29]

In the case of the first conference, the majority of those invited to Nuffield Lodge (excluding Baty, Todd and Morris) were from university Classics departments. On this occasion there were also two representatives from UDEs and two school representatives, neither of them from the maintained sector. In the case of the second conference, the participants were predominantly from schools (four from maintained and four from the independent sector). At these conferences Kenneth Todd was the only Classics HMI present.[30]

In response to the concerns raised by the Nuffield Trustees, Baty and Todd must have had some difficulty in identifying individuals who could advise first on new ways of teaching pupils to read Latin, and second on courses which did not include a classical language element. Those invited to the first conference included individuals who might be expected to support initiatives aimed at developing new approaches to Latin teaching but it would appear that there was only one person present who had been involved in such a venture already and this was still at a very early and tentative stage of development. It is unlikely, at that date, that classical scholars from Oxford and Cambridge would have needed to apply their minds to ways of teaching the Latin language *ab initio*. Probably the only conference member present on the first occasion who had any such experience was one of the UDE representatives, Sharwood Smith, who had already set up a small-scale experimental project in a school with some specialist linguistic assistance. The other UDE representative present, David Morton, had been in contact with some pioneering work which was being undertaken at that time in a Bradford comprehensive school, though he did not himself have any direct involvement.

At the second conference, a substantial contribution was made to the discussions by C.W.E. Peckett, who besides being a lifelong exponent of the direct or oral method of classical language teaching and the joint author of *Principia* and *Thrasymachus* had continued to interest himself in ways of improving the middle school Latin course.[31] With regard to the second area of concern, the development of what were to be referred to as 'non-linguistic' courses, strenuous efforts were made to involve one particular secondary modern school teacher, a neighbour of Peckett's in Shrewsbury, who had developed a version of the 'Humanities' course already well established over many years at the Priory School.[32] Miss M.W. Gough of Monkmoor Girls' School was the only person present at either conference who had experience of teaching a non-linguistic Classics course across a wide ability range.

Baty's original list included a note to the effect that both Peckett and Sharwood Smith were especially interested in 'Ancient World for also-rans'. Two UDE classicists with progressive views who were among the most enthusiastic advocates of Classical Studies for all in the junior high schools were W.B. Thompson and D.J. Morton. It is curious that neither of their names is asterisked on Baty's list, especially as Baty was already working closely with Morton on the JACT reorganisation pamphlet and would have seen Morton's interests as much wider than the provision of Latin. Thompson was the only contributor to the pamphlet on Classics and reorganisation who was not invited to attend either of the two conferences. No representative of classical teachers in Wales was included, although one name was suggested as an afterthought.[33]

Conference 1: the pundits

The first conference was held on 27 November 1964 at Nuffield Lodge and included some names well known outside as well as inside the world of Classics teaching. Those present included: Mr Brian Young, by now in post as Director of the Foundation, who chaired the conference and who had been involved in the preliminary discussions (together with Todd, Baty, Morris and Becher). From university Classics departments were Professor C.O. Brink, R.G.G. Coleman and E.J. Kenney from

Cambridge, D.A. Russell and J.T. Christie from Oxford and Professor T.B.L. Webster from University College, London. From university departments of Education were Sharwood Smith from the London Institute and Morton from Nottingham. School representatives were J.C. Dancy, Master of Marlborough College, and Miss J.E. Pharo, Senior Classics Mistress at Croydon High School.[34]

Baty went to some lengths to secure the presence of suitable people at this conference and to brief them in advance. The correspondence between Baty and J.T. Christie, the Principal of Jesus College, Oxford, illustrates this point well. [35] Christie was an obvious choice from Baty's point of view. Not only was he an august figure from the world of university Classics teaching, but he had been a near contemporary of Baty's at Oxford and was a distinguished classical teacher who moved with ease between the more prestigious public schools and academia. Besides his long and distinguished career teaching Classics to university undergraduates and public school boys, he had in fact been Headmaster of Westminster School, of which Baty was an alumnus. Although Christie was the kind of person in the academic world whose support was needed at the outset, this did not mean to say that he was aware of the problems that faced Classics teachers beyond the confines of Westminster School and the University of Oxford. In fact, it does not even appear that Christie was at this stage a member of JACT. Baty's approach to him was two-fold. Firstly, he was anxious to allay any fears that he might have regarding the proposed systematic enquiry into the teaching of Latin: 'Let me explain . . . that it is by no means a mere repetition of the old question of direct method, or of no-prose-composition, or anything like that'.[36] Baty was also at pains to point out that the Kenneth Todd, by way of 'the Department', had been fully involved in the preliminary discussions.[37] Secondly, the threat of imminent comprehensive reorganisation in state schools and even perhaps a hint of governmental intervention in the independent sector, were used to impress on Christie the urgency of the situation:

> But matters of secondary re-organisation (Leicestershire Plan, Bristol, Liverpool and all that, impending in many parts of the country) are making the future of Latin in grammar and other schools very problematic; and some of us are most keenly anxious that Classics should not be neatly penned in to the public school enclosure, there to be fenced in until it can be isolated and finished off. And I do not think it is an exaggeration to say that there is a danger of this.[38]

Correspondence from that time provides some indication of the concern felt by those who wanted very much to make progress but who were anxious not to arouse fears that reform might imply a lessening of the rigour traditionally associated with a study of Classics. For example, Baty, acting on the advice of Dancy, proposed to Becher that the final document presented to the conference on 27 November might make a mention of 'intensive reading'. This was suggested in order to 'conciliate the pterodactyls'.[39]

The stage was now set for the first conference. All participants had been sent a copy of the discussion paper before the meeting. The need for reform of the middle school Latin course was by now long overdue. It was already four and a half years since Brink's Southampton speech and here at last was the possibility of financial support for a systematic enquiry into a more worthwhile study of Latin for the non-specialist student.

The conference did not run as smoothly as Baty and Todd had hoped. They had wanted a clear endorsement of the principle that reform should go ahead with the financial support of the Nuffield Foundation. Todd expressed surprise that the conference lasted until 5 p.m. Disagreement among the participants and the protracted nature of the discussion initially filled them both with deep pessimism. Todd felt that discussion was both lengthy and diffuse and expressed strong misgivings about a successful outcome.[40] Baty had placed high hopes on what he termed 'the bigger guns' who had been invited to the first conference. He confessed to feeling let down, however, and began to look towards the next round for something better.[41]

From a study of the official report of the proceedings it is not easy to establish precisely which were the major points of disagreement that clearly troubled Baty and Todd so greatly.[42] A scrutiny of the letters exchanged following the meeting suggests that the cause of their despondency was the inability of even this hand-picked assembly of classicists to agree on the principles underpinning the proposal. Instead, they had insisted on trifling over details of implementation.[43] A concentration on ends rather than means would have helped the meeting to expedite its business. This experience appears to have guided the Chairman in his opening remarks at the second of the two conferences.[44]

An initial cause for contention was sparked off by Professor Webster in his quest to replace Latin with Greek as the first classical language to be studied in schools. The conference concluded, with some regrets, that those who knew no ancient language should in general concentrate on Latin, although there might be some scope for a middle school Greek course also. Having cleared away this issue, the conference went on to range over a number of issues related to courses with linguistic content. The report of the meeting suggested that there was a fair measure of agreement and the following points were recorded.

Firstly, there was a concern to develop the practice of reading Latin aloud. The prevailing emphasis upon silent reading was felt to be caused partly through lack of time and partly by the uncertainties which some teachers had about the correct pronunciation. Secondly, there was a recognition that the grammatical understanding acquired as the result of translating from English into Latin is only of marginal value. However, the conference did not feel that composition should necessarily be abandoned altogether. Thirdly, a drastic reduction in time spent on composition should enable pupils to read more widely and in greater depth. Comprehension should be elicited by the use of careful questioning rather than by translation. Formal translation was not thought to be necessary in the middle school. The task of selecting suitable reading texts would be difficult but crucial. Fourthly, there was agreement that grammar should be taught inductively, although it was felt that formal grammar would have to be tackled later, at sixth-form level.

The conference showed caution in relation to the proposal that a middle school Latin course to 16 should include the reading of some Latin literature in translation and should be supplemented by further studies of the history, social structure and values of classical Rome. The document had also proposed some study of classical Greece along similar lines but with the addition of art and mythology and including some carefully selected Greek literature in translation.[45]

Many of those present were said to be sceptical about 'background courses per se' and felt that the pupil's acquaintance with the worlds of Greece and Rome should arise directly out of reading classical texts. Accordingly, the proposal was made that studies of life in classical Rome, its history and social structure and values, should develop out of the reading.[46] Webster again appears to have been in the minority in arguing the Hellenist cause.

One major area in general where the conference was less than helpful was in relation to non-linguistic courses. Only three individuals are recorded as having made a contribution to this part of the discussion. Yet the paper being prepared by Morton, Baty and others for JACT during that very period placed great emphasis upon the new style of course which would be appropriate in schools reorganised along comprehensive lines.[47]

It is unlikely that the conference spent long discussing the development of non-linguistic courses. There was little experience of such courses in schools at that time and it seems inconceivable that the university representatives at that date would have been convinced of their value unless they could be shown to be crucial to the survival of Classics in schools. These kinds of argument do not appear to have been advanced. In fact, the comprehensive 'threat' is not referred to either directly or indirectly in the report of this conference, although it is mentioned in the discussion paper which the conference was asked to consider. Besides, there was plenty to discuss on the linguistic side to which the university representatives felt more able to contribute. It is perhaps strange that Baty is not recorded as speaking in support of what he refers to elsewhere as 'Classics without the Classical languages', despite having seen for himself Miss Gough in action at Shrewsbury.[48]

Conference 2: the practitioners

The second conference was also held at Nuffield Lodge a month later on 30 December 1964. The report of the conference indicates that on this occasion the Chairman Brian Young endeavoured from the outset to focus discussion on ends rather than risk the conference becoming embroiled in arguments about means.[49] He began on this occasion by posing the following three questions:

1 Was the present middle school Latin course satisfactory for the very large number of pupils who would drop Latin after 'O' level?
2 If not, what kind of course should be offered instead?
3 What could be dropped from the present curriculum to make available the extra time required for a course such as was outlined in the paper?

The conference first considered how the Latin course might be changed before going on to consider non-linguistic approaches to the teaching of Classics. On this occasion, progressive opinion about broadening the nature of the Classics course from a narrow linguistic programme for able linguists to a course suited to pupils from a wide range of ability played a much bigger part in the discussions.

Peckett declared that unless the proposed new Latin course was valid for our civilisation he (as a headmaster) would take it out of the curriculum. He preferred to talk of Classics rather than Latin. Morton suggested that while linguistically able pupils might have to be confined to Latin, they should also be given the opportunity of studying Graeco-Roman civilisation. On the linguistic side, Morton questioned the need for translation into Latin, arguing that accuracy could be achieved through reading and comprehension. The Chairman was, however, sceptical. Peckett, challenged by the Chairman as to what new ground needed to be broken, argued that Kennedy's Latin Primer was no longer completely valid, a fresh analysis of Latin grammar was required and a different description of the Latin language was needed. Unlike the first conference, the second spent some time discussing the possibilities of Classics without a linguistic element, although the balance of time was still weighted towards discussing linguistic study. Peckett afterwards regretted that more time had not been spent on 'background' study.[50]

Miss Gough outlined her experimental work in Humanities with A, B and C streams in her school, in which she explored History, Literature in Translation, History of Art, Architecture and Archaeology. The pupils were strongly motivated and inspired to engage in a great deal of imaginative work of a practical nature. One result had been the very great improvement in written and spoken English.

A strong plea was made by Morton for preparing to meet the challenge of comprehensive reorganisation and he developed at length a number of concerns which should be taken into consideration if Classics were to survive the imminent upheaval. These included the following points:

1 Classicists must be prepared for changing circumstances including changes in traditional age divisions.
2 Classics should be offered to all pupils.
3 Problems of staffing would arise but non-specialists must be trained.
4 Reading skills in Latin should be developed in pupils aiming at 'O' level and CSE.
5 In the new schools, which would contain a range of ability, Classics would have to become multiply based.[51]

Referring to Morton's points, Becher thought that they must bear in mind both the needs of grammar schools and the type of work that Miss Gough was doing. It was important not to have too much of a dichotomy between the kind of Classics taught to the abler pupils and that taught to the slower ones. There should in fact be a strong continuum from one to the other.[52]

The Nuffield Trustees met in mid-January 1965 and were presented with two proposals for an enquiry which might benefit substantially from 'relatively modest' financial support along similar lines to the School Mathematics Project based at Southampton University.[53] The first general proposal, in the name of Professor Brink, was for a small curriculum development which would be located within the University of Cambridge and would be concerned to develop an alternative middle school course with greater emphasis than at present upon rapid reading skills in the Latin language, leading to a broader study of classical civilisation than that now undertaken. This proposal had not yet been formulated in detail, but the Trustees were informed that Brink hoped to submit an application 'subject to the discussion of the present meeting'.[54] The second proposal was from Professor D.M. Balme of Queen Mary College, London, for 'rather similar research'.[55] The Trustees indicated their readiness to hear more about the two proposals. Baty wrote to John Dancy of Marlborough College on 19 January 1965, giving the 'encouraging news' from Nuffield and asking his advice about the possible alternatives.[56]

It seems likely that Baty had also raised some doubts as to whether Brink would be the best person to take responsibility for the proposed curriculum development in view of his likely absence from Cambridge in the near future. Dancy's advice to Baty was that if Brink was not in a position to do it, there were three other possibilities: someone else from Cambridge (Oxford was not felt to be sufficiently in sympathy), someone at London working under Webster or Balme or in the London Institute of Education under Sharwood Smith in the Institute of Education, or JACT itself.[57]

By the time that the Nuffield Trustees' January 1965 meeting took place there were only two realistic alternatives. The possibility that JACT might have acted as direct sponsor does not seem to have been seriously considered and would not in any case have fulfilled the School Mathematics Project model envisaged by Becher which the Nuffield Trustees had already endorsed at their January meeting.

The London initiatives

In the meantime, Balme's bid was by now established, not only with Baty but also with Nuffield. Since the end of October 1964, Balme had been considering establishing a new research post in his Classics department; although some teaching duties would be involved, the major part of the work would be devoted to research into Latin teaching method. Balme wrote to Baty on 31 October. He was clearly aware of discussions that had taken place with Nuffield and raised the possibility that Nuffield might support the proposed new post, either wholly or in substantial part.[58] In the same letter he set out the advantages of locating such research in London and in the Queen Mary College Classics Department in particular. In making this proposal he reported the favourable reaction of Sharwood Smith.[59]

Of the other possible London sponsors mentioned by Dancy, it is unlikely that Professor Webster who had attended the first Nuffield conference would have made a bid to sponsor a curriculum development project in Classics unless there had been a general agreement that Greek would be the preferred first classical language as a focus for research. Sharwood Smith, on the other hand, had made no secret of his own developing plans for a controlled experiment in Latin teaching methods. In a letter written to Becher immediately following the first Nuffield conference, Sharwood Smith outlined a proposal for using the research of Dr John Wilkins, whom he described as 'our Cardiff general linguist-cum-Latinist' in a pilot scheme at Watford Boys' Grammar School. He also referred to the possibility that Balme might find a home for Wilkins.[60] Wilkins at this stage held the post of Lecturer in the Classics Department of University College, Cardiff and he had recently completed his doctorate in the field of linguistics. Sharwood Smith had established a working relationship with him and clearly thought highly of his work and of his potential as a linguistic consultant.[61] Sharwood Smith, it would seem, had already thought out his scheme in some detail and the plan was ready to put into operation on an enlarged scale. 'A sound basis of language theory is crucial', he argued.[62]

Arrangements for locating Wilkins permanently in London at Queen Mary College would have suited Sharwood Smith's plans well. If Balme were to find a home for Wilkins, and early trials at Watford proved promising, he and his collaborators planned to extend the project to include teacher secondment and at a later stage to make use of a language laboratory. Even the matter of a publication by Longman projected for 1967 had been considered.[63]

Balme, on the other hand, would find in Wilkins just the kind of specialist linguist he was seeking to undertake research into Latin teaching method, though other candidates were not excluded.[64] The appointment of Wilkins to a post at Queen Mary College would thus enable both Sharwood Smith and Balme to proceed with their plans. The support of the Nuffield Foundation for such an appointment would ensure both that the cost of the new post at QMC would be met and that the school-based experimental work planned by Sharwood Smith would be extended and developed into a larger scale operation.

No separate formal bid was submitted to Nuffield by Sharwood Smith, and Becher clearly did not feel obliged to treat Sharwood Smith's letter as such a bid. Balme, on the other hand, did submit a formal request for the research to be located in his department. Although Balme received a cautious reply, his bid was presented as a formal offer to the Trustees along with that submitted by Brink.[65]

The genesis of Sharwood Smith's and Balme's proposals were distinct and separate, but it is clear that they were in close touch with each other and that they had certain objectives in common. Nuffield sponsorship could ensure that a London-based Latin project came about. It is also clear that a project based in a department of Education would not have met with Nuffield's approval. A majority of the Trustees were senior and established academics with traditional views about 'Education as an academic subject'.[66]

The Cambridge proposal

At this point it is necessary to return to the first suggestion in Dancy's letter to Baty, namely that the project should be located at Cambridge. It will be apparent that Cambridge was throughout the favourite candidate for the location of a curriculum development project. This is likely to have been Becher's preference.[67] It was Brink, the Kennedy Professor of Latin at Cambridge, who had first raised the banner on the issue of 'O' level Latin reform in 1960 and he would probably be seen as the front-runner in any competition for sponsorship of an appropriate curriculum project. Brink also attended both conferences. Baty appears to have seen Cambridge of the two older universities as offering the better prospect. His preference may have been influenced by his observations of reactions at the first Nuffield conference.

Following the meeting of the Nuffield Trustees, Becher contacted Baty and informed him that he had 'authorization to negotiate with Cambridge by way of Professor Brink'.[68] It may be assumed that Brink had also had a telephone call from Becher that same day. A meeting of Classics dons at Cambridge took place in Brink's rooms at Gonville and Caius College on 26 January 1965 at which a detailed proposal for a curriculum development project to be located at Cambridge was hammered out.[69] Brink and Baty were both sent a set of 'rough notes' by Becher in advance of the meeting scheduled for 3 p.m.[70] However, Becher did stress to Baty that the notes were simply to be regarded as a starting point. There is no official record of what took place on that January day in Brink's rooms at Caius. It is possible, however, to compare the notes prepared for the meeting by Becher with the actual proposal document that subsequently emerged and which was presented to the Faculty Board of Classics for their consideration in the name of Professor Brink and his colleagues, Messrs Bamborough, Coleman and Kenney.

As a result of this meeting a proposal emerged which covered two sides of foolscap paper. The document set out the proposal for a new school Classics 'programme' together with an appendix detailing an estimated budget for the programme to run for three years from October 1965 to September 1968. The proposed programme aimed at improving the teaching of Classics in the middle school. It was presented to the Faculty Board of Classics on the afternoon of Friday 11 February. If accepted, the proposal would have gone forward to the Nuffield Foundation with a request for a grant amounting to £11,500 per annum to cover the costs of the programme.

Under the terms of this proposal, the main research would be undertaken by a team of seconded school teachers and others with experience of pupils of the appropriate age; it was thought that university teachers of Classics would have much to contribute and that Cambridge would provide a particularly suitable centre for this work.[71] The programme would be two-fold. Firstly there would be the development of a scientific investigation into the problems of teaching Latin in the light of recent developments in linguistics; the emphasis would be upon achieving reading fluency without sacrificing accuracy of comprehension. Secondly, a wider study of the possibilities of classical civilisation should form part of the study and should be properly related to actual texts read in Latin.

It would be relevant to consider the part which might be played by translations of both Greek and Latin authors.[72] The draft budget in Becher's rough notes for the meeting with Brink and Baty is identical to that which was actually submitted to the meeting of the Faculty Board of Classics. However, there was much that had disappeared from Becher's notes and from the earlier discussions at Nuffield Lodge during the formulation of the final proposal. The concept of a Classical Civilisation course aimed at a broad ability range, which Becher's paper proposed, would appear to have vanished.[73]

In the proposal which went to the Faculty Board of Classics, all reference to classical courses without the language for 'less academic pupils' and to the 'needs of a wide range of pupils in the middle school' had disappeared. Reference is made to the needs of pupils in the sixth form and at university who would be studying subjects related to Classics such as History, English and Modern Languages; no mention is made of Classics for the less able or Classics 'without the language'. Whether in response to the concern expressed at the first Nuffield Lodge conference about 'background courses *per se*', or whether as a tactical device, the proposal is confined to a linguistic course presumably directed at the traditional clientele who might be expected to study Latin in secondary schools.

With the ground prepared and the proposal carefully framed in the light of earlier discussions, it was hoped that approval by Faculty Board would enable the proposal to go forward to the Nuffield Trustees in the succeeding week.[74] However, this was not to be. In the words of one of the proposal's sponsors, the proposal received a 'rather rough handling'. Although there was general support for the idea, it was felt that no formal decision could be made without a formal consultation with the University's Department of Education.[75] The outcome of the meeting, agreed by a very narrow margin, was that the Department of Education should be asked to make an application similar to that proposed and that the Faculty Board of Classics would cooperate actively in implementing the proposed programme.[76]

There was now a great danger of an impasse. The Faculty Board of Classics did not want to approach Nuffield alone, but wanted the proposed programme to have the blessing of the Department of Education; Nuffield, on the other hand, was reluctant to locate curriculum projects in university departments of Education and had reacted favourably to the idea that this project might be sponsored by the Faculty of Classics. The prospect of establishing a project in Cambridge from the 1 October 1965 now looked extremely bleak, especially to Baty. Hasty exchanges of letters took place with a view to retrieving the situation by arranging cooperation between the Faculty Board of Classics and the Department of Education. Earlier concerns expressed privately about university departments of

Education are echoed in Becher's concern to keep the Classical Faculty as the sponsor of the scheme[77] and in his proposal that, if possible, the Faculty Board of Classics should be the 'senior partner'.[78] There was concern at Nuffield to involve university teachers of Classics as well as 'schoolmasters'. Geoffrey Hunt, the UDE lecturer at Cambridge, was apparently unaware of the proposal which had come before the Faculty Board of Classics until after the meeting had taken place.[79] Baty played a major part behind the scenes in seeking to unravel the local political difficulty which had arisen in Cambridge. Baty's extreme irritation is shown in a letter to Geoffrey Hunt:

> It all seems to the outsider very complicated; and, if I were not exceedingly anxious for something to get done, I should derive some cynical amusement from watching related bodies graciously giving way to one another so as to avoid the responsibility of having to be given a large sum of money for a purpose which one would imagine to be of interest to both![80]

The outcome was a joint approach to Nuffield by the Faculty of Classics and the Department of Education acting together. It was agreed that a committee of four members, two from the Board and two from the Department of Education, be set up to initiate the scheme and to manage the appointment of staff and to exercise a general advisory power without too much interference with the detailed work of the staff. The four members of the committee were to be Professsor W.S. Allen, Mr E.J. Kenney (Classics), Professor W.A. Lloyd and Mr A.G. Hunt (Education).[81] The Faculty Board's approval was said to have been unanimous only because it was understood that its two representatives were to be Kenney and Allen. Professor Brink, who held the Kennedy Chair of Latin in the University and who had kindled the first flames of public interest in reforming school Latin teaching, was not included.[82]

A formal proposal was now jointly submitted to the Nuffield Foundation on 8 March and this was duly approved at a meeting of the Nuffield Trustees on Friday 19 March.[83] An early meeting was arranged between members of the Cambridge Project Committee together with Charles Baty at Nuffield Lodge on 13 April, and David Morton was approached and asked to take a major part in the Project.[84] A press release was issued by the Nuffield Foundation on 29 April 1965 announcing that a grant of £34,500 would be given to finance a three-year project to be based at Cambridge University on the teaching of Classics in schools.[85]

The extraordinary difficulties which had arisen in relation to the Faculty of Classics and the Department of Education at Cambridge were summed up by Charles Baty as follows: 'It took two visits by Tony and me to introduce those two august bodies to one another . . . but now they seem firm friends, with the prospect of jointly getting a grant of £35,000'.[86] Baty added wryly that the part of the application that he had not himself written was drafted by Becher and commented: 'So hard is it to give away money!'[87]

The original intention of Nuffield was that the grant should go to the Faculty Board of Classics which would be responsible for establishing and managing the Project. The initial proposal had been formulated and presented by the small group of Classics dons led by Professor Brink. There is no evidence of any attempt to involve or even inform the Department of Education, although the Department's cooperation would be vitally important for the practical implementation of the proposals. Hunt, as well as being a UDE lecturer, was himself Director of Studies for Classics at Fitzwilliam College; yet he did not know of the proposal until after it had been presented to the Faculty Board.[88] Baty subsequently criticised himself for not having discussed the proposal with Hunt earlier, ascribing his error of omission to overwork.[89]

Baty's apologetic letter to Hunt, written after the event, stated that in any operation it was 'taken for granted that the Faculty would consult other interests concerned in the University, first of which would be the Department of Education, and in particular you'.[90] Such a statement is difficult to reconcile with the seemingly complete lack of even informal soundings between members of the Classics Faculty and members of the Education Department. The failure in communication by omission would have been all the more remarkable in view of Hunt's association with both the Faculty and the Department and his well-established links with those Classics dons who contributed to his teacher training programme. More broadly, but for the strenuous intervention by outside agencies, serious delay might have resulted; it is even possible that Cambridge University might have missed the opportunity altogether. The net result was that the proposal was delayed by only one month and the Department of Education became an equal partner with the Faculty Board of Classics in the enterprise.

Further confirmation that Cambridge had all the time been the desired locale for a Classics project comes from letters written by Baty after the initial refusal of the Faculty Board of Classics to process the Nuffield application. In his anxiety to ensure swift cooperation from the University Department of Education, Baty, in correspondence with Hunt, referred to the 'beginnings of a similar scheme at QMC'.[91]

In fact Balme, the only other serious contender for Nuffield funding, had announced to Becher before 1 February 1965 that he was planning to go ahead with his own scheme independently of Nuffield.[92] It is likely that he had heard of the meeting which had taken place in Brink's rooms in January. He proposed to go ahead with the appointment of a linguist by the end of February. Balme confessed to Baty that he felt he was getting the brush-off from Nuffield, as their letters were 'brilliantly meaningless': 'One feels like an Austin 7 faced by a fully loaded and euphoric lorry: one can only back.'[93]

Baty was keen, however, to keep open his lines of communication with Balme and Queen Mary College. This was to prove an important factor in future developments. Despite the difficulties surrounding the introduction of the Cambridge Project proposal to the Faculty Board of Classics, the scene was now set for curriculum change on an unprecedented scale.

The Project Committee's view of the twin tasks ahead, as set out in a job description provided for applicants for the post of Director, suggests very clearly that the possible non-linguistic developments were to be aimed at older pupils and that the Committee did not have in mind the broad ability range. Their statement did not in fact acknowledge changes taking place in secondary schools.[94] The press notice released by Nuffield, on the other hand, added the following rider: 'Account will be taken of current developments in secondary education and the ways they are likely to affect the subject.'[95] The press release referred firstly to the linguistic task of examining the elementary stages of teaching Latin in the light of modern language teaching and secondly to the possibilities of a wider 'background' study of classical civilisation and culture.

The *Times Educational Supplement* commented on its front page that changes were needed to Classics teaching in view of changes in school organisation:

> traditional methods of teaching, perhaps mainly because of their long and honourable history, die even harder in classics than elsewhere. Yet now that secondary education is being reorganised, classics teachers must not only consider how to teach the languages, but also look afresh at the actual civilisations to see what could be made useful, interesting and exciting to a wider range of people than ever—no longer just to those who discover the background in the traditional way through learning the languages.[96]

Comprehensive reorganisation: a catalyst for change

The large 11–18 comprehensive school undoubtedly had the potential for offering a broad curriculum with a wide range of subject options including Classics. However, there was limited awareness in the early 1960s of how the traditional classical curriculum might be adapted to the needs of a fully comprehensive clientele.

The organisations which predated the birth of JACT had failed to offer a lead in reforming the Classics and were unsuited to providing the kind of forward thinking and information service that Classics teachers under pressure from reorganisation now required. The successful inauguration of JACT ensured that a vehicle existed through which ideas could be shared and proposals for reform formulated.

Long-standing views in favour of transforming traditional Latin into a broadly based programme of Graeco-Roman study aimed at the 'non-specialist' had, since the crisis of 1960, found favour with the more pragmatically inclined and now became official orthodoxy in the context of Crisis Two. With the extension of comprehensive reorganisation, the dissemination of Classics teaching in new forms to a wide range of ability became attractive to those whose prime interest was the survival of classical language teaching in state schools.

Even before the General Election of 1964, and a full year before *Circular 10/65* emerged from the Department of Education and Science in July 1965, crucial moves were set in train which were to be of immense importance to Classics teachers facing reorganisation. As described earlier, the Leicestershire Plan conference had resulted from a decision by the JACT Committee. It was this conference that proposed the preparation of a JACT pamphlet on reorganisation and Classics which became JACT Pamphlet 2. David Morton and Charles Baty ensured that this blueprint for classical courses under various reorganisation plans was available by the spring of 1965. Its publication very satisfactorily anticipated both the government circular and also the variety of patterns of reorganisation which that circular permitted. Sales of the pamphlet suggest that there was widespread demand for it.

The second development, carried out more covertly by Baty as Honorary Secretary General of JACT, was concerned with moves to establish a curriculum project for Classics. Classicists were fortunate that the interest of Morris and, through him, Becher in eliciting Nuffield support for their subject coincided with the urgent need to face the implications of comprehensive reorganisation. The need to reform Classics teaching was already urgent. Although developments since Brink's 1960 speech had been slow, the advent of comprehensive reorganisation now provided a much needed argument for acceleration.

Disappointed at the traditionalist reaction shown in the Leicestershire Plan conference, some individuals used comprehensive reorganisation as a means of emphasising the urgent need for reform. A reference to the Leicestershire Plan was interpolated into the text of the document prepared for the two Nuffield Lodge conferences. Baty was not afraid to use reorganisation as a means of concentrating minds. Morton made a strong bid at Conference 2 for comprehensive reorganisation to be taken fully into account. Even before the first conference he was emphasising the urgency to Becher:

Many of us are convinced that there is an urgent need to engage in radical rethinking about both content and teaching methods and that this rethinking needs to be based on controlled experimentation. The situation is rendered all the more urgent by numerous current plans to reorganise secondary education with new age divisions that cut across courses that are at present contained within a single school.[97]

At the Nuffield Foundation, the Trustees were informed that the situation for Classics was urgent.[98]

Whereas Morris, Becher, Baty and Todd were sensitive to the need to develop non-linguistic Classics courses for a broad range of ability within comprehensive schools, Cambridge dons concerned with the needs of non-specialists in the sixth form were apparently thinking on more conventional lines. The proposal which went to Nuffield suggests that the Cambridge dons were principally influenced in their thinking by Crisis One and its likely impact on grammar and public schools. Unlike the group of people that had undertaken the preparatory work, they were not unduly concerned with the implications of Crisis Two.

CHAPTER FOUR

The Project's First Year: An Agenda for Change

The political climate in the mid-1960s

It has already been shown how the prospect of comprehensive reorganisation played an important part in the decision to establish a curriculum development project for Classics. Where grammar schools were reorganised into a comprehensive system of schooling, Latin seemed destined to become at best an option for a minority of pupils; timetabled hours for language teaching would be reduced and the starting age for Latin would be postponed. The need to reconsider the nature of a middle school Latin course was therefore paramount and very urgent. At the same time, other challenges existed. For those teachers who were prepared to consider the possibility, there were opportunities for considering the part that Classics might play in a general Humanities programme for all pupils in the lower secondary school.

The Labour government in Britain had survived with a tiny majority since October 1964, during which time *Circular 10/65* had been issued (in July 1965) and a commission to consider the future of independent schools had been established under the chairmanship of Sir John Newsom. This body, which later became better known from the name of Newsom's successor as the Donnison Commission, was established in December 1965 with a brief to advise on the best way of integrating the 'public' schools with the state system.[1] Evidence from public opinion pollsters at this time suggests that there was widespread and consistent support for comprehensive schooling among the British electorate, despite some local cries of anguish which greeted specific reorganisation plans.[2] The General Election of 31 March 1966 gave the Labour Party a landslide majority of ninety-seven and a clear and secure mandate to continue with their policies.[3] Comprehensive reorganisation was now set to continue apace and the possibility of changes in the independent sector also during the next five years could not be ruled out.

The Cambridge School Classics Project is born

The Cambridge Project officially came into being on 1st January 1966, three months later than originally envisaged. The temporary setback arose from the difficulties which the Project Committee had encountered over securing the right personnel.

David Morton appears to have been 'marked out' as the obvious person to direct the Project, well in advance of the formal interviews for the post held on 19 May 1965. Morton cut an impressive figure on account of his energetic style and sense of urgency together with his considerable powers of eloquence. Combined with the progressive views that he had come to hold about the potential role of Classics within a reorganised system of secondary education, these qualities recommended David Morton as a potential leader who would command credibility and inspire confidence in the prevailing climate of educational change. It is clear that his appointment was favoured and canvassed privately by Baty.[4] He almost certainly also enjoyed the support of Brink.

The choice of a Director may have seemed obvious to some. However, a serious difficulty lay in the path of the Project Committee faced with the need to find a suitably qualified linguist. The advertised appointments were for a Director with educational qualifications and experience, and an Assistant Director with specialised linguistic qualifications. The Project Committee stipulated that the Director should have responsibility for the direction of the programme within a general framework laid down by the joint Committee. The Assistant Director, on the other hand, was to be responsible (under the supervision of the Director) for research into the problems of teaching the Latin language in the light of recent developments in linguistics.[5] Even before the interviews for Director were held, the Committee realised that their search for a suitable linguist who might also fulfil the requirements of an Assistant Director was in vain.[6] It might therefore be necessary to reconsider the whole staffing structure of the Project and to postpone even the appointment of a Director. This decision was taken immediately before the Committee proceeded to interview two candidates: Messrs D.J. Morton and P.H. Vellacott, the author of a recently published Latin textbook, for the post of Director.[7]

The Committee decided to explore a solution which was favoured by Baty, that they should discuss with Nuffield the advantages of a closer link with Queen Mary College, London.[8] Interviews for the post of Director were held but no immediate appointment was announced. Candidates were told officially that 'there were difficulties with other aspects of the Project'.[9] Privately, Morton was informed by a member of the Committee

46

that the problem centred on finding a deputy 'equipped both as a classicist and in modern linguistic theory'.[10] Although Baty had technically ceased to be directly responsible for getting the Project into being, once Nuffield funding had been granted to the joint applicants at Cambridge, he nonetheless continued to play a major role behind the scenes. He had continued to pursue the possibility of support from the Gulbenkian Fund for the Queen Mary College scheme and was anxious that the two schemes at Cambridge and London should complement rather than duplicate each other.[11]

Soon after the interviews for Director had been held, Baty, acting as a diplomatic channel between the Project Committee and Balme, explained the situation in which the Committee now found themselves.[12] John Wilkins, who had already accepted the post at Queen Mary College from October 1965, and was still at University College, Cardiff, was referred to by Baty as 'almost the only eligible person for the linguistic job'.[13] Having accepted the full-time post at QMC, Wilkins was not in a position to apply for the post of Assistant Director. It might, however, be possible to secure him for the Project as a consultant. The Project Committee was informed on 28 May that Professor Balme was prepared to consider the matter further.[14]

The Committee then made arrangements to explore the Queen Mary College link in more detail with Balme, Baty and the Nuffield Foundation. At the same time it was agreed to inform Mr Morton that the Committee intended to offer him the job of Director as soon as they were assured that the Project could go forward, but that they would not now expect him to take up his duties before 1 January 1966.[15] By 1 June 1965, Morton had been offered the post.[16]

Geoffrey Hunt representing the Project Committee met Professor Balme, Charles Baty and David Morton at Queen Mary College on 8 June to consider ways in which they believed a link with John Wilkins' research might work. According to a memorandum of the meeting which Hunt prepared for the Committee, Wilkins' research programme was to undertake a general description of the Latin language, with the limitation that this was to be concentrated on the literary language of the 'best Latin authors' (down to Suetonius).[17] Although there was no obligation for him to keep in his mind the pedagogic implications of his work, it was known that Balme himself was keenly interested in using oral methods in teaching Latin to his undergraduates and that Wilkins had already himself in mind plans for experimentation in conjunction with the London Institute of Education.[18] Throughout the discussion the importance was stressed of safeguarding Wilkins' 'academic freedom to carry on [or not to carry out!] his research in his own way'.[19] In view of the uncertainty it seemed inappropriate for Wilkins' time to be paid for on the basis of so many days per week. During discussion the idea began to emerge that the amount of consultation should gradually be increased during the three-year life of the Project. Morton and those present at the meeting were under no illusion that the early stages of the Project's work would be able to benefit from Wilkins' research and in fact it might transpire that no scheme emerged from the research at all:

> The fact that his new scheme, if any, will not be ready for experimental testing until the second/third year of our project, does not prevent our making some initial experiments on the basis of both the traditional description and some of the more recent ones.[20]

Despite the possible limitations of what Wilkins' research might be able to offer, Morton appears to have been undaunted. He suggested that the Project's own early experience might in fact be helpful to Wilkins and could well be significant for their later stages of experimentation.[21] In the meantime there was much to be done in examining the 'purely pedagogical aspects' of current methods and teaching aids. David Morton clearly had some doubts about basing the whole linguistic programme on a new schema which might not become generally accepted for a number of years. He felt, however, that the advice of John Wilkins on the lines discussed at the meeting on 8 June should prove to be sufficient for the Project's needs.[22]

At a specially augmented meeting of the Cambridge Project Committee held on 2 July 1965, at which both Balme and Wilkins were present as well as Baty, Becher and Morton, it was agreed that the link between the work of Dr Wilkins at Queen Mary College and the Cambridge School Classics Project could best be established on a part-time consultancy basis.[23] Following a suggestion by Wilkins the full-time post of Assistant Director as originally advertised was left unfilled.[24]

The Director designate's attention was now turning to the kind of personnel he wished to join him on a full-time basis. The original staffing structure of the Project was to have involved two posts established for three years, those of Director and Assistant Director, together with a number of short-term appointments using secondment where appropriate. The removal of one of the two three-year posts meant that the rest of the staffing structure of the Project had also to be looked at afresh. Once the role of the Linguistic Consultant had been established by the Project Committee, arrangements were made for the recruitment of a second full-time member of the Project team. It was agreed on Morton's recommendation that this post should be advertised as 'Assistant to the Director'. The person appointed would be expected to share the work of preparing material for trial in schools.[25]

Clarence Greig was appointed to this post on 4 October 1965.[26] Greig, who had been an Assistant Classics Master at the Cambridgeshire High School for Boys, was seconded to work on the Project for a period of three years. Greig's appointment was to provide a model for all but one of the future academic appointments to the Project team, each new person appointed being designated 'Assistant to the Director'.[27] By late in 1965 a secretary had been recruited to work for the Project.[28] University premises were made available on a short-term basis and a cleaner was appointed.[29]

So it was that the Director, David Morton, and an Assistant to the Director, Clarence Greig, together with the Project's first full-time secretary, began work at 21 Silver Street, Cambridge in early January 1966. This was not the first occasion that they had met to consider the task ahead. The Director's report to the first meeting of the Project's Advisory Panel, held in December 1965, indicates that a certain amount of preliminary thinking had already been done by the Director in conjunction with both the Linguistic Consultant and with his recently appointed Assistant. It is during these preliminary discussions that an important shift in emphasis may be seen to have taken place with regard to the programme of the Project.

To recapitulate earlier developments, the document which had been discussed by the two Nuffield conferences and the 'rough notes' produced by Becher as the basis for a project proposal had identified two main strands (see above p. 28). There was a concern to provide a study of Graeco-Roman civilisation appropriate to a wider ability range as well as linguistic study for a somewhat narrower spectrum of ability. And yet the document which emerged from deliberations in Professor Brink's rooms in Caius College contained a significant departure from these earlier formulations with regard to the 'wider study of Graeco-Roman civilisation'.[30] The proposal which emerged, and which was consistently followed in the paper presented to the Classics Faculty, in the joint proposal submitted to Nuffield, and in the earliest declarations of intent published by the Project Committee, was as follows: firstly, a scientific investigation into the problems of teaching the Latin language in the light of recent developments in linguistics, with an emphasis upon the achievement of reading fluency in Latin without sacrificing accuracy in comprehension; secondly, an investigation into the possibility of a 'wider study' of classical civilisation, subsidiary to the linguistic investigation but complementary to it.[31]

The concept of a programme of study for a wide range of ability does not feature in the documentation. The proposed 'wider study' now evidently refers only to a wider study for those studying Latin. However, the evidence of the early discussions between the Director of the Project and his colleagues show clearly that a conscious decision was made from the outset to reformulate the Project's programme in such a way that the

49

needs of a wide range of ability could be accommodated. This constituted a restoration of the *status quo ante* and represented a reversion to the earlier Nuffield formulation. In a paper presented to the Advisory Panel on the first occasion that it met, the Director set out the Project's tasks as follows:

1 To investigate ways of improving the teaching of Latin at the early stage, ie. up to 'O' Level, with special reference to the task of improving reading fluency.

2 To investigate courses of a non-linguistic kind for pupils who lack the ability or opportunity to take a linguistic course. We shall also devise non-linguistic foundation courses to precede, in some cases, the language based course.[32]

Both tasks were presented against the background of 'contemporary difficulties and problems'. The Director's paper recognised the widespread anxiety among Classics teachers over the effects of secondary reorganisation. However, there was also a recognition that even if the survival of Classics were not at stake, there would still be an urgent need for the radical reform in the teaching of school Classics.

Task (a) was consistent with all the discussions which had taken place since Brink's Southampton clarion call in 1960 and in particular during the gestation period which led to the establishment of the Project. The Director's paper proceeded to flesh out the detail a little further:

The emphasis must be on reading from the outset. Reading must dominate the linguistic training. While this does not preclude composition activities, we insist that composition is a means and not an end and indeed, that it must be a proven means. In fact, the concept of composition should be changed to that of the manipulation of the language in such ways as to bring the pupil to reading success as quickly as possible. Oral work is likely to play a significant part at the beginning of the course.[33]

Task (b) recognised the long-espoused view of many forward-thinking Classics teachers that the Classics had something to offer to pupils as part of 'general education' and that the justification lay in the major part played by the classical world in our own cultural history as well as in the intrinsic ability of classical culture to stimulate taste and sensibility.[34]

The Director not only made a firm commitment to the traditional range of ability for which Classics teachers have always had to cater, but also resolved to take advantage of the opportunities offered by comprehensive reorganisation.

for the first time, they will teach in schools containing the full range of ability. Will they have anything to offer to children below G.C.E. ability? I regard it as a matter of great importance that teachers should offer classical courses of varying types to children of modest ability.[35]

Referring to JACT Pamphlet 2, Morton declared that they regarded a three-year Latin course as the minimum time allowance and that this should preferably be preceded by a foundation course of the 'Thompson' type.[36]

It was to be expected that a progressive-minded project director would recruit fellow team members to the Project who broadly shared his views about ends, if not about the means by which those ends might be accomplished. Greig appears to have been in full sympathy with the strategy which was worked out from the beginning of the Project's existence. Wilkins had not been directly recruited by Morton but the nature of his research was likely to be broadly in tune with the Director's views on the linguistic task.

With regard to the Advisory Panel, a list had been prepared of possible members in the autumn of 1965. The Project Committee was advised by the Director to select all the members themselves rather than invite nominations from other interested bodies. Members of the Advisory Panel in the early days of the Project were as follows: Professor D.M. Balme, Mr M.G. Balme, Mr C.W. Baty, Mr R.A. Becher, Professor C.O. Brink, Mr C.H. Craddock, Mr E.O. Furber, Miss M.W. Gosling, Professor L.A. Moritz, Mr C.W.E. Peckett, Mr W.B. Thompson, Mr K.G. Todd, Mr B.M.W. Young, together with the four members of the Project Committee. Meetings were normally chaired by a member of the Project Committee. Professor Balme was elected Vice Chairman at the first meeting of the Advisory Panel.

Membership was almost entirely male, the only woman being Miss Gosling, a Classics teacher from a north country grammar school. Members were recruited from universities, grammar and independent schools and had been selected to represent a wide spectrum of interests. There was no representative, even in the later stages of the Project's full-time existence, with experience of teaching in comprehensive schools. The Panel did, however, include all the contributors to JACT Pamphlet 2, including William Thompson. Thompson, along with Cyril Peckett could be expected to press for the non-linguistic developments as forcefully as they argued for a radical reform of Latin teaching. Peckett had also many years of experience as the co-author of Latin and Greek language courses (see p. 30).

Other members of the Panel included university teachers Professors David Balme and L.A. Moritz (the latter from University College,

Cardiff), together with some experienced schoolteacher authors of classical textbooks such as E.O. Furber, C.H. Craddock and M.G. Balme, who could be expected to take a particular interest in the linguistic developments.[37] Furber and Craddock taught, as did Miss Gosling, in maintained LEA grammar schools which would in due course be the subject of reorganisation schemes; however, Maurice Balme taught at Harrow School and was less likely himself to be feeling the immediate effects of government policy. When it came to considering the needs of teachers who were already undergoing reorganisation, and the detailed response of the Project team to those needs, there was no one with direct experience to offer realistic advice. There was, however, much general sympathy and support for the Project team as it attempted to meet the urgent needs of schools with the offer of Classics through English for the many and a reformed Latin course for the few.

David Morton had skilfully set the Project's revised agenda against the current background of radical educational change, and no one appears to have challenged him, either on the Cambridge Project Committee or at the first meeting of the Advisory Panel. By now there was acceptance among Classics teachers that whatever their preferences might be in normal circumstances, something had to be done now if Classics was to survive. In the face of crisis, there might be much to be gained from a radical change and the Project Director and his team deserved their support. Miss Gosling was one Classics teacher who brought a generally positive attitude towards curriculum change in the prevailing climate to the discussions of the Advisory Panel and she already had a proven track record for forward thinking. In view of the various forms of secondary reorganisation impending, she had looked at sixth-form work from below as well as from above. Both the future demands of the universities and the possibility of drastic reorganisation of schools had to be faced.

> *'Stant litore puppes'*. We should not watch helplessly, like Dido,
> the final departure of all that we had most valued, but should
> rather, like Aeneas, sail to found a new home; and there was
> much in the old that would be better burnt![38]

Priority to Latin

Although the agenda had been altered to ensure provision for the broad ability range, from the outset priority was given to the development of a new Latin course. During the first year of the Project's existence, the energies of the Director and his Assistant were for the most part devoted to the development of draft Latin teaching materials.

By May 1966, arrangements were in hand for some pilot materials to be tested in about ten schools and a text was beginning to emerge for both pupils and teachers.[39] Morton and Greig chose Pompeii rather than Rome as the location of this early material. The grounds they gave for choosing Pompeii included 'compactness and greater comprehensibility' in contrast with the 'complex structure of Rome itself' and the abundant opportunities for visual illustration and specific historical detail arising from archaeological excavation. A further very practical reason was that a short unit of study lasting one term could be abruptly ended with the dramatic eruption of Vesuvius.[40]

From the very beginning, Caecilius Iucundus, the successful Pompeian business man, was chosen as the central character in the introductory unit, since his house, his many financial dealings and even his facial appearance have been revealed by the archaeologist's spade. The real *praenomen* of Caecilius's son Quintus was adopted, but other members of his *familia* were invented by 'pedagogical licence'. A similar degree of licence was exercised in writing the story material. An apology was offered in advance to the *manes* of Caecilius and members of his family; the hope was expressed that they would approve of the Project's attempt to confer upon them 'posthumous notoriety'.[41]

Handsome red ring-binders contained the duplicated prototype material for Unit I of the future Cambridge Latin Course. The pupil's materials were entitled 'The Romans: people and language'. These took the form of eleven 'stages'. Each stage was subdivided into three sections: Part One contained illustrated model sentences which were followed by information about the language, Part Two comprised a Latin reading passage followed by a list of words and phrases, and Part Three consisted of exercises aimed at practising the language. A final section at the back of the ring-binder offered 'paralinguistic material' entitled 'Pompeii' which related to various topics that formed the basic subject matter of the text. Teachers were supplied with a set of notes in addition to the pupils' text.

Even when a second Assistant to the Director, J.A. (John) Jones (of Tudor Grange Grammar School, Solihull) joined the Project team on 1 September 1966, there was little evidence of attention being turned towards the promised 'broader' courses in Classical Civilisation.

At the first meeting of the Advisory Panel, Morton had promised that the first few months would be devoted to preliminary design of material embodying new ideas in language learning. The team would seek to devise a method that was appropriate to the particular objectives laid down and would probably include:

(i) Oral/visual experience from the outset;
(ii) Induction of rules of inflexion and syntax from the linguistic phenomena;
(iii) Complete sense groups of words to be used from the beginning;

(iv) Statements, commands and questions to be introduced at once;

(v) The verb and the noun, possibly [sic], to be introduced horizontally rather than vertically;

(vi) Oral drills, both in the classroom and where possible in the language laboratory to establish the basic features of the language, but these oral drills will be designed for a reading, not a conversational, purpose.'[42]

The team would need to know more about the frequency and structure of basic syntactical patterns in order to determine the best sequence of presentation and with this in mind the link with John Wilkins' research at Queen Mary College, London had been established.[43] A programme was drawn up by David Morton in the early days of the Project which in retrospect appears breathtakingly unrealistic; nonetheless it gives some indication of the enthusiasm and idealism with which the Project team began work in January 1966.[44] Such an action-packed programme also reflects the urgent need which was felt at the time by the Director to help teachers undergoing reorganisation or contemplating the prospect thereof.[45]

Morton had originally told the Advisory Panel in December 1965 that arrangements for testing the Project's material would be set up in schools in September 1966, and that if the 'main problems' were overcome by spring 1967, larger-scale testing would begin in September 1967.[46] In his report to the Advisory Panel in October 1966, the Director suggested that his original plans had been too ambitious and that plans for a testing programme in about ten schools lasting about twelve months from September 1966 had had to be postponed. In a lengthy *apologia* Morton suggested that the team had felt dissatisfied with the draft material as it had stood at the end of June 1966, and that there had been a need to make further study of several major problems.[47] Having formulated the best provisional principles possible, the team would create all the material for the first year of a three-year course and would put it out for testing in September 1967, to about forty schools. The second-year materials would be written and put out for testing in like manner in as many of the same schools as possible. There would, however, be a problem in that the Project was due to come to an end by 1968 and they would not be as advanced as had been originally hoped.[48]

This 'official' account of the first major upset in the lifetime of the Cambridge School Classics Project needs to be supplemented from the records of the Project Committee and from correspondence written at the time in order to establish the divergence of views between the Director and the Linguistic Consultant. Wilkins had indicated to Morton that the draft material that was being prepared for September trials in schools did not reflect his linguistic formulations clearly enough and that he expected that substantial modifications would need to be made in the light of probable developments in his own research programme. He had therefore advised a postponement of testing until further basic work had been carried out. After rehearsing the arguments for and against postponement, the Director recommended to the Committee that they postpone the proposed testing programme, cancel arrangements with schools and revise their overall schedule accordingly.[49]

This episode is important for a number of reasons. It illustrates the divergence between the interests of the Linguistic Consultant, John Wilkins, and those of the Project Director, David Morton. The interests of the two men coincided in so far as they both wished to reform the teaching of Latin in schools and to develop teaching materials, based upon recent linguistic theory which would assist the rapid acquisition of reading skills. Morton was dependent upon Wilkins for supplying linguistic formulations which could be used as the basis for writing Latin learning materials; Wilkins would have the opportunity for testing out in schools the formulations which resulted from his research.

The major divergence arose in relation to timescale. Wilkins had taken up his post in October 1965 at Queen Mary College, and was only at the outset of his research and there was no ready-made 'off-the-peg' list of linguistic features that could be handed over to the Project once it began work in January 1966. However, the Project clearly could not afford to wait if its own three-year life span was to be adhered to. Furthermore, as has been seen, the situation for many Classics teachers who faced reorganisation schemes was now becoming urgent. The Project had been given a task to do within a limited timescale and it was the Director's job to ensure that this task could be accomplished. There can be little doubt that members of the Project Committee were right in their recognition of Wilkins' ability as a potential Linguistic Consultant to the Project, but their decision to structure the Project in the way they eventually did, contained serious built-in contradictions. If the pressing needs of schools were to be met, the Linguistic Consultant would be placed in an impossible position.

The problem of differential timescales was not unrelated to the way in which the Linguistic Consultant's services were used. Wilkins' complaint that his linguistic formulations were not sufficiently clearly reflected in the early draft material suggests that there was little direct communication, except perhaps on a social level, between Wilkins and Morton's assistant, Greig, whose task it was to draft the teaching material.[50] In fact, it was a long-standing cause for complaint on the part of Wilkins that on his regular weekly visits to the Project during the first eighteen months of the Project's lifetime he did not have direct access to members of the writing team.[51] Instead, Wilkins engaged in regular dialogue with

Morton, who in turn passed on linguistic formulations in a form which he considered appropriate to the writing team, with a brief to convert them to teaching materials.

An important knock-on effect of these difficulties was that tensions within the language programme from the middle of the Project's first year of existence delayed development of the non-linguistic side of the Project's work which was as vital to the future of Classics in the maintained sector as the proposed Latin course; it remained a long way behind in terms of personnel and resources, at a time when a new impetus was desperately needed in schools. The twin prongs of the Project's programme, facetiously dubbed 'Morton's Fork', had both been seen as vital by Morton himself, and it was through the Director's own efforts, as seen earlier, that the concept of non-linguistic courses had been broadened to cater for future patterns of comprehensive reorganisation.

The realities of life after 1 January 1966 were that the Project was committed to two major undertakings: the preparation of a new Latin reading course to 'O' level with sufficient teaching material to last a minimum period of three years, and materials for non-linguistic courses in Classical Civilisation for a range of abilities and at different levels. It was realised very early on that the implications for resources were considerable, especially in regard to personnel and in a number of other respects, not least in respect to the training of Classics teachers in the new approaches which the Project hoped to develop. Within three months, at a meeting of the Project Committee, it was agreed to approach the Nuffield Foundation with a view to obtaining further financial support.[52]

Since the supplementary estimates submitted to Nuffield following the meeting of the Committee included the cost of appointing a fourth member of staff to 'develop rapidly the non-linguistic side of the Project's work', it must be surmised that the Project Committee had quite deliberately decided to give priority to the production of the new Latin course and would stake any sizeable future non-linguistic developments upon future funding. The team would in September 1966 consist of a Director, a Linguistic Consultant, and two writers. All would devote their energies to the production of a new Latin course. Although this task included preparation of the cultural content as 'background' to the linguistic study, it did not assist with the process of developing Classics for a broad ability range within reorganised secondary schools. Little more progress was made in this direction until full-time staffing was obtained.[53] The Director's report to the Advisory Panel records the following admission:

> The non-linguistic aspect of the Project's programme would require the services of at least one further full-time member of the

56

team, if it were to be developed with the speed and thoroughness that was called for. The present staff would have little time to spare from their duties on the linguistic side.[54]

At this stage in the Project's life there was already a recognition of some of the problems involved in maintaining a rolling programme with schools. A commitment to large-scale testing of materials in trial schools had by this time become a regular feature of curriculum projects which followed a Research, Development and Diffusion model. Whilst testing on a wide front was expected to ensure a sound basis for developing the final version of the material, there were other benefits to be gained. The Project's thinking could be disseminated more widely at an early stage, especially with a view to helping those schools which were under pressure to change. In addition, larger quantities of materials produced could help to ensure that the trial budget was self-supporting and in some cases to realise profits which might be ploughed back into the Project.

The trial programmes of the Project in later years sometimes proved to be a millstone around its neck which meant that everything in the Project had perforce to be subordinated to the meeting of deadlines. The Classics Project was not the only curriculum development project to find itself in this situation. M.D. Shipman, commenting on the Integrated Studies Project based at the University of Keele in Staffordshire, has referred to 'materials madness' in describing the way in which the production of materials for publication came to dominate the life of the Project.[55]

An important feature of the first year of the Project's full-time existence was the commitment undertaken by the Project Director to tour the country in response to invitations, meeting groups of Classics teachers who were concerned about the future of their subject and seeking to reassure them that deliverance was at hand. The Project's contribution to in-service courses continued throughout the lifetime of the Project as a full-time enterprise and has continued ever since; and during the first eighteen months of the Project's existence, the nationwide programme of speaking engagements was at least as intensive as in any subsequent year.[56] Speaking engagements involved visits to North Wales, Scotland and Northern Ireland. There were contributions to conferences held by the Classics Committee of HMI held at Oxford in July 1966, to the ARLT Summer School at the University of Keele and the standing conference of lecturers in university departments of Education held in September at Hull. These were all crucial occasions when key individuals could be given an up-to-the-minute account of developments on the Project front.

Most of the meetings to which the Director contributed during 1966 and the first half of 1967 were for classroom teachers. Some were convened to provide Classics teachers with a realistic appraisal of the prospects for Classics in the context of comprehensive reorganisation. A conference organised by Miss E.P. Story of the University of Oxford Department of Education, at which forty to fifty teachers were expected, was clearly envisaged as such an opportunity: 'I think they [Classics teachers] need to be told the hard facts of life about re-organisation'.[57] A conference organised under the *aegis* of the University of Liverpool during April 1966 was entitled 'Classics and Comprehensive Schools' and included David Morton as a guest speaker. It was arranged in response to the urgent need to prepare Classics teachers for comprehensive reorganisation in Liverpool. The staffs of grammar schools in the Merseyside area were invited and some thirty teachers attended.[58]

The Project Director had also received early on an invitation to speak at Bristol, a second area in which controversial reorganisation plans had been introduced even before the change of government in 1964. This was the one conference to which the Project Director was invited during the first year of the Project that was entirely devoted to developments in Classical Civilisation. There was already growing interest in the possibilities of Classics syllabuses for the new system of examinations for the Certificate of Secondary Education (CSE). This conference was entitled 'Classical Studies in the CSE'.[59]

The conference mounted at the University School of Education attracted over fifty members, although only thirteen were teachers working for the Bristol authority and only six were teachers in schools fully maintained by the authority.[60] It is worth noting, however, that the conference aroused much interest in the possibility of Classical Civilisation as a subject at CSE among teachers from schools in the adjoining counties (Somerset, Wiltshire and Gloucestershire) as well as in some of the local independent and voluntary (Roman Catholic) schools. There was little at this stage however, to offer teachers apart from the syllabus already developed for CSE in Classical Studies by the East Midlands Board.[61] These conferences set the pattern to be followed in the years ahead. Initiatives were taken in the main by university departments or institutes of Education, by university Classics departments or by local branches of the JACT and the CA. Where there were invitations forthcoming from LEAs, this was usually due to the presence of a classicist or someone strongly sympathetic to Classics occupying a fairly senior position within the authority.

A further indication of the Project Director's desire to adopt a high profile approach was the decision to include advertisements in the first *JACT Bulletin* of 1966 and in the *Times Educational Supplement*, inviting teachers to write to the Project and offering interim bulletins on the Project's progress.[62] In spite of the pressures under which the Project was operating during the first year, the exhilaration of the early months comes strongly through in reports of progress given to various interested groups at the time:

Mr Morton gave an exciting survey of the work of the first seven weeks of the Project and outlined the various questions that had bubbled up at the beginning of the enterprise—the length of the GCE course in future, should a non-linguistic foundation course lead (a) to study of the language and (b) to CSE-type examinations, what standard of reading fluency was possible in a three-year course, how to get pupils to ask the sort of questions that lead on to literary criticism, what parts of Latin grammar are required for recognition as distinct from composition?[63]

Public reaction to the new Latin course

Early reactions to the Project's trial Latin course materials cannot be easily gauged from reports of meetings at which the Project featured. These reports confine themselves to close factual accounts of the Director's presentations. On 13 April 1966, Morton addressed the Annual Meeting of the CA with Baty in the chair.[64] Morton's address, it appears, was particularly concerned with the first few months of the Project's work on the Latin course and there was also some speculation about the future of Classics in reorganised schools. The Project would need to take account of schools which might have no more than three years for an 'O' level Latin course.

The meeting followed hard on the heels of the decisive result of the General Election, and teachers are likely to have been receptive to some practical guidance as to how their subject might best survive in schools. They did not necessarily greet the Project's proposals with wild enthusiasm. No reactions to Morton's address are recorded.[65] The account in *Latin Teaching* of David Morton's progress report to the ARLT Summer School held at Keele University is similarly presented without comment.[66] Evidence of the reactions of rank and file teachers to the initial proposals from the Project is mainly anecdotal. Whether they were shocked by what they heard from the lips of the Project Director or whether they were exhilarated as they listened to his exposition, audiences of Classics teachers were stunned into silence.[67]

Classics through the medium of English

At the end of the first year, the Project had not a great deal to show for the second half of the programme that it had originally set for itself. On the linguistic side, the team had already put out a set of draft materials for testing in seven schools. Feedback was available from the trial schools and the third full-time member of the team, John Jones, had now been in post for four months. The scene was set for an all-out assault on the linguistic course from January 1967, with a view to a full-scale test programme in the autumn of 1967. On the non-linguistic side, by contrast, there had been relatively little progress.

Morton's talks frequently explained the Project's overall strategy and contained the promise of future developments on the non-linguistic side, although the main emphasis was on the linguistic developments. The one exception to the normal pattern was at Bristol. Here the conference on Classical Studies and CSE was the first of its kind to be mounted in association with the Project anywhere in the country; it arose from an attempt made on the initiative of the local UDE lecturer, Miss M.E. (Margaret) Jervis, and sought to offer a constructive way forward to Classics teachers facing comprehensive reorganisation.

The debt to William Thompson's pioneering work with teachers in the north of England had been acknowledged by Morton in his first address to the Project's Advisory Panel, when he referred to courses of the 'Thompson type' preceding a study of Latin in reorganised secondary schools.[68] Thompson had contributed a chapter on the possibilities for a foundation course in JACT Pamphlet 2, but his contribution to this early development did not rest here. A whole year before the Project began work, in January 1965, Thompson had directed for the University of Leeds Institute of Education a course for Classics teachers specifically aimed at the new possibilities for Classics under various forms of comprehensive reorganisation. The course was entitled 'Classical studies: a new approach for the junior high school'.

This course was essentially concerned with promoting general courses in Classics taught in English. Included in the programme were contributions from C.W.E. Peckett and Morton.[69] Thompson recalls how teachers came from places far and wide, including from the other side of the Pennines in the most inclement of winter weather conditions, to hear the new message of hope that was being offered to teachers of Classics in comprehensive schools and to participate in deliberations about a positive approach to the future.[70] A second course with the same title was held in April 1966.[71]

The one solid achievement of the Project in relation to non-linguistic developments during 1966 was a modest one, and involved what were to become known as 'foundation courses' or 'foundation courses in Classical Studies'. Here, David Morton succeeded in establishing one experimental foundation course at Heriot's Wood Girls' Grammar School in Harrow, where the Classics enjoyed strong support from a scientist head. Following an encounter between the Head of Classics, Miss B.J. (Betty) Trollope, and the Project Director in April, the possibility of an experimental course at the lower end of the school was put forward. Harrow's proposed reorganisation plans helped set the stage for this piece of curriculum development:

At present, we are a 3 FE [form entry] grammar school, of fairly high academic standard. Our buildings may, in Harrow's Re-organisation Plan, either house a 12–18 mixed school, or a 6th form college, but we shall probably have two years! We shall certainly have to rethink our Classics teaching![72]

It was agreed, with the support of the Head, that a foundation course experiment should be undertaken with three unstreamed first-year classes. They would each have two periods of thirty-five minutes and one twenty minute homework.

Morton's original proposals to the Advisory Panel had suggested that curriculum renewal would involve introducing into the curriculum 'more active methods which involve the discovery of ideas and principles and appeal to the imagination and feeling as well as the comprehension of the adolescent'.[73] In terms of concrete proposals for content in Classical courses, he suggested that they should give a 'reasonably coherent treatment to such themes as myths, legends, history and social patterns, art and material culture' and that they would 'seek to put much more material in the hands of the teacher'.[74] With David Morton's encouragement, the first non-linguistic trial school used material from the *Odyssey* and *Iliad* as the basis for a 'foundation course' and this was to set the pattern for future developments in succeeding years.

At the October meeting of the Advisory Panel, Morton was able to report that this experimental work had been successfully established and to confirm that a further full-time post had been secured with assistance from the Schools Council.[75] Interviews for this post which was aimed at developing the non-linguistic side of the Project's work would be held the following week.[76]

It had been clear that the initial grant from the Nuffield Foundation was insufficient to meet the needs of the Project, and the financial support of the Schools Council had been sought.[77] Interviews for the newly established post were duly held on 25 October 1966 when M.St.J. (Martin) Forrest (the author) was offered the post of Assistant to the Director with special responsibility for non-linguistic classical courses. After some initial uncertainty about the starting date of the appointment, Forrest began work as an additional Assistant to the Director from 1 January 1967.[78] Money for this newly created post came entirely from the Schools Council and not from the original Nuffield grant. Although the job description was particularly related to non-linguistic developments, there was an understanding that the person appointed might also be expected to contribute to the Latin language programme.[79]

A traditionalist voice

Whilst most teachers of Classics were coming to terms with the two crises of the early 1960s and were prepared to listen carefully to the reformers, at least one individual was prepared to speak out against what he believed to be a betrayal of traditional values. T.W. Melluish is still acknowledged even by those who were his fiercest opponents as a fine teacher of Classics. His biting wit and sense of fun are well remembered by many people along with his scholarly contributions to the teaching of traditional Classics. When it came to proposals for reform, however, Melluish was uncompromising. He used his position as President of the ARLT during 1966 to launch a savage attack on the new order in an address to the same summer school which was also addressed by David Morton. Melluish claimed that classicists were now acting so defensively that he had sometimes looked at the end of *Didaskalos* for a free gift of cyanide issued to all its readers.[80]

In an article published in *Latin Teaching* in the same year he again criticised the reform movement as follows:

A suicidal chorus of young teachers mount the band-wagon which is to prove a tumbril, proclaiming their strong attachment to Latin by saying that there should be less of it, that translation from English to Latin should be abolished, that Latin Literature is better studied in translations, and that the linguistic excellences of Latin are negligible. So a Christian martyr in the arena should pat the lion on the head for its nice sharp teeth.[81]

CHAPTER FIVE

Quid Novi? A Prototype Latin Course

After the initial small-scale trial of Latin course material conducted in the autumn of 1966, work continued on the preparation of materials for the first large-scale school trial due to start in September 1967. The task of the writing team was to develop the language materials in a form which was appropriate to and which would appeal to adolescent pupils. This task involved the creation of story material which would provide a vehicle for introducing linguistic features step by step, according to the syntactic gradient of difficulty designed by the Linguistic Consultant. The writers worked intensively at their task from September 1966 to the exclusion of much else, and the first stages of the Latin course were produced in pamphlet form (as opposed to the ring-binder format used in the earlier material). A printer based near Cambridge (the Layston Press) began to turn out what were to become the familiar orange covered booklets containing elements of a new language course. There began to spring to life for the first time in printed format Caecilius Iucundus, his spouse Metella, his son Quintus and other members of his *familia*, Melissa and Grumio.

The first stages of the course were again located in Pompeii immediately before the eruption of Vesuvius in AD 79 and the team began to explore the possibility of setting later stages of the material in other parts of the Roman Empire at the time of the Flavian Emperors (AD 69 to 96). The quality of the materials was greatly enhanced by the recruitment to the Project's services of a husband and wife team of illustrators, Leslie Jones and Joy Mellor. A photographic expedition by some members of the Project team (comprising John Wilkins, who, in addition to his skills as a linguist, was a highly accomplished photographer, Morton and Forrest) to Pompeii, Herculaneum and Naples in February and March 1967 also ensured that a rich supply of colour transparencies and some negative film was available to support the linguistic materials. The worst of the winter weather was by now over and there was an unbroken succession of

Figure 1. The author and attendant remove brambles from a Pompeian shop front before it is photographed by John Wilkins (March 1967).

clear, sunny and pleasantly warm days in which to photograph the houses and public buildings of the ancient cities. Even in the mid-1960s however, signs of neglect were evident. The amphitheatre had been temporarily closed for reasons of public safety and a number of sites had to be tidied up with a little judicious gardening before the camera work could begin!

Another important development during 1967 was the appointment of an Evaluation Officer. From September 1967, the staff of the Project was augmented by Miss E.P. Story, an experienced teacher of Classics in schools who had recently been working at the Department of Education in Oxford University. Within a month of her arrival, the new Evaluation Officer was outlining plans to evaluate the large-scale trial programme which had just started. By the autumn of 1967 there were five former Classics teachers employed full-time by the Project, including Martin Forrest, the author, who had joined the team in January 1967.

In the autumn of 1967, trials of the Latin language course involving 3,800 pupils began in 74 schools, with the intention that the first pupils would reach 'O' level in the summer of 1970. These schools included some comprehensives but also many grammar and independent schools where there was an interest in reform. The front-runners who would take their GCE first were from those schools where a maximum of three years was allowed for the course, but this represented a small minority. The team's original expectation was that 13+ would soon become the standard age at which Latin was started in reorganised schools. In practice, however, the move towards a shortening of the middle school Latin course came about more slowly than expected. In-service training was provided at Cambridge for teachers in the trial schools. Teachers were informed that the second year's material would be ready for school trial in September 1968, and that it was hoped the first part of the course, revised in the light of school trials, would be published by September 1969. There was the proviso, however, that this would depend upon no major problems being encountered during the first twelve months of testing.[1] In the event, the revised material appeared on the market, published by the Cambridge University Press, in 1970.

The trial materials presented Classics teachers with a number of major departures from tradition. The Linguistic Consultant outlined these differences between the new Latin material and traditional courses in an explanatory bulletin. These points may be summarised as follows.

Firstly, the objective of the new course was defined as *Reading skill*. This distinguished the course both from traditional Latin courses (whose objectives included composition as well as reading) and from modern language learning which involves skills of listening, speaking, reading and writing.

Secondly, the linguistic thinking behind the Project's material had been influenced by the modern schools of grammatical analysis of Noam

Chomsky in the United States on the one hand and M.A.K. Halliday in England on the other. In the new analysis that had been undertaken for the Project, the Latin sentence was seen as 'the most valid analytical entity'. Sentence patterns were compared with one another and all other parts of the language were treated with reference to their typical place in the sentence structure. One important result of this was that 'formal paradigms and sets of inflexions', both of which were prominent features of traditional courses, received a 'more realistic assessment'.

Thirdly, second language learning had been viewed as 'mapping a new language on to the existing patterns of the native language'. In the construction of the course material, therefore, devices had been used to highlight similarities between Latin and English. Although it was recognised that such devices did some violence to Latin, only those features which occur quite frequently in 'good' Latin were utilised and these devices were gradually reduced as the material developed.

Fourthly, the heavy burden of grammar that was formerly handled openly with the pupils had not vanished completely, but overt grammatical drilling had been replaced by a 'programmed grammatical experience' in the reading passage.[2]

Morton, the chief author of the explanatory Bulletin No 1, stressed several differences between the Project's approach and the traditional Latin course. He emphasised the importance of the 'model sentences' which were placed at the beginning of each stage of the course which carried the new linguistic feature to be introduced. He stressed the need for pupils to read passages of Latin aloud, the use of accompanying techniques such as question and answer, and the use of supporting audio-tapes as reinforcement, all as a means of encouraging comprehension rather than grammatical analysis of a traditional kind. Morton continued: 'Grammar begins at the level of what the pupil observes, is confirmed by successful interpretation of meaning and only afterwards is organised into general statements'.[3] Teachers were also alerted to the fact that the conventional case labels had been replaced, temporarily, by literal designations; for example, Form A represented the nominative case, and Form B, the accusative.

Other unfamiliar features of the new course were 'manipulation exercises'. English-Latin composition was excluded from the course; manipulation exercises required the pupil to complete a sentence by selecting words from a given pool initially on the basis of sense. Selection on the basis of grammatical criteria was introduced gradually as the course progressed. Paralinguistic material was a term used to replace the traditional concept of 'background' to the linguistic study. Whereas Classics teachers had often regarded 'background' study as an optional extra to be treated if time allowed, the new terminology was coined to emphasise that the cultural context of the Latin learning materials was an integral part of the whole experience. The Project's linguistic objectives were defined clearly as: 'The development of materials and techniques which will accelerate and improve pupils' ability to read classical Latin literature and widen their knowledge of classical civilisation'.[4]

Members of the Advisory Panel were the first people to have a chance to react to the course as each stage of its development unfolded. Reactions to the new course proposals reflected the wide range of interests of the Panel members. For example, at the first meeting to take place in 1967, extensive discussion took place on four issues:[5]

1   Stabilisation of the word order in the early stages of Latin learning in order to reinforce the functional structure of basic sentence types.

2   Use of personal pronouns as a temporary measure when the first and second persons are introduced.

3   The absence of *macron* signs to mark long vowels in the pupils' texts; this matter had also been raised at an earlier meeting of the Panel in 1966.

4   The amount of linguistic ground to be covered during the first year of the course.[6] Some Panel members had commented at an even earlier meeting that the gradient of difficulty in the pupils' material might be too easy.[7]

The internal dispute

Reference was made earlier (p. 54 ff.) to the first methodological tensions between the Linguistic Consultant and the Project Director during 1966. What made matters more serious this time was that the Project had by mid-summer 1967 taken on major long-term commitments to sixty trial schools. For some months during that year it became apparent to those working full-time on the Cambridge Project that a major crisis was brewing over production. The original intention following the 1966 crisis had been that 'specific linguistic and methodological models' would be adopted by the end of December which would enable the team to base a year's material on them.[8] Advisory Panel members were informed in October of that year that there would be available by 31 December 1966, a 'reasonably complete schema of linguistic development over at least the first two years of a three year course' and that by then a framework of linguistic and methodological principles would have been worked out in substantial detail.[9]

Unit I was sent out to schools in time for the beginning of the autumn term 1967, although by that time difficulties in completing Unit II were acknowledged.[10] By March 1968, members of the Advisory Panel had to be told that it had not been possible to maintain the original rate of progress, the production timetable had to be revised and that more staff were needed to help with the task in hand.[11] A letter was sent in April to teachers in the trial schools urging them to 'moderate the pace' if they had already reached stages 18 or 19. The final stages of Unit II were at the printers and they could expect to receive the final stages of Unit III by the beginning of November.

To the Project team the production crisis was becoming all too apparent during the later months of 1967, but the crisis was discreetly concealed to avoid undermining the confidence of teachers in the trial schools. Few, if any, outside the Project team were aware of the position.

The year 1968 was to prove the most difficult in the full-time life of the Cambridge Project. The emergent crisis of 1967 dominated the work of the full-time Project team throughout the following year. By the end of 1967, the two Assistants to the Director who were employed to draft the pupil's material for the Latin course had become convinced that they were rapidly being sucked into an impossible situation. Their mood was one of extreme frustration. Production of the trial material was behind schedule and the increased complexities of writing a new course were becoming apparent. Despite this, the Project Committee, including the Chairman, was apparently oblivious of the situation. The large scale of the trial programme added to the difficulties.

Following the Christmas break, the Assistants to the Director decided to petition the Project Committee and to acquaint members with their position as they perceived it. One moonlit January night, when crisp snow covered the land surrounding the old rectory near Haverhill in which Professor Lloyd lived, a memorandum was delivered to the Chairman by some members of the team. The team members felt that their action in setting out the salient features of the impasse would bring matters out into the open and that the Committee would be forced to make a decision which would somehow resolve an increasingly difficult situation.[12]

Shortly afterwards the Project Committee met Morton and subsequently the rest of the team. The Committee made it clear that they fully supported their Director and the production programme. The only alternatives would be to close down the Project. It was made clear to Morton that all his colleagues must either be prepared to trim their unrealistic expectations or expect the Project to be terminated.[13]

By the time spring 1968 arrived, two important developments had taken place which Morton was able to use to bolster his position. Firstly there was the long-awaited outcome of negotiations with the Schools Council for fresh funding which would enable the Project to continue to August 1970 and thus (in theory) to honour its obligations to trial schools. There can be no doubt that the prospect of leaving these schools in the lurch was a powerful argument deployed by Morton in seeking to persuade the Schools Council to provide additional funding.

Secondly, successful negotiations had been concluded with the Southern Universities Joint Board (SUJB) to conduct a pilot GCE examination which reflected the aims of the newly developed Latin course. Earlier attempts to interest other examination boards, including the most obvious candidates, Cambridge Local and the Oxford and Cambridge Boards, during 1967 had met some resistance. The positive response from SUJB based at Bristol, therefore, came as a welcome relief, not only to the Project team. It would also be the cause for rejoicing among teachers who were now committed to the Project's trial programme. Despite these promising developments, the output of material was now at crisis point and Morton reported to the Project Committee that there would be a breakdown in production within four weeks.[14]

During a confused period in the lifetime of the Project when one resignation threat followed another, there can be little doubt that Morton's successful negotiations for further funding, and an appropriate GCE examination for the trial school pupils, helped strengthen the resolve of the Committee to back their Director in his attempts to speed up production rates and bring the Project back on schedule.[15] Despite this, the crisis was not resolved for many months and in fact rumbled on until early 1969. Morton sought the assistance of the Project Committee in his attempts to establish production schedules which would meet the requirements of trial schools.

In his dealings with members of the Project team Morton deployed both the 'carrot' and the 'stick'. During May 1968 positive steps were taken by Morton to respond to a request by the Linguistic Consultant for a renegotiated agreement, in consultation with his Head of Department, David Balme. As a result of the award of further funding, the way was also clear for extending the contracts of the two Assistants to the Director who formed the linguistic writing team and the Linguistic Consultant beyond 1968. In addition, the prospect of further funding meant that it was possible to go ahead with a further full-time appointment on the linguistic side from September 1968.

At the same time it appears that Morton made it known to Wilkins during May that the situation within the Project had been reported by a member of the Committee to the Faculty Board of Classics. 'Discreet consultations' were said to have taken place with the Project's financial sponsors the Nuffield Foundation and the Schools Council, and Morton had declared his intention of letting both Wilkins and his Head of Department know that in the event of any further serious challenge to the Director and the Committee over matters of policy, time schedules etc., the Project would be wound up quickly and no more exhausting efforts made to save it.[16]

In order to understand why, despite Morton's strenuous endeavours to speed up production, the trial programme was brought to a near standstill, it is necessary to return to the position of the Linguistic Consultant vis à vis the writing team.

During 1967 an important change had taken place in the relationship between the writing team and the Linguistic Consultant. The latter came to spend more and more time in Cambridge in order to work more closely with the writers. Following the 1966 crisis the Director had tried to insist to the Committee that the Linguistic Consultant's advice should always be communicated in the first instance to himself. The Consultant should not at any time give instruction to or press advice on his assistant staff. Wilkins, he insisted, was to accept deadlines which he as Director prescribed. In saying this, the Director was attempting to clarify the 'chain of command' within the Project. As he saw it, the Committee had structured the Project in a particular way. The Linguistic Consultant was there to offer advice (which would be accepted or rejected), not to try to control policy within the Project.[17]

By the end of 1967, however, it appears that the Director had come to accept that a close working relationship between the two writers and the Linguistic Consultant was necessary and without it further progress with new material would be impossible. The two writers and Wilkins came to enjoy a very close working relationship during the later stages of 1967 in which there was extensive and detailed discussion about the linguistic input for each stage of the material as they reached it.

The early stages of what was to become Unit II were developed reasonably smoothly. The new location for the story material was Roman Britain and this gave fresh impetus to the writers. The author Martin Forrest, who had a particular interest in Romano-British archaeology, contributed to this area by researching some of the prosopographic and archaeological possibilities for linking up the storyline of Unit I with the 'distant Britons'. Historical characters like C. Salvius Liberalis and others whose inscriptions have been found in Britain, such as the legionary soldier Modestus and the *haruspex* Memor, provided inspiration for some lively and imaginative story writing. An important contribution to the quality of the content of the Latin course had always been the contacts established and maintained for a period of time with specialist scholars. For example, Dr M.W. Fredriksen had been extremely helpful during the formative stages of Unit I in the early part of 1966. Such contacts constituted a major stimulus to the writing team. In 1967, the three Assistants to the Director travelled to Southampton in order to discuss with Professor Barry Cunliffe how they might take account of his recent archaeological discoveries at Fishbourne whilst they were writing Stages 15 and 16 of Unit II. The team members were able to hear at first hand details of the work undertaken and to receive from Professor Cunliffe dyeline drawings showing a proposed reconstruction of the Fishbourne Palace which would be helpful to the Project's artists. Many other scholars generously gave their time: in Cambridge, Dr M.H. Braüde advised on the wearing of the toga, Miss Joan Liversidge loaned the proofs of a forthcoming book, *Britain in the Roman Empire*. Miss Joyce Reynolds and Mr A.G. Woodhead advised on epigraphic sources.

For a time, steady progress was maintained on the linguistic front, with the writing team grappling with the increase in complexity. However, the rate of progress was insufficient to keep up with the demands of schools.

In April 1968, in an effort to speed up production, the Director issued a memorandum to the Project Committee and staff of the Project in which he sought to solve the existing problems and set out a proposed production schedule which would, if followed, meet the needs of schools. He rejected any suggestion that the existing 'rolling programme' should be broken off and existing trial pupils abandoned; in this rejection, he had the support of the Project Committee. The Director's view was that present difficulties arose mainly from the problem of producing material of 'sufficient quantity and quality'; he pointed to differences of opinion about what should be the appropriate remedy in the short and long term.

According to the Director's memorandum, delays in production were now said to be so serious that several measures needed to be applied at the same time.[18] These included (1) economising in the quantity of material for each stage by reducing the number of pages in some cases and by reducing the amount of paralinguistic material; (2) restricting research into the cultural and historical validity of the content to what was possible in the limited time available; (3) accepting a tightly defined timetable for the production of each pair of stages with a proposal to 'guillotine' the production where necessary in order to meet deadlines. Those schools whose Latin course began at 13+ were on a three-year course to GCE 'O' level and could not reasonably be asked to slow down by very much; their needs were to be separately considered. A schedule set out the dates by which each pair of stages would be written, up to and including Stages 31–32, which would complete Unit III by 23 July and continuing to the production of the first pamphlet of Unit IV by 3 September. In addition supporting materials were listed, including posters, slides, tapes and the handbook for Unit III which would be written concurrently with the stages. The schedule allowed three weeks holiday for each team member but was described as 'austere' with scope for modification being 'extremely small'.[19]

The proposed schedules were discussed at a meeting of the Committee on 26 April 1968 at which Dr Wilkins was in attendance. To judge from the minutes of that meeting a positive approach to the future was adopted by all concerned. Additional grants to the Project of £43,745 were reported. This included £11,000 from Nuffield which complemented the Schools Council's funding. A revised schedule was approved by the Committee, which it was hoped the Project could keep to and which would also reduce the inconvenience to schools to a minimum.[20] The revised schedule differed significantly from that drafted by Morton on 1 April. The deadline for completion of Unit III had become 15 November 1968, 23 May 1969 for Unit IV, 12 December for Unit V, and by the end of June 1970 Unit VI and ancillary material would have been prepared.[21]

The Project Committee minutes also show that plans were at this time put in hand to appoint an additional member of staff from 1 September 1968 to assist with production of the language material, to appoint an administrative assistant who would help expedite the production and distribution programme, and to issue renewed contracts for the two existing members of the writing team. The Linguistic Consultant's earlier concerns to have both travelling expenses and honorarium renegotiated were met and it was agreed to approach Queen Mary College about the possibility of extending his links with the Project from 1 October 1968. The issue of the Director's participation in the work of the Project after 31 December when his original three-year secondment was due to end was 'remitted for informal discussion'. As for the six schools following a three-year Latin course, the Director was to consult with colleagues about possible options.[22]

But storm clouds were soon gathering once more. Following the Committee meeting on 26 April, the two members of the Latin course writing team were formally requested to agree to the revised schedule. Morton's letter, sent on 30 April, made their agreement a condition of accepting the recently awarded grant.[23] Morton had also been instructed to draw up letters of contract for the two writers, Clary Greig and John Jones. In a letter to the Committee Chairman, Greig and Jones agreed to the schedule for the stages to the end of Unit II, but expressed in very strong terms their objection to more distant items in the timetable (Unit IV, V, and the ancillary items).[24] This letter to the Director reveals their deep unhappiness over publication of 'ancillary materials', in addition to the creation of each new stage of the language course. They felt unable to make any commitment to the future until a proper working relationship had been established within the Project. They had no guaranteed position to which they could return. They both had family commitments and they wished it to be known they intended to look for posts elsewhere. They concluded by stating that they desperately wished the Project to continue and desperately wished to stay with it.[25]

Greig and Jones were right in thinking that there was a crisis in Project leadership and they were right to feel less secure than some members of the team. The author (Martin Forrest) had recently been appointed to a post in Bristol and would be leaving his full-time project post at the end of August. As for the Director, it was by now clear that his presence would be required back at the University of Nottingham from 1 September

72

1968, since his temporary replacement had found a permanent post elsewhere. The successful outcome of a proposal to secure some timetable relief for Wilkins appears to have improved working relationships within the Project for a while. The Director reported to the Committee in October that Dr Wilkins was to be released for two days per week for his work in Cambridge from 1 October.[26]

The Director reported to the Committee meeting at which Dr Wilkins was also present, that despite the backlog in production, the team had been greatly helped by the resolution of policy difficulties and the arrival of a new team member (David Chandler, who was experienced in using the Project's materials in Queen Elizabeth's Grammar School, Carmarthen). A renewal of contract had been accepted by John Jones and was being prepared for Clary Greig. The difficulties of keeping schools supplied with trial materials was again referred to. Schools doing the three-year course would be helped by the offer of temporary bridging material written by Pat Story and Morton, consisting mainly of simplified selections of Pliny, from December 1968.

At the October meeting also, the future of the Project Director was discussed. The Committee took the view that the appointment of a new director from outside was not practicable and that the present Director should be invited to continue to give general supervision. He would make one visit to Cambridge per week during the first six months of 1969 and thereafter probably come on a fortnightly basis. The Director's first visit to the United States, aimed at disseminating the Project's work there during the summer of 1968, was postponed until a future date.[27] There was evidently some feeling among team members that this visit should not go ahead whilst a serious backlog in production remained.[28]

By mid-November 1968, there was a further eruption of the long-running difficulties between the Director of the Project and the Linguistic Consultant. This time it was to be the beginning of the end of Wilkins' long-standing relationship with the Project. By the end of that month, Wilkins had tendered his resignation and this time, after some exchanges of letters between members of the Committee, it was accepted.

At the heart of the disagreement between the Linguistic Consultant and the Project Director lay Wilkins' concern that his linguistic consultancy was being treated as a 'fringe "academic service"', when in reality he was now devoting an increasing share of his time to the Project.[29] This point had first been made to the Committee Chairman in May 1968 when Wilkins argued that the linguist should now be placed at the centre of the team that was creating the language course. It was inevitable, he concluded. that the linguist should form an integral working relationship with the Assistants to the Director, whereas the Director of the Project himself would be better employed, since he 'could not lay claim to having any specialist linguistic expertise', in administering the Project overall and maintaining good relations outside the Project.

This was in fact the main source of disagreement between the two men. Morton was not a specialist in linguistics but he always insisted on the importance of good school teaching experience and knowledge of what would work in the school classroom. This caused him to question Wilkins' linguistic formulations on pedagogical grounds. Greig and Jones on the other hand, who were also experienced teachers of school Classics, had a high regard for Wilkins and were eager to cooperate closely with him. For example, Morton challenged Wilkins' claim that it was possible to introduce structures of the '*est mihi*' type into both Si and Sii sentences at the same time. Whilst intellectually tidy and appealing, it presented difficulties for the pupils.[30] In the final exchange of letters, Wilkins set out in detail to Professor Lloyd an explanation for his resignation.[31] He continued with his plea for there to be a suspension of the production programme and included in his letter the following statements:

> I think we should all now agree that the haste with which the Classics Project was originally created, permitted all too little consideration of the likely research commitments . . . Full-time educationalist and writing staff were appointed with the brief of producing new teaching materials, public commitments were entered into, while the linguistic burden was relegated to a part-time consultancy. The application to the Schools Council for an extension afforded an opportunity to redress this imbalance, but no effort was made in this direction.'[32]

Morton commented in detail on Wilkins' letter by writing to Lloyd immediately. Morton's letter contradicted a number of points made by Wilkins. He fiercely repudiated Wilkins' contention that the Project would be best served by a period of intercalation: 'A major extension of time and funds has already been negotiated. The human tendency for one extension to lead to another must be restrained in practice'.[33]

To Morton it was doubtful whether production would ever be resumed after a period of intercalation. The new grant had been awarded for the 'express purpose of safeguarding the needs and interests of pupils who are at present using the Project's material'.[34] There can be no doubt that the patent risk of leaving trial school pupils in the lurch was a powerful determining factor when the Schools Council made their decision. There would be few schools willing to embark on a second trial programme having once been let down, public money would have been withdrawn and 'there would be no writers and no director!'.[35]

In a letter sent by Clary Greig and John Jones to the Committee

Chairman in a mood of profound frustration early in January 1969, a compromise solution was put forward.[36] Progress had been extremely slow during 1968 as a whole and they had currently been bogged down in writing Stage 26 for the past six weeks. They were now seemingly rudderless, with the Linguistic Consultant now gone and the Director only able to visit Cambridge on a part-time basis. They saw the cause of the breakdown as entirely 'linguistic', resulting from the departure of John Wilkins. They believed that neither they themselves nor the Director could resolve their difficulties. Indeed they were convinced that they lacked the competence to undertake detailed linguistic planning. They pointed out that there was now little hope of completing the remaining twenty language pamphlets in as many months, let alone the required handbooks, grammar and vocabulary pamphlets and ancillary materials such as slides and tapes. The likely increase in complexity of writing new language materials made this a totally unrealistic schedule. They also spelled out their belief that the quality of the material was now suffering as a result of economies being exercised within the Project. An example quoted was Stage 25 which had gone to press without the usual linguistic controls in the hope of increasing the speed of output. This pamphlet, ironically entitled *Pax*, did not in fact contain the usual 'practising the language' sections. The proposal contained in this letter was that the Project should identify two distinct objectives: firstly, the supply of material to trial schools; secondly, the creation of the 'Project course'.

The first of these objectives would involve accelerated production of material which would enable schools committed to the trial programme to take their pupils up to GCE. The Director had already 'ably demonstrated' that such material could be produced with 'facility and speed'.[37] Such an emergency programme, however, could not be regarded as a continuation of a course of the quality they had in mind and they suggested a parallel operation involving 'the creation of the Project course', treated as a separate objective. Further production of language material would be postponed, while adequate research under proper direction was carried out. Such a provision would involve a further extension of the Project beyond the finishing date of 1970, but they were convinced that this was the only way to achieve quality.

The rescue operation

Members of the Project Committee evidently had no intention of listening at this stage to compromise proposals of this kind. They adhered to the line previously enunciated, that the commitment to trial schools must be paramount. Those working for the Project must be prepared to stifle their feelings of disappointment and endeavour to boost production. Professor Lloyd wrote to Morton on 17 January 1969 in a letter which suggests the New Year had duly brought new resolution on the part of the Chairman and his fellow Committee members:

> My impression is that members of the committee will want to take a tough line with such members of your team as seem unable to cooperate with the Project and I expect that the committee will probably want to discuss with you a very firm line of action after the meeting.[38]

In a letter which appears to have crossed with that from the Chairman, Morton also declared himself to be keen to take firm action against recalcitrant colleagues. He reported that he had told them in writing of his expectations. As a basis for future action Morton proposed to develop the linguistic scheme for future stages himself and to discuss it with two classics dons who had close relations with the Project, Professor W.S. Allen, who was still a member of the Committee, and R.G.G. Coleman.

By May 1969, the Project had moved to new premises at 17 Panton Street, Cambridge. At this point Morton also chose to adopt a new strategy over the day-to-day direction of the Project. He had already given some hint of his intention in his letter to Lloyd written in January and referred to above.[39] Clary Greig was promoted to the role of leading the production team and in due course came to be known as 'Production Director'; he was soon said by the Director of the Project himself to be proving a 'tower of strength'.[40] John Jones on the other hand, who had been profoundly upset by Wilkins' departure, announced his intention of taking up a post elsewhere.[41] His place was taken in September by R. M. (Robin) Griffin, another trial school teacher from Crown Woods Comprehensive school in London and who like David Chandler had first hand experience of teaching the new course. The withdrawal of John Wilkins during the winter of 1968–9, this time for good, had undoubtedly left a huge vacuum in the design and day-to-day working of the Project.

The arrangement whereby the Director passed on his own linguistic formulations to busy members of the Faculty of Classics was unlikely to provide a suitable basis either for forward planning or for a permanent *modus operandi*. In addition the Project was by this time beset by enormous problems on the production front, and the criticisms of the Advisory Panel, previously voiced politely during formal sessions, were now becoming increasingly strident. The knowledge that Wilkins was no longer Linguistic Consultant opened up huge areas of doubt in the minds of several Panel members over the whole basis on which the course was being constructed. After the Panel's meeting in February 1969, the first salvo was fired by Cyril Peckett. Peckett wrote a letter to the Project Committee Chairman, Professor Lloyd, in March.[42]

Peckett's first complaint was that Wilkins had based his work for the

Figure 2. Members of the Project team at work in Cambridge in 1969 (from left to right, John Jones, Pat Story, Clary Greig, David Morton and David Chandler).

Project on linguistic 'hunches' rather than upon a computer analysis of Latin literature. As examples he referred to the 'misuse of *est*' and 'the too frequent and often grotesque use' of the dative of possession. Secondly, he complained about the slow pace of production. The original intention, he recalled, had been to produce seventy-two stages covering six terms in the first two years of Latin study.[43] The materials produced so far had failed to introduce grammatical patterns at a steady pace or in a systematic way. In Peckett's view, teachers in the trial schools were enthusiastic, but most did not know where they were going. They regarded the Project as something magical which would produce success for them if only they had faith. It seemed to Peckett that history was repeating itself; he saw in the Latin course trials the ingredients of the disaster which fell upon Rouse's direct method. The greater the teachers' enthusiasm, he wrote, the greater will be the disaster. He saw himself and A.R. Munday as having taken twenty years to rescue Rouse's work. He was concerned that a similar disaster should not recur and offered several pieces of advice. As he put it, 'For the sake of the Classics as a whole, the Project must not founder'.[44]

The second person to write to Professor Lloyd was Charles Baty. Spurred on as a result of a recent conversation with Peckett, Baty was undoubtedly deeply perturbed and appears to have been convinced by Peckett's arguments that something needed to be done with great urgency. He offered his support for a rescue operation to retrieve the Project and its Latin course from a dangerous situation.[45] He referred to Peckett's contention that the former Linguistic Consultant had 'made no proper analysis of the language': 'the Course . . . has no future unless someone takes it firmly in hand, with a clear awareness of where it is to lead and at what pace it is to advance'.[46] Baty gave his unqualified support to making the Director's position more tolerable and to making some drastic changes in the interests of tackling 'weaknesses of scholarship' and the 'slow pace of work'. Baty further emphasised that he felt the Advisory Panel had not been used to best effect hitherto and that properly used, they could have 'saved the course from many errors both of method and of scholarship'.[47] Baty referred to the part he himself had played in establishing the Project and felt doubly responsible for what had happened.

Professor Lloyd replied to both Peckett and Baty following close consultation with members of the Project Committee and with the Director in particular. In both replies, Lloyd was at pains to head off any attempt to press for an abandonment of the linguistic principles underlying the course. He referred to the Project's recently appointed Linguistic Consultant, Dr P.A.M. Seuren of the Department of Linguistics in the University, who was said to have a favourable view of the Project's course so far and to the evidence of viability that was emerging from schools.[48] Peckett's expressed view that what had been produced so far was 'not a course but a very good reader which could supplement other courses' was firmly rejected.[49] Whilst there were undoubtedly difficulties, the process of revision would be greatly enhanced by the 'valued contribution' of the Advisory Panel members. In the long term the Project Latin course would prove to be a 'somewhat larger achievement', Lloyd continued; 'We do not, however, wish to advise the Director to change the main linguistic hypotheses on which it has been constructed, and prefer that these should go forward to be fully tested by experience over the next few years'.[50]

A dinner party to be held in Cambridge at Peterhouse was proposed by the Chairman of the Committee on the evening before the next meeting of the Advisory Panel in May/June. The purpose of the dinner party was to enable Baty and Peckett to have some discussion with members of the Committee, the Director and Dr Seuren. Professor Balme was invited to join them as Chairman of the Advisory Panel.[51] In the event, Peckett was unable to attend the dinner party, but a meeting with Lloyd and Peckett was arranged to take place immediately before the Advisory Panel meeting. The dinner party was seen as 'tactically useful' in bringing together Baty and the new Project linguist. The exercise of securing the support of Baty was also seen as a 'useful preliminary' to countering Peckett's criticisms.[52] The strategy was clearly successful and went some way towards assuaging those who sought a change of linguistic approach. Following the Advisory Panel meeting, Peckett admitted to being impressed by Seuren and confessed to feeling 'a little less unhappy'.[53] Even before the dinner party took place, Baty showed signs of backing down:

> It may well be that I, for one, have been unduly troubled by much obviously unsound latinity, and disturbed by obvious personal incompatibility. And it is certainly true that I hear good reports of actual experiences in the schools in which Project material has been in use.[54]

One of Peckett's persistent complaints was that computer analysis should have been undertaken on the target literature. This was closely related to his concern that the synthetic material put too much emphasis on sentence patterns which did not frequently occur in original Latin. At the May/June Advisory Panel meeting, Peckett suggested that a computer count could be done relatively quickly and that the results should be incorporated in the revised material.[55] In fact computer analysis of the target literature was one of the areas that John Wilkins had hoped to investigate in detail. During the latter part of his time as Linguistic Consultant, he had secured access to a computer at the University of Essex. However, Dr Seuren, the new Project Linguistic Consultant, expressed the view that computer techniques had not yet advanced beyond the analysis of fairly simple linguistic data and that useful results, in terms of phrase and sentence structure, were not yet obtainable.[56] The Director reassured the Panel that when the new structural patterns were introduced careful sample checks were made in the literature to ascertain the most frequently occurring forms.[57]

Full involvement of the Advisory Panel in the revision of the Latin course materials proved to be a sound tactical move. At the Advisory Panel meeting held in February 1969, this constructive involvement was particularly important since it distracted members' attention away from the gravity of recent events. The full extent of the turmoil in the Project had been revealed to the Panel for the first time in the Director's report. At that meeting it was reported that Dr Wilkins had tendered his resignation at the end of the previous November. New arrangements entered into by the Committee had led to the two most experienced members of the writing team proposing to withdraw from the Project by the end of August 1969.[58]

As a distraction from the negative and depressing aspects of the Director's report, Panel members became absorbed in the preparation of reports on Unit II of the Latin course. The general recommendations of these 'revision groups' echoed what were by now familiar concerns:

1 The word order should be less stereotyped, particularly in relation to the verb 'to be'.
2 More use should be made of pronouns to reduce repetition of the noun.
3 *Macra* should be inserted in the text: most members wished to see these in the story passages as well as in the lists of words and phrases.
4 Traditional terms for noun cases should be adopted in place of the Project's 'A' form, 'B' form etc.

The last point was again the subject of unanimous approval at the May/June meeting of the Advisory Panel following receipt of a report that the trial school teachers had voted narrowly on the issue. In fact forty-eight voted 'for' with forty-eight against and five abstentions on a proposal to retain letters for the traditional cases.

At the May/June meeting members were invited to submit a note of those features of word order and latinity which they felt to be particularly doubtful. In a letter to the Chairman of the Project Committee dated 23 May 1969, the Director stressed the extent to which he, together with the Evaluation Officer, were taking account of the Advisory Panel's suggestions in their revision of the materials. Such attention to the wishes of the Advisory Panel members is confirmed in the Director's Report to the

Panel dated 31 May: 'When you see our proposals for the text, I am sure you will feel that the contribution of the Advisory Panel has been carefully considered and in many cases acted upon both in Unit 1 and Unit 2'.[59] The nature and extent of the rescue operation which he had planned as Director together with the assistance of the Evaluation Officer Pat Story was outlined for the benefit of the Panel members.[60]

There was altogether better news for Panel members at this next meeting. Morton reported that Greig had now decided to stay with the Project and had accepted an invitation from the Committee to supervise the daily running of the production team, although John Jones had persisted in his intention to withdraw from the full-time Project team in September. He was subsequently appointed to a teaching post in a Cambridgeshire primary school.

A gradual improvement in the production rate had taken place. At this point Stages 33 and 34 were seen as the final pamphlets of synthetic Latin in which there would be consolidation of what had preceded them, although Stage 32 could mark the end of the synthetic material if need be. The fourth booklet of supplementary material based on the letters of the younger Pliny and designed for pupils undertaking the three-year course had been despatched. These pupils would be taking their GCE examination in the summer of 1970. A first book of *Carmina Latina* had been produced by Pat Story and David Morton and would be despatched soon. Further booklets of poetry and prose were in preparation, whilst work on the handbook for Unit III was proceeding 'as quickly as other calls allow'.[61]

Public reaction to the new Latin course

Some early printed comments appeared in 1967, when a short article on the main Latin trial materials (published with the title *Quid Novi?*) was published in *Latin Teaching*. The author issued a disclaimer that this was 'in no sense a review', but rather a note intended to give members an idea of what was going on and also to wish the Project every success in its work.[62] Although some criticisms are evident in relation to errors of pronunciation on the language tape and to the English style in which the teacher's handbook had been written, the article is generally not unfriendly. The author is at pains to minimise the differences between the new course and the direct method. Referring to the section of the teachers' handbook contributed by Wilkins, the author commented that there was far less difference between the two methods than Classics teachers might have been feared or Wilkins perhaps thought. The basic difference was the removal of sentences from English into Latin and the learning of grammar by rote.[63]

The report of the 1968 Weekend Refresher Course held on 1 and

2 March, includes the first report of a demonstration lesson given by a teacher using the Cambridge Latin material. In a review of the lesson given by Miss Beachcroft of Berkhampsted School for Girls, the following comment reveals the doubts of at least one Association member: 'Interest was sustained by discussion of background and by varying the method of approach, but one could not help wondering if this interest could be sustained indefinitely in a course almost entirely devoted to translation'.[64]

The possibility that an oral or 'direct' method of learning Latin might ultimately give way to a new approach was entertained by the reporter who recorded events at the ARLT's 45th Summer School in 1968, held at Durham:

> most members of A.R.L.T. concede the possibility of other roads to reformation. Evidence of this flexibility was given by the inclusion among the guest lecturers of Mr D.J. Morton, Director of the Nuffield Research Project in Classics, whose explanation of the theory, aims and techniques of the reading course being developed at Cambridge helped dispel some misconceptions as to its nature, if not to remove all reservations as to its probable efficacy as an alternative to Direct Method.[65]

Reports on the weekend refresher courses held in the two years that followed, again suggest a reasonably positive response by those who attended.

The demonstration lessons in 1969 included not only the Project's linguistic material in use but also a Classical Studies lesson given by a teacher associated with the Project's non-linguistic developments. Much of the rest of the Saturday programme was devoted to hearing about and discussing the Project's work on both the Latin course and on the non-linguistic side. The report is again positive towards the Project, although some nagging doubts still remain about the Project's ability to deliver.

> In the discussion which followed, it was evident how excited teachers are with the work being done—it has provided a real shot in the arm for many—but there were reservations. The 'characteristic sentence structures' around which the course has been built will no doubt enable pupils to tackle certain authors with confidence, but will they be able to cope with verse, or Tacitus, or many others, without practically having to learn the language again? Miss Storey's [sic] measured replies to this and similar questions did much to soothe doubts.'[66]

At the 1970 Weekend Course, where the audience was broken up into about a dozen study groups, the Cambridge Project attracted larger numbers than any other group.[67]

A Classical Studies Foundation Course

At the time of Martin Forrest's appointment, it was expected that non-linguistic developments would be concerned with the CSE age range (14–16) on the one hand and foundation courses (which would precede the learning of Latin) on the other. It quickly became apparent that the most urgent need was to consider the needs of teachers facing reorganisation by helping them to establish the latter type of course, which would be aimed at the full ability range and which was intended to offer a contribution to general education at the junior end of the secondary school. Contacts were established early in 1967 with five schools. Two were grammar schools and three were comprehensive including one 11–14 junior high school.

Reference to these early contacts with schools, like that referred to in the previous chapter, give some insight into the feelings of Classics teachers as they sought to transform their subject in a comprehensive system of schooling. One of the comprehensive school teachers, Roger Frost of Bray's Grove Comprehensive School, Harlow, approached the Project with the following request:

> I thought I would write to you to find out if we could in any way help or more particularly be helped as I feel a great rethink is necessary about the place of Latin in the Comprehensive School and the method of teaching.
>
> At present we teach Latin to the top two streams in an 'eight-stream' entry school. This is done for the first three years. In the 4th and 5th years there are small groups. There is little prospect of teaching the subject to 'A' level.
>
> Projects such as the one you are concerned with are probably the only hope and this is why I am writing to you.[1]

This Classics teacher negotiated with his headteacher and obtained the necessary resources to introduce a classical foundation course to be taught entirely in English for all pupils in Year 1 in September 1967. He clearly saw this as an urgent priority. The decision was made to postpone the introduction of Latin to Year 2. He first corresponded with Forrest in April 1967, indicating his special interest in discussing the approach to be employed with groups of 'completely mixed ability' and from that point onwards detailed collaboration began.[2]

A second school, the Westwood High School, Leek, had introduced a non-linguistic Classical Studies course for the first time in September 1966, when the intake first became comprehensive. The new course was followed by all Year 1 pupils except the 'remedial' group and was taught in mixed ability classes. The school planned to continue with Classical Studies for all in Year 2 and to offer Latin or possibly Greek as an option in the third year. Three teachers, including the Head of the lower school, Miss J.S. (June) Wrathall, contributed to the teaching of Classics in the school. There was evidently contact also with the University of Birmingham School of Education. One of the Classics teachers wrote to the author in February 1967: 'From what I can gather, this approach to the Classics is fairly novel. Miss Wrathall spoke at a Midlands conference at Birmingham University last week and most of the people there were quite shattered to hear about the things that go on!'[3]

A third participant was an independent Roman Catholic boys' grammar school which was about to become a comprehensive school. The plan was for the school to change to voluntary aided status and be housed on a new site in Stevenage where there had recently been large-scale housing development. As early as February 1966, the Head of the Classics Department, John Murrell, wrote to the Project asking to be kept in touch with developments. Having explained the changing circumstances of his school he continued:

> I am, therefore, particularly interested in the Cambridge Project. We intend to pursue as vigorously as ever the traditional courses and also to provide a course in Classics for all those who do not study the Classical Languages. May I wish you success in your Project and say how important those of us who are faced with reorganisation consider it to be.[4]

Contacts with these three and two other schools had already been established before Forrest joined the Project; his task was therefore to strengthen the Project's link with schools. The five schools, in the event, were to provide a ready-made cluster of trial schools in autumn 1967, in which some materials for a Classical Studies foundation course could be given a preliminary test. Three of the schools were already reorganised as comprehensive schools or were in the process of transition. Two could expect to change in the near future. Teachers in the schools that had already been reorganised all accepted the view that Classical Studies for all should be the first priority for their schools and that the provision for Latin should take second place. Once the concept of a foundation course was in place, there was the expectation that some interest would be generated in learning the Latin language, perhaps even Greek. The two other schools were still unreorganised and the intake in both schools remained a selective one; but in each case the Classics staff were interested in introducing a Classical Studies foundation course for all in anticipation of reorganisation.

The newly appointed Head of Classics at Westwood High School, Nigel Slater, had deliberately moved from his traditional grammar school to promotion as head of a department within a new comprehensive school which offered strong support and considerable potential for Classics.[5] It soon became apparent that for teachers who were facing a period of rapid and intensive change in their schools, the publication of guidelines or handbooks of ideas would simply not suffice. There was an acute dearth of suitable material on the market which was attractively presented and suitable for a wide range of ability. Whilst it was possible to suggest class libraries of books drawn from a wide variety of publishers, it appeared to Forrest that there was a clear need for resource packs of individual items which could be shared by a number of pupils at one and the same time.

All the teachers in these schools had responded positively to a proposal that they should adopt what came to be known as a 'story-centred' approach. A variety of 'response activities' could be explored. Although there was an expectation that much of the response would be creative activity, including non-verbal forms as well as the written and spoken word, books and other resources for the pupils to investigate were regarded as essential.

Forrest's own experience of using '*Jackdaws*' which he adapted himself for secondary school History teaching had convinced him that resource packs containing photographs, line drawings and written texts could provide resources in a highly convenient format. By focusing on certain topics, it would be possible to prepare purpose-made packs of material suitable for the very wide range of ability that was now to be found in some reorganised schools. Furthermore, resource packs could involve investigative approaches to the classical world. The provision of work cards or work sheets, sometimes in multiple copies, could assist teachers in initiating group activities.

A series of mock-up folders was produced on a small scale for trial in the first group of associated schools. Black and white and colour photographs, line drawings and sheets of written text were mass produced, from the Project's own resources, for use in schools from September 1967. The Project's electric ink duplicator and picture scanner were fully stretched for many days on end. Feedback from the trial schools was enthusiastic, although the appearance of the materials produced by the Project was sometimes indifferent. It was the concept of resource packs which won general approval, as a means of assisting teachers of Classical Studies to get their new course off to a good start. Plans were therefore laid for a larger-scale trial which would employ a professional illustrator and a commercial publisher and aim at dissemination of a more professionally produced article in the autumn of 1968. An agreement had been concluded between the Project Committee and Cambridge University Press to publish the Project's teaching materials in Latin, but this did not prevent initial exploratory talks taking place with other publishing houses about the non-linguistic materials. Thomas Neurath of Thames and Hudson showed considerable interest in what the Project was trying to do and provided valuable assistance in the form of illustrative material, especially coloured photographs.[6]

An investigation into the attitudes of pupils undertaking the school trials was carried out by a Classics teacher, Brian Middlebrook, who was at that time studying at the Cambridge Institute of Education. His conclusions were that the project had generally been well received by pupils in the trial schools. However, it was stressed that for the course to have maximum chance of success, the school administration and the teacher in the classroom must be fully committed to the ideals, aims and teaching procedures of the course as outlined in the teacher's handbook.[7] It was important to have ample space for drama, plenty of working and storage space, and if possible a sink. The allocation of a double period on the timetable was also seen as highly desirable. The teacher was faced with the tasks of considering how to organise the class for group work, providing a wide variety of follow-up activities and careful planning of resource-based learning. The report of this investigation appeared to indicate (among other things) the need for considerable in-service training. A further point emphasised as a result of the investigation was the expression of some doubts as to whether the course was making provision for the needs of more able pupils.

Large-scale school trials of four initial folders of material on the ancient Greeks and a teacher's handbook began in September 1968. The number of trial schools expanded dramatically to sixty. Within a short period of time, this number had risen to over one hundred and the Project had to make arrangements for a reprint. Many of these schools had written to the Project seeking help with the introduction of a Classical Studies foundation course in the 11–13 age range. In a few cases, schools intended to use the materials with an older age group. The Project itself published the trial materials but the combination of a commercial printer, good quality photographic originals and a professional illustrator, Eric Thomas, ensured that schools could draw upon materials that were at the same time innovative and competently produced. As in the case of the Latin course, Cambridge classical dons generously provided advice: Dr F.H. Stubbings on the background to the Homeric poems, Mr J.S. Morrison on Greek ships, and others on particular points of detail.

An analysis of the schools which took part in the main non-linguistic trial reveals that the majority were maintained or voluntary secondary schools which were reorganised already along comprehensive lines or might expect to undergo reorganisation in the near future. These were the schools where help was most urgently needed and for which the Project was able to provide some support. The Project willingly supplied trial materials to all those teachers who wrote in requesting assistance from the late summer of 1968. Remarkably little interest was kindled among Classics teachers in preparatory schools. In general, however, it would seem that preparatory school Classics teachers were more concerned with the requirements of the Common Entrance Latin examination than with the possibility of a broadly based foundation in general Classics through English, which might among other things whet the appetites of potential students.

A notable exception was Malcolm Young, who was in charge of Classics in Westminster Under School, who not only became firmly convinced of the value of a Classical Studies course for his boys before they started Latin, but also went on to make an important contribution to the development of non-linguistic courses generally. A number of independent secondary schools, however, did feature in the Project's list of trial schools. As the possibility of integrating independent schools within the state system increased (arising from the recommendations of the Public Schools Commission) some Classics teachers in the independent sector had their eyes on the implications for Classics in their schools in such circumstances. The concept of a Classical Studies foundation course preceding the learning of Latin was seen by some teachers as an important way of stimulating interest in Classics at an early age.

As early as March 1967, it had been realised that the two-year appointment of a single person to develop the non-linguistic side of the Project's work was grossly inadequate if the needs of schools were to be met. The need to extend this part of the Project's work was identified as 'desirable' in a report from the Director which argued also for an extension to the linguistic staffing and to the evaluation.

The proposal for supplementary funding which was submitted to the Schools Council (p. 68) was prioritised by Morton in the form of a series of options. Of these options the most optimistic was the appointment of a second team member to share with Forrest work on the non-linguistic developments until 31 August 1970. The worst option was that the non-linguistic side of the Project would be cancelled at the end of December 1968 and future funding be concentrated on the linguistic programme.[8]

In the event, the Schools Council awarded the Project a further grant. The non-linguistic side of the Project would thus have the necessary funds to continue, although no further expansion of personnel could be expected. In the meantime Forrest, in the expectation of the most pessimistic outcome of the Project's application, had applied for and been offered a post at St Matthias College of Education in Bristol. It was therefore proposed that the non-linguistic side of the Project's work should be transferred to Bristol and that that part of the extension grant allocated to non-linguistic developments (£6,250) should be used to support the continuation of this programme. Instead of advertising for new personnel to continue this part of the Project's work, Forrest would be asked to continue to work for the Project in his own time.[9] The Project Committee agreed that outstanding work should be completed and that teacher contact should be maintained with a view to revising the materials for publication. This decision paved the way for establishing an advisory group of trial school teachers, the Teachers' Advisory Group (TAG). Teachers appointed were all strongly committed to the Project's approach and this ensured a smooth transition from the trial stage through to final publication.

The production and widespread distribution, to schools stretching from Stornoway to Penzance, of trial teaching materials was one way of ensuring that the Project's approach was disseminated well before the final publishing stage, and there were many schools seeking urgent help. A second way of disseminating the Project's ideas was to respond readily to all requests received from a variety of agencies concerned with in-service education and training. The Project was able to sponsor only one conference of its own in connection with the non-linguistic side of its programme while Forrest was employed full-time at Cambridge. This conference, held in early January 1968 at Churchill College, Cambridge, included opportunities for Classics teachers to explore some Greek legends through drama. From 1968 onwards Forrest was involved in a steady stream of one-day events and short in-service courses in many parts of the United Kingdom.[10] There was a variety of sponsors: the Department of Education and Science, university Education and Classics departments and a number of Classical organisations arranging meetings at national and local level. The number of sponsoring LEAs was surprisingly small.

It may be useful also to consider the different kinds of course on offer. In some cases the occasion was confined to the formal lecture in which progress on the non-linguistic side of the Project could be described together with some opportunity for questions and discussion. On other occasions, teachers who had hitherto little experience of teaching anything other than traditional Classics were given the chance to gain some experience at first hand of activities which might arise from story-telling: art and craft activities, drama, movement and music-making. The experience of primary teachers was seen as being particularly relevant to the needs of secondary Classics specialists as they sought to develop cross-curricular approaches to their subject.

Attendance at all these in-service events during the later 1960s was encouraging. The contribution of David Morton and Martin Forrest to a conference organised at Beatrice Webb House by the London Association of Classical Teachers in December 1967 was described in positive terms in a conference report. This was later felt to be worth reprinting.[11] There were also reports in *Latin Teaching* of developments on the non-linguistic side of the Project.[12] Interest was shown by Independent Television in the Project's story-centred approach and a series of ten fully networked broadcasts entitled *Heritage* was transmitted to schools during the spring term 1969.[13]

CHAPTER SEVEN

The Cambridge School Classics Project in a Period of Educational Change

Among Classics teachers there were some for whom comprehensive reorganisation offered an unprecedented opportunity to transform their subject from its narrow linguistic base in the grammar school into a subject available to all pupils irrespective of ability. There were some in the past who had argued that the Classics form such an important element in our culture that they must be brought within the reach of all members of the community; but this aim had failed to become a reality under tripartism. Here at last was an opportunity to be seized by all who thought in this way. The climate of change in secondary education encouraged especially those Classics teachers who were sympathetic to the comprehensive philosophy, to strive to ensure that Classics in its transformed state played a full part in the new age that was dawning. Classics for all, followed by a classical language for those who elected to study it, would ensure that the subject could contribute fully to the school curriculum in a way that had not previously been possible. Moreover, it seemed to eliminate the embarrassing and indefensible problem of drop-outs from compulsory Latin.

Along with the changes that were introduced into school Classics teaching in the 1960s went a spirit of optimism and idealism that transcended some of the mundane realities of school and classroom life. As one former comprehensive school classicist recently remarked, 'bliss was it in that dawn to be alive'. It was believed by those in the van of reform that Classics for all in Years 1 and/or 2 of the secondary school would generate a vigorous demand for optional classical language study, and in a number of trial schools this was in practice what happened.

It seems likely that the need for Classics teachers to address the comprehensive age was, at least for some, sustained by the hope that the new Cambridge Latin language course would be able to provide a

90

worthwhile linguistic experience for a much wider clientele than anything previously written. It is significant that despite the vigorous arguments that persisted throughout the Project's full-time existence, none of the team members has ever sought to abandon the principles upon which the Latin course had been founded.

Seldom was the voice of dissent heard in the land during these early years. Strongly held views about the new Classics there undoubtedly were. No doubt many simply preferred to wait and see. One exception was T.W. Melluish (see p. 62) who continued to castigate the new developments in the teaching of Classics and to preach the continuing virtues of prose composition. Melluish, who retired from teaching in 1967, was not afraid to go public with his views on comprehensive reorganisation, politicians of the Left, directors of education and intransigent heads. A letter from Professor Lloyd-Jones to the *Times* in 1969 showed a similar eagerness to attack comprehensive reorganisation 'head on'.[1] There is evidence, from private correspondence, of some teachers who were minded to express their views publicly on the issue of reorganisation and who sought advice from JACT as to what strategy they should adopt. Advice from JACT to avoid publicly rocking the boat was, it seems, generally heeded and the plaintiffs remained silent.[2] Some must have left the profession, while others remained at their posts and carried on as if nothing had changed.

For most Classics teachers, however, the response was a pragmatic one. It appeared that comprehensive reorganisation was likely to come sooner or later and their subject must therefore adapt to changing circumstances or disappear from the curriculum. There was private acknowledgement that some reorganisation schemes might be disastrous for Classics or educationally unsound, but the wisest counsel was to press on with the strategy of Classical Studies for all in Years 1 and 2 followed by Latin.

Attempts at reforming the teaching of Classics since 1960 may be characterised as essentially 'top down'. The moves to establish JACT and the initiatives to create a Cambridge Project had been achieved through the endeavours of a small number of influential classical activists. Traditionalist opinions were effectively squeezed out on both occasions and the reformers won the day. With the exception of Melluish's two articles in *Latin Teaching*, it is difficult to find openly hostile reactions to the new developments in teaching Classics during the period of the Project's full-time existence. However, the witty and satirical *agon* in the style of an Athenian Old Comedy presented by the Director of the Nuffield foundation, Brian Young, to the AGM of JACT in May 1967, managed to encapsulate some of the traditionalist sentiments towards change.[3]

The moves which laid the foundations of reform in the second half of the decade also encouraged a new generation of activists who would speak up for reform of classical teaching in schools and who would disseminate the new thinking. The Schools Council Classics Committee, in common with JACT Council, was firmly controlled by individuals who favoured changes in school Classics teaching and both could be counted on to press for reform. As far as evidence of rank and file reactions is concerned, those teachers who volunteered or agreed to take part in the Project's trials were usually those who wanted change for one reason or another.

What has been described above relates primarily to teachers from the maintained sector who were in grammar or comprehensive schools, or in schools which were in a state of transition. However, the lists of schools undertaking the Cambridge Project's trial programmes include a number of independent secondary schools and a few preparatory schools. Teachers in independent schools, like their colleagues in maintained schools, had a vested interest in the production of a reformed Latin course. In their own schools they were by no means free from the pressures that arose from the changes in university requirements, although generally speaking the commitment to Classics in these schools remained strong. Looming in the background, however, was the possibility that independent schools, particularly direct grant grammar schools, would not escape any thorough-going plans on the part of the government to integrate them into the comprehensive system. There was therefore a strong incentive for innovative Classics teachers in independent schools to take part in the Project trials.

Crisis One had provided a spur to both independent and state schools alike to reform their approach to Latin. There was a need to make the Latin course to 'O' level more interesting and worthwhile (and perhaps to precede it with a Classical Studies course). The emphasis would be on reading for understanding and on exploring the social context of the Latin language. However, Crisis Two, which followed hard on the heels of Crisis One, caused a divergence of interests between teachers in independent schools and those in maintained schools. Crisis Two affected many schools in the state sector, where reform was now urgent if Classics was to survive. A Classical Studies foundation course was needed for all which was capable of interesting, informing and motivating pupils; a rapid Latin reading course was needed that could be studied within the hours now available for Latin. For the independent school teacher, however, the urgency seemed less great. This divergence is well illustrated by the fact that independent schools could often assume a study of Latin as beginning at 11 at the latest.[4]

As the 1960s drew to a close, the impetus for curriculum change was no longer confined to a small band of activists dedicated to transforming their subject. By now, there had emerged a substantial groundswell of support from Classics teachers for the initiatives taken first by JACT and then by the Project with JACT's support. The prospect of comprehensive reorganisation had acted as a catalytic force, concentrating the minds of Classics teachers. The editorial in *JACT Bulletin* 20 praised teachers for the enormous strides they had made within a comparatively short space of time.[5] In the state sector, there was much evidence not only of a willingness to follow the lead given by the Project, JACT and other agencies, but of teachers taking their own initiatives in the light of local circumstances.

Some thirty years earlier, the Spens Report had advocated courses of Classical Civilisation for all, together with a streamlined Latin course; these two reforms were now becoming a reality. On the other hand, despite the positive support for the 'new' Classics shown by JACT and the Schools Council's Classics Committee, the provision of in-service support at local level was extremely variable. In-service events were sponsored in the main by local branches of JACT (or the CA) or by a university or by both in collaboration. There were far too few LEAs which regarded Classics as a priority area.

CHAPTER EIGHT

Publication, Dissemination and Consolidation 1970–4

The political climate

A significant feature of the political scene in Britain in the late 1960s had been the losses of government-held seats in parliamentary by-elections. To a government originally elected with a majority of nearly one hundred, these defeats were unlikely to be felt as more than a glancing blow. A much more serious set-back for the Labour government of Harold Wilson were the local election disasters of 1968 and 1969. However, the government was still very much in power and there were other means by which its objectives might be pursued. From 1965, there had been calls for the government to make the nation's schools, including the independent sector, comprehensive by law.[1] After losing control of most LEAs, including the traditional Labour strongholds of Sheffield and Coventry, the Party Conference in 1969 unanimously voted that the Labour government should immediately enact legislation to implement the principle of comprehensive education.[2]

However, there had already been considerable movement towards reorganisation. In 1965 there had been only 262 comprehensive schools; by 1969 there were 900. The number of pupils attending comprehensive schools had increased during this period from 240,000 to 771,000, an increase from 8.6 per cent to 26.9 per cent of the total school population.[3]

Only eight LEAs had refused to submit reorganisation plans to Whitehall and nine others had had their proposals rejected.[4] The Public Schools Commission's *Second Report*, published in March 1970, recommended that the 178 direct grant grammar schools and independent day schools should be integrated into the comprehensive system, with further recommendations that negotiations for such integration should begin as soon as possible.[5]

Caroline Benn and Brian Simon's study *Half way There* was published

94

during the election campaign on 9 June 1970. This report surveyed the progress towards comprehensive reorganisation to date, and concluded that a much more aggressive approach was required. It called for legislation to push through comprehensive education for all 11–18 year olds.[6]

After 18 June, however, it was too late to expect the government to make a positive response to such a request, for a Conservative government under Edward Heath was now in place with a majority of thirty, and in the words of the *Times Guide to the House of Commons*, 'A new era had begun'.[7]

The incoming Secretary of State, Mrs Margaret Thatcher, was quick to withdraw *Circular 10/65* and made it clear that there would be a mixed system of all kinds of schools with us for many years to come.[8] She also gave a strong message of support for direct grant schools and for independent schools which she saw as safeguarding all children against a 'state monopoly' in education.[9]

It is now a matter of record that Margaret Thatcher presided over the implementation of more reorganisation schemes than any of her Labour predecessors, a fact that rankled with her own party activists and helps to explain the centralist approach adopted some years later by her own administrations towards local authorities. For a large number of LEAs which had already begun the process of reorganisation, there was no turning back, irrespective of local political control, and the move towards comprehensive reorganisation continued uninterrupted.[10] The need for Classics teachers to take account of the changes which were taking place in their schools was greater than ever before.

Under a Labour government direct grant and independent schools had been the subject of proposed radical changes in the Donnison Report; this report was now a dead duck. Teachers in these schools could be reassured by the words of the incoming Secretary of State at her Party's October Conference. They were no longer in danger of being forced into change by government actions. The *Times Educational Supplement* called it a 'reprieve'.[11]

Publicity and support for changes in school Classics

As the decade drew to a close, both JACT and the Schools Council Classics Committee had begun to adopt a more confident, less defensive, even an evangelistic stance in proclaiming the virtues of middle school Classics in their reformed state. This new air of confidence was first perceptible in 1969. What was on offer to pupils studying Classics in secondary schools had begun to look very different from the old-style Classics programme criticised by Brink in 1960. The publicity drive stemmed from three main sources: the Project itself, JACT, and the

Schools Council Classics Committee. Project personnel, in particular David Morton, had from early 1966 adopted a high-profile strategy as an integral part of the Project's curriculum development programme. The Schools Council Classics Committee had already published *An Approach Through Classics* in 1967 as a contribution to the discussion of Humanities programmes for the young school-leaver. The target audience of *Teaching Classics Today: a Progress Report* (Working Paper 23) was not only Classics teachers but also those with responsibility for planning the curricula of secondary schools. It was not intended as an *apologia* for Classics. Rather it was seen as a vehicle for outlining current curriculum developments and the changes that were taking place in the teaching of Classics in schools.[12]

An initiative of the JACT Committee at its March 1969 meeting had some swift and positive results. A press conference was called to which a principal contributor was David Morton, who gave an account of the Project's work.[13] The Committee also secured a favourable article from Dilys Powell and hoped for other contributions from prominent journalists.

'Classics cleansed of drudgery,' was the headline in the *Times Educational Supplement* in November 1969:

> The traditional methods of teaching the Classics—the endless learning of case endings, the grappling with sentence structures with rewards offered for a correct rendering of bonus-bona-bonum, are on the way out, thanks to a new and experimental way of teaching Latin and Greek.[14]

The Classics Committee of the Schools Council had agreed to encourage Classics in all types of school by stepping up of publicity to schools all over England and Wales. In this members were spurred on by the conclusions of a report prepared by Professor B.R. Rees of University College, Cardiff, on behalf of the Schools Council Classics Committee which noted: 'Change is clearly preceding comprehensive reorganisation, not necessarily in anticipation of it but sometimes producing developments which represent valuable opportunities for the subject before the arrival of reorganisation'.[15]

At the same time, the Committee sought other ways of publicising new developments. Two articles appeared in *Dialogue*, the Council's own organ which contained an account of the new developments generated by the Cambridge Project.[16] These built on an earlier article written about the Project in 1969 which had adopted as its title the motto of ARLT, *Tempora mutantur*.[17] A working party of the Classics Committee volunteered a contribution on the Classics for inclusion in a working paper on the middle years of schooling (8–13) which would be linked with the work of the 'middle school' curriculum project directed by Professor Alec Ross and based at the University of Lancaster. The committee was anxious that any consideration of the whole 8–13 curriculum should not omit Classics.[18]

The Cambridge Latin Course

The experimental phase of the Latin course eventually gave way to publication in the light of revision. The published course began to emerge gradually from the Cambridge University Press from 1970 onwards. Most of the original trial group of schools continued to use the course in either its experimental or in its published form and prepared their pupils for the Project's 'O' level examination. The first trial-school pupils, the very small group which had started the course at 13+ in 1967, sat their examination under the auspices of the SUJB in 1970; the percentage of pupils passing was very encouraging at 75 per cent.[19] Pupils from two much larger groups of schools were entered for the examination in 1971 and 1972. The published course was first reviewed for *Greece and Rome* in 1972 by the head of a Classics department in a direct grant grammar school, where the Project's materials had been used in their trial form. Further reviews of the material continued to show a generally friendly and sympathetic attitude towards the newly fledged course.

In the public presentation of the new thinking in classical teaching, a positive outlook was necessary; it was inevitable that the Project would adopt an energetic marketing approach in the dissemination of the new Latin courses. Both JACT, with its original involvement in the genesis of the Project, and the Schools Council Classics Committee, as a sponsor of the project, could be expected to stress the positive achievements of the Project during the relatively short time that it had been in existence. Despite the difficulties experienced by the Project in keeping trial schools supplied with a regular flow of materials, there was much evidence of goodwill. Progressive-minded classicists and pragmatists alike were desperately anxious that the Project should be successful. To the traditionally minded, the new course was a betrayal of a long and glorious tradition, but such criticism did not appear publicly in print in the late 1960s, at a time when everything appeared to depend on the Project's success and most teachers who were aware of the Project's existence were prepared to put their faith in the Project team.

The positive achievements of the Cambridge Latin Course (CLC) were stressed in all the reviews of the material which appeared in the educational press and classical journals. The task undertaken by the Project was recognised to have been 'enormous', but the effort was seen as more than justified by the results.[20]

At a discussion session held at the CA AGM in 1971 entitled: 'How is

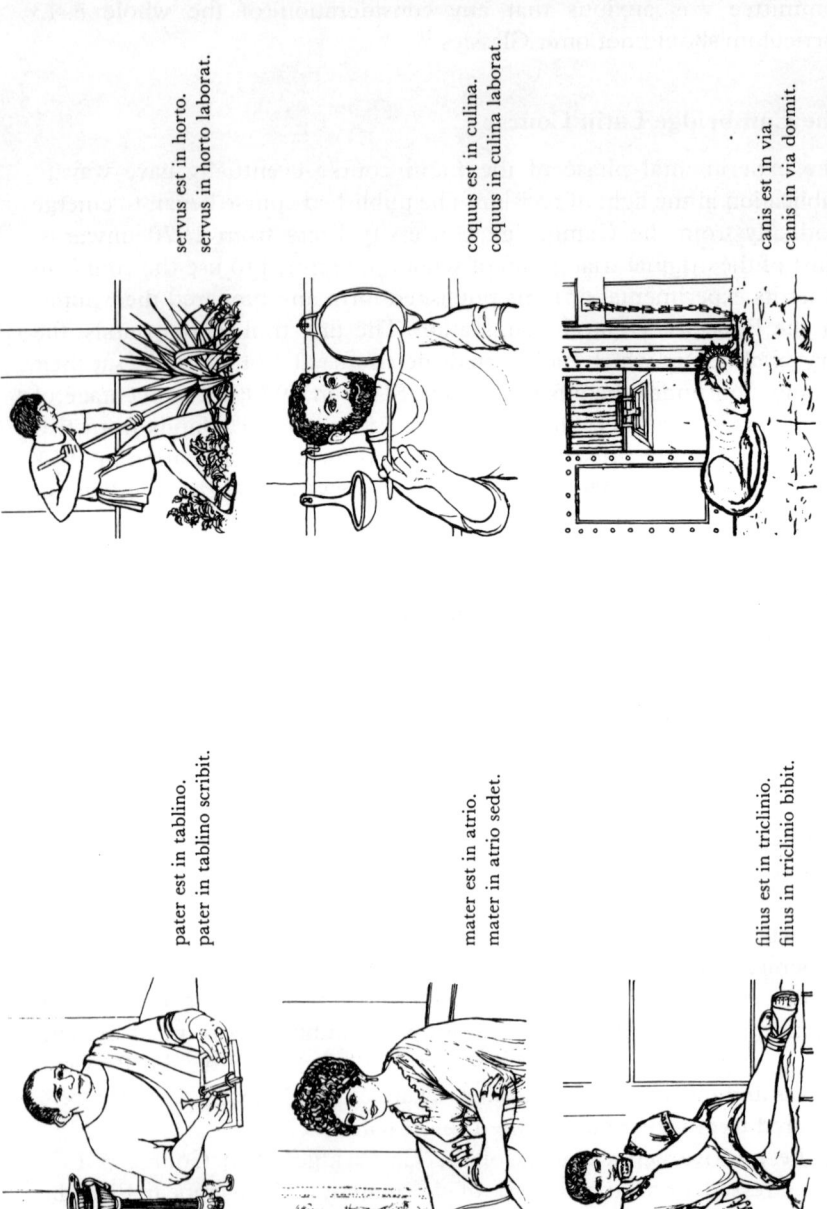

servus est in horto.
servus in horto laborat.

coquus est in culina.
coquus in culina laborat.

canis est in via.
canis in via dormit.

pater est in tablino.
pater in tablino scribit.

mater est in atrio.
mater in atrio sedet.

filius est in triclinio.
filius in triclinio bibit.

Figure 3. A double page spread from Unit 1 Stage 1 of the Cambridge Latin Course (First Edition 1970).

the CSCP linguistic course faring in schools?', pupils were said to enjoy the course greatly, were thoroughly interested and acquired confidence in reading Latin at an early stage.[21] 'Few of those who have used the Project material show any inclination to return to the traditional type of Latin course.'[22] From the early 1970s, however, criticism that had gradually been building up among those teachers who had taken part in the trials began to emerge in print.

In the words of Mr M. (Malcolm) Ricketts, a head of department at Manchester Grammar School, at that time a direct grant grammar school, and a strong supporter of the CLC, put it: 'Not unexpectedly, the first wave of enthusiasm for the course has given way to some doubts— and those not only among diehard traditionalists—particularly with regard to the treatment of formal grammar'.[23] The following points of criticism emerged publicly at the CA AGM discussion, chaired by Kenneth Todd HMI: the Project should not be regarded as having achieved all its objectives and criticism and revision were still needed; there was much less formal grammar than in the traditional course; formal grammar was reserved until too late in the course with the result that there was a sudden congestion at about Stages 30 and 31. Three years should be regarded as the absolute minimum for those beginning Latin at the age of 13+ and four years for those at 11+.[24]

Despite the criticisms of the Project for lack of formal grammar, it also had its loyal friends. A demonstration lesson at an ARLT conference provoked the following comment:

> for the benefit of those with traditionalist qualms about the Cambridge Project's approach to learning the linguistic material, I will record that the grasp of Latin shewn by this class seemed to me to be a good advertisement for the Project, for Mr Thorpe, or both.[25]

At the same refresher course, however, a number of reservations were also raised in the discussion group devoted to considering the CSCP course. These included anxiety over pupils' ability to make the transition to 'A' level and their level of accuracy in translating.[26]

Concern about the lack of formal grammar in the course was a constant preoccupation of reviewers: 'As always the theory of language teaching as set out is pretty persuasive, its practice is less successful; but any good teacher who has reached this stage will have had some ideas on how to supplement or reinforce grammar.'[27] The same reviewer commenting on Unit II at an earlier stage remarked: 'The handbook is less 'apotreptic' about grammar learning than in Unit I, but there could have been more emphasis on it in the actual material'.[28] There was an acknowledgement by the reviewer that some modifications had been made as the course progressed from the earlier stages, but he did not feel the modifications had been sufficient.

There were, in fact, two major criticisms of the course, conveniently summarised by Ricketts. Firstly, the assumption that the learner would gradually acquire personal competence in grammar by his or her own unaided efforts had proved to be too optimistic, and there was a feeling that teachers should make a positive effort to draw the attention of the class to essential morphology and syntax, whilst at the same time avoiding any serious slowing down of pace in the reading programme.[29]

The second criticism, regarded by Ricketts as more serious, was the concentration of new morphology and syntax in Unit III of the course, though there was a recognition that some attempt had been made to spread this more evenly in the published version.[30] Similar criticism had also been publicly voiced by a colleague of Ricketts speaking at the ARLT Summer School.[31]

The Project's strongly market-orientated approach in dissemination has been referred to above. It is understandable that those responsible for writing the materials should feel a strong commitment to their products, feeling them to be superior to any that had been previously produced. However, too aggressive a policy of 'hard sell', perceived by potential consumers as bordering on the intolerant, sometimes proved to be disastrously counterproductive. Clary Greig, who was closely identified with the development of the CLC materials and latterly served as Production Director, became well known for his fiery denunciation of traditional courses.

For example, Greig aimed some fierce polemic at Cyril Peckett for deliberately avoiding the cultural background in a language course (*Principia*) and at one of the authors of a widely used traditional Latin course *The Approach to Latin* for aiming at reading skill on a largely compositional base, where Greig commented: 'Nothing could be more absurd, nothing more inefficient'.[32] Stung by Greig's 'fusillade of pejorative words', E.G. Macnaughton, one of the two authors, vigorously counter-attacked. The advocacy of wholesale change couched in uncompromising language, urging teachers to reject many of the ideas and approaches with which they had been brought up, was not the kind of language designed to appeal to Classics teachers in the prevailing climate of the 1970s, particularly those who occupied the 'middle ground' and who might be persuaded but would not be railroaded into change.

N. Critchley provides a perceptive view of the attitudes of Classics teachers to curriculum change in this period:

> In between the conservatives and the reformers are very many who, while slightly repelled by the self-flagellation which sometimes marks the pronouncements of the latter, are uneasily aware that it is

hard to justify the present system as it affects the average pupil taking O Level Latin and then dropping the subject. Yet the proposals of the reformers often fail to carry conviction and I think it is worth considering why this should be so.[33]

Critchley went on to suggest the following reasons for this state of affairs. Firstly, there is a natural conservatism on the part of many Classics teachers who have themselves been educated in the traditional pattern. These teachers feel that they can give at least satisfactory service in educating others according to the same pattern and may be forgiven for doubting whether they would be capable of giving as good a service if the pattern were completely changed. Secondly, the proposals of reformers are often based on a 'somewhat unrealistic notion of what can reasonably be expected of pupils below the sixth form stage'.[34]

A former Classics teacher who held the post of Assistant Secretary to the Oxford Delegacy of Local Examinations, N.C. (Colin) Dexter, was invited to address the ARLT Summer School in 1973. Dexter (better known latterly as the creator of Inspector Morse) was also irritated by the advocates of radical change, and he was equally critical of teachers who had adopted the new approaches. He asserted his belief that: 'propaganda for the newer teaching methods has been over-shrill, and that some teachers have assumed that new ideas must necessarily replace old ideas instead of implementing them and complementing them.'[35] Dexter went on to deliver a strong attack on a number of recent trends in the teaching of Classics in schools. In particular, he attacked the CLC, using evidence from the latest available examiner's report with which to do so. He recognised the Project's important achievement in creating 'attractive and vigorous reading material capable of holding the interests of children more strongly than most, if not all, traditional material;[36] however, he saw the greatest weakness as the failure to give the learner very much in the way of grammatical and syntactical knowledge so necessary to under-standing languages so highly inflected and so highly complex as Latin and Greek. Success in the Project course at 'O' level, he argued, was no guarantee of a firm basis for 'A' level studies. For all the emphasis on rapid reading, 'Have we really, in the SCP, discovered a dramatic short cut to the summit of Olympus?'.[37]

Dexter's attack represents a bold statement of the traditionalist position, ranging over key areas of classical teaching. The objects of his attack were: the pruning of grammar to the fewest possible rules and paradigms, abandonment of separate grammar sections in the GCE, the concept of encouraging literary appreciation in pupils, the abandonment of English-Latin composition, the use of comprehension questions, and the increasing amount of additional material now read in translation at 'A' level.

The brute fact was that by the 1970s there was now generally less time available for the study of Latin than had previously been the case. It was now too late for any return to the traditional form of Latin course, particularly in the maintained sector. The same could be said of the independent sector too, although it was no longer overshadowed by Crisis Two. Since the inception of Crisis One a decade earlier, even the independent sector was not entirely protected from the changing climate of opinion and the high status traditionally enjoyed by Latin was being increasingly challenged. Many preparatory schools had already taken the opportunity to change their Latin curriculum. A new style Common Entrance Examination introduced in 1968, which had offered alternatives to prose composition, encouraged a Latin reading course approach in schools and a number had adopted the CLC.

Classics through the medium of English

The early 1970s are distinguished by three developments in non-linguistic courses. Firstly, there was the rapid and remarkable growth in Classical Civilisation courses through the medium of English at the lower end of the secondary school. This was to be contrasted with the comparatively slow development of examinable non-linguistic courses in the CSE. Secondly, came the revision, in the light of school trials, of the Project's foundation course materials and their dissemination. Thirdly, an epistemological debate began about the nature of Classical Studies courses through the medium of English.

For a new subject less than a decade old, Classical Studies had become widely established in secondary schools by the early 1970s. A survey of sixty-seven schools carried out by the London Association of Classical Teachers (LACT) in 1971 suggested that 42 per cent of them had some kind of foundation course.[38] A detailed survey carried out in 1973–4 by HMI, while showing widespread local variation, indicates that courses in Classical Studies were followed at 73 out of 309 comprehensive schools in a random sample.[39] The enquiry's findings suggest that Classical Studies as a separate subject was to be found overwhelmingly in the first two years of the secondary school, where it was taught to a substantial proportion of the pupils, if not to all of them, mainly in mixed ability groups.[40] The enquiry also revealed the continuing dominance of GCE 'O' level as an objective of the comparatively few courses in Classical Studies so far established in the upper classes of the secondary school.[41]

During this period, Martin Forrest was devoting a good deal of the time that he was not employed in initial teacher education, to monitoring the responses of schools in which the CSCP trial materials were being used. This included some visits to schools, but much of the work was carried out in conjunction with the Teachers' Advisory Group (TAG). For most of the time, this group consisted of four comprehensive school teachers (including two from schools which had recently been re-organised) together with one representative from a preparatory school. The TAG met regularly in Bristol at weekends from 1969 until all the revised foundation materials had been prepared for publication; the members of the group had all taken part in the 1967–8 trial programme and had mostly been involved also in the 1967 trials. Each of them was following a programme of his or her own devising, but was using the trial materials and closely following the story-centred approach as outlined in the teacher's handbook.

When the first batch of foundation material was ready for publication, some members of the TAG assisted in a major dissemination conference held at the College of St. Matthias in Bristol and attended by more than fifty teachers from a wide geographical area. Members of the group also became involved in in-service activities in various parts of the country during the early 1970s.

The Project's foundation course folders received a favourable press. Reviewers welcomed the fact that, for the first time, materials had arrived on the market which were designed for use in Classical Studies courses with mixed ability groups.[42]

In the early 1970s, the whole concept of Classical Studies foundation courses came under critical scrutiny from classicists themselves. The debate over the nature and purpose of such courses was fuelled from a number of quarters. Clary Greig, who had left the Project in 1970 and returned to full-time teaching, this time in a Norwich comprehensive school, challenged the unquestioning way in which many schools had taken up and developed the idea of Classical Studies through the medium of English as a survival strategy for their subject, with scant thought for what the appropriate rationale might be for a non-linguistic course offered to a wide range of ability. He stigmatised CSE Classical Studies courses as having all the characteristics of 'Robinson Crusoe's raft'.[43] Classical Studies courses had been useful in helping Classics to remain afloat in comprehensive schools and had a greatly enhanced potential for offering the subject to a greatly expanded clientele, but now the time had come for frank discussion of the part played by Classics in the school curriculum.

Differing views over aims and objectives were also evident in the Project's foundation course handbook, which included accounts from all members of the TAG of the way in which they saw Classical Studies within the curriculum of their own schools. Sometimes the emphasis was upon creative activity; sometimes there was a tendency to stress the importance of children acquiring knowledge about the ancient world.

Stephen Sharp wrote a very positive account of the part that Classical Studies had come to play in his school curriculum at Dinnington High

School in South Yorkshire. He began by taking issue with some currently held views:

> For a number of years, JACT has offered to the nation's panicking classicists a solidarity which has, in my opinion, hindered frank discussion of the part Classics should play in our schools. I give the boat a gentle rock at this stage because, since the result of the 1970 election halted many reorganisation plans, I suspect that many of us have breathed a sigh of relief that we shall not, after all, have to pretend that we welcome change.[44]

The widespread reorganisation of the 1960s had provided a fine opportunity for Classics to contribute more widely to the curriculum. But Sharp felt that in many cases, to judge from reactions in teachers' meetings up and down the country, Classics teachers had simply constructed impregnable defences on undisputed territory. Too little evidence had been shown of an urgent desire to use Classics in the education of children. Sharp suggested that classicists felt the storm had been weathered, but in his view the improved courses which had been produced were mostly for an academic elite. JACT Ancient History and Cambridge Latin were, he believed, only marginally relevant to his school. Sharp went on to explain in some detail the contribution that Classical Studies was now making to general education in his school's core curriculum.

The school was an 11–18 comprehensive school with 2,000 pupils, situated in a community which was part dormitory, part agricultural but centred on a mining village. The particular story-centred course in Sharp's school had been devised for the whole ability range with a view to developing skills; it firmly emphasised the general contribution (as opposed to the specifically classical) that Classical Studies might make to education. Cognitive skills included the need to comprehend the stories and to learn to articulate opinions and emotions and to sustain sensible discussion. But there was a strong emphasis upon the affective also: pupils learnt to cooperate with other children of different abilities and temperaments in the production of group assignments.[45]

The course was mainly based upon Greek content with the first year of the course built around the stories of Troy and Odysseus, whilst Year 2 moved to Greek drama and stories from classical Greece. Throughout his description of the course, Sharp emphasised that the development of certain skills was much more important than the 'learning of facts'.[46] He preferred to avoid the term 'foundation course' in that it led many to use the time as a foundation for Latin in the later years rather than a course which was valuable in its own right.[47]

Sharwood Smith, in his discussion of Classical Studies foundation courses, drew a distinction between education *through* Classics and education *in* Classics.[48] The Dinnington course clearly fell into the category of education *through* Classics. Among the teachers in the Project's trial schools there was a general consensus in favour of combining both education in and education through Classics. Most Classics teachers would appear to have seen the former as being of paramount importance. However, their non-specialist colleagues may have inclined more to education through Classics rather than education in Classics. There was wide variation, ranging from schools which emphasised the development of skills and attitudes to the virtual exclusion of specific knowledge about the classical world, to those schools which consciously placed most of the emphasis upon the acquisition of knowledge about Greece and Rome.

An example of education in Classics is described in two articles by Hollinghurst, published in *Latin Teaching*.[49] Hollinghurst's comprehensive school used the Project's trial material. He developed his own story-centred approach using content ranging from prehistoric Crete to Roman Britain, and he became a keen advocate of the new part that Classics should play in the general education of all. In contrast with Sharp, Hollinghurst stressed the uniqueness of classical content and the importance of pupils having an appreciation of the ancient world, in view of the heritage we have derived from it. He saw some form of classical education as 'essential for a real understanding of our languages, literature, history and thought'. He also allied himself with other progressives, seeing comprehensive reorganisation as an opportunity for developing Classical Studies rather than as a recipe for its decline: 'Classics teachers until recently have been too much concerned with imparting their treasures to an elite. Now compelled to widen their appeal, there are opportunities for teaching the complete range of ability'.[50]

Dissemination of the Project's work

During this period both JACT and the Schools Council Classics Committee were major disseminators of curriculum change. JACT's interest in the twin Project developments of a Latin reading course for the middle secondary school and a Classical Studies foundation course, found practical expression in its continuing efforts to disseminate new thinking in Classics teaching and to seek opportunities for fresh developments which might sustain the cause of Classics and support teachers in schools:

> the campaign . . . to secure a place in British Education for the study of Greece and Rome is scarcely begun. Certain things have

been lost . . . But it is not mere bravado to say that these losses are compensated by the new versatility and range of Classics courses, and by the remarkable adaptability and tenacity shown by Classics teachers in facing their difficulties.[51]

The Schools Council Classics Committee's role in the early 1970s became much more of a proactive one than had been the case in the Council's early days. It had a considerable overlap in membership with JACT Council and also with the Project's Advisory Panel. Under the leadership of John Dancy, members of the Committee agreed to engage in critical reflection on their role, rather than simply reacting to the plethora of papers presented to them by the central Schools Council committees. By this stage the initial burst of curriculum innovation had taken place and the most immediate needs of schools undergoing reorganisation had been met.

Comprehensive school Classics on the map

By 1971, the number of comprehensive schools was showing a steady increase, though the pattern across the country varied greatly. In Staffordshire, for example, there were by now sixteen grammar schools, twenty comprehensive schools and fifty secondary modern schools. JACT took the important and unprecedented step of choosing as its President Miss Muriel Telford, the Head of a comprehensive school, Westwood High School in Leek. Muriel Telford was not a classicist herself, but she had given strong support to the curriculum development that had taken place in the Classics Department of her school. Westwood had been an early pioneer of Classical Studies, providing a foundation course for all pupils including the 'remedial classes' and had been closely associated with the Cambridge Project since early in 1967. Some Greek was taught in the school as well as the CLC and the Classics were generally flourishing. Not surprisingly, therefore, Miss Telford was regarded by her sponsors as 'an embodiment of various desirable qualities in a president of JACT'.[52] The appointment of Miss Telford was seen as tactically important, and there was a deliberate effort by the JACT Council itself to ensure that the media education correspondents, including a representative of the *Times Educational Supplement*, were present when the new President's inaugural address was delivered at the AGM.

Miss Telford did not disappoint: her commitment to Classics for all in a comprehensive school was clear and unwavering. She agreed with her classical colleagues that the Classics must not be divisive, but unifying. She went on to describe the role that non-linguistic Classical Studies was making to the general education of slow learners in her school, and she described her joy on hearing a 'problem child of a problem family, maladjusted, IQ about 80, say "My favourite subject is Classics"'.[53]

In-service training courses for teachers

The Cambridge School Classics Project, in common with other early Nuffield and Schools Council funded projects, had no built-in financial element to assist it with dissemination and teacher training. Indeed, the Schools Council's own original constitution did not even include teacher training. The Project saw that in-service training was crucial for teachers participating in the school trials, or using the materials in their published form. Clearly, in dealing with a new language course which departed to such an extent from traditional courses, such training assumed especial importance. Consequently a great deal of in-service training was directly generated by the Project itself but this training had to be financially self-supporting. The first major trial of the CLC was launched with an in-service course held at Cambridge in the summer of 1967, at which all trial schools were expected to be represented. A small conference of early trial schools was also held in conjunction with the Project's Classical Studies developments in January 1968.

From 1967 the Project continued to provide, at one or other of the Cambridge colleges, conferences for teachers who were already using or who were intending to use the CLC. These courses included lectures and practical sessions dealing with the content of the course, the linguistic scheme, teaching method, the use of tapes and slides and the 'O' level examination.[54] In 1972, the Project also organised a conference for experienced teachers who had begun using the Project's material during the trial phase. The reflections of teachers who spoke at this conference were subsequently published in a booklet.[55] The Project continued to provide periodic bulletins for teachers with updated information and guidance on the use of the CLC in its published form.

The Project's foundation course materials in their revised form were launched in September 1972, at a course attended by more than fifty teachers. This course, held in Bristol at the College of St Matthias, a college of education where the majority of students were prepared for primary school teaching, was directed by the author, Martin Forrest. In an attempt to meet the needs of Classics teachers undertaking Classical Studies courses for the first time, the course drew upon some of the primary school expertise and resources available in the College and had two main aims:

(a) that serving teachers of Classics, history and general subjects should be able to familiarise themselves with various creative media through which Classical story material can be interpreted in the classroom: drama, movement, art and craft. There are plans for those attending the course to experience these media at first hand by personal involvement in interpreting selected themes from Greek myth and legend;

107

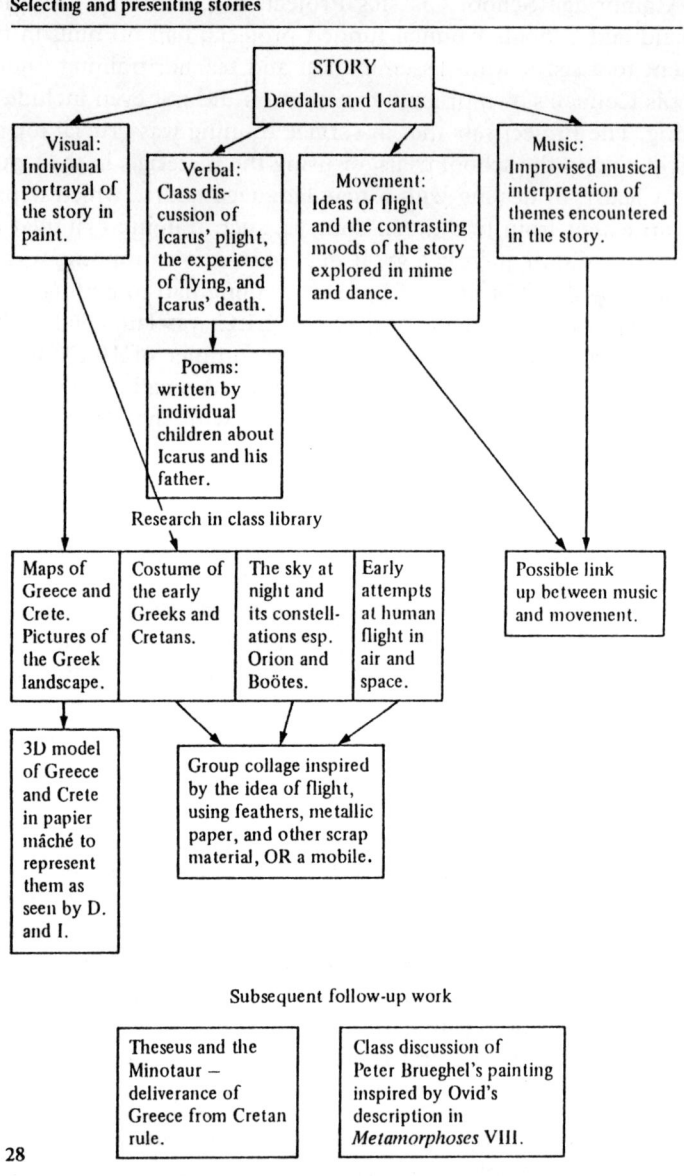

Selecting and presenting stories

STORY
Daedalus and Icarus

Visual:
Individual portrayal of the story in paint.

Verbal:
Class discussion of Icarus' plight, the experience of flying, and Icarus' death.

Movement:
Ideas of flight and the contrasting moods of the story explored in mime and dance.

Music:
Improvised musical interpretation of themes encountered in the story.

Poems:
written by individual children about Icarus and his father.

Research in class library

Maps of Greece and Crete. Pictures of the Greek landscape.

Costume of the early Greeks and Cretans.

The sky at night and its constellations esp. Orion and Boötes.

Early attempts at human flight in air and space.

Possible link up between music and movement.

3D model of Greece and Crete in papier mâché to represent them as seen by D. and I.

Group collage inspired by the idea of flight, using feathers, metallic paper, and other scrap material, OR a mobile.

Subsequent follow-up work

Theseus and the Minotaur – deliverance of Greece from Cretan rule.

Class discussion of Peter Brueghel's painting inspired by Ovid's description in *Metamorphoses* VIII.

28

Figure 4. A diagram from the Classical Studies Teacher's Handbook (1972) to show how a story-centred approach to ancient Greece might be organised.

(b) that course members should have an opportunity to examine the practical implications of mounting a course in Classical Studies for pupils of all abilities in the 10 or 11–13 age range.[56]

The course provided an opportunity for Classics specialists who had spent much of their previous career teaching classical languages, to experience at first hand a story-centred approach to the world of ancient Greece by participating in art and craft activities and by interpreting the stories through movement and drama. Each day a different theme was chosen: Wednesday—the Trojan War; Thursday—the upper air/underworld; Friday—the Greeks and the sea.

Throughout this period, members of the Project team, all of them now returned to teaching posts, continued to take part in in-service events mounted by bodies other than the Cambridge Project. Sometimes programmes were arranged to incorporate both linguistic and non-linguistic developments of the Project.

As has been noted earlier, the universities and the subject associations initially made the running in promoting the Project's work. By 1973, however, the public sector had begun to take an interest in these developments. Sponsorship was thenceforth largely dependent upon the Department of Education and Science and (to a much lesser extent) upon the LEAs. The continuing low level of LEA response reveals one of the most serious difficulties for Classics, namely the virtual absence of specialist support provided by local authorities. Some LEA-sponsored events were mounted only after pressure had been applied by the local branch of JACT.

The role of HMI

The Inspectorate had been associated with the movement to reform the middle school Classics course from the outset. As Staff Inspector, Kenneth Todd was keenly interested in all that emerged from the Cambridge Project and as a member of the Project's Advisory Panel he was in a good position to observe each stage of the development as it unfolded. Both Todd and his successor, Brian Kay, served in turn as HMI assessors on the Schools Council Classics Committee in the early 1970s. Here they witnessed various attempts to extend the Schools Council's role in the dissemination of new ideas on the teaching of Classics. By 1968, all the Classics HMI were beginning to learn at first hand about the CLC. In this year the standing conference of Classics lecturers met jointly with the Classics HMI at Nottingham University to be given a detailed exposition of the Project methods by David Morton and Pat Story. In December of the same year Forrest was invited to outline the Project's non-linguistic developments for HMI when they met in committee at Somerville College, Oxford. Individual members of the Inspectorate had been closely associated with a number of in-service events mounted by agencies other than the Department of Education and Science (DES). Forrest's first invitation to take part in a DES-sponsored course came in April 1973. This course was directed by the Staff Inspector and took place at a Liverpool college of education.

By 1972, the concept of Classical Studies through the medium of English had become absorbed into HMI thinking and had become a standard ingredient in the type of middle school Classics programme advocated by the Inspectorate. An article appeared in *Trends in Education* by Mr John Graham HMI as an *apologia* for Classics without the languages. In this article, Graham contrasted contemporary popular interest in the Classics with traditional Classics teaching:

> On the other hand, from the traditional school Classics course as we have come to know it in the last quarter of a century these mainsprings of interest so often have been absent. In the minds of most people the study of Classics still remains almost a synonym for the study of a Classical language, usually Latin, concerning itself largely with a sub-structure of grammar and syntax upon which only a few pupils ever raise any sort of edifice.[57]

Graham was given particular responsibility within the HMI Classics team for Classical Studies courses and in April 1974 he was asked to direct the first DES course to be devoted entirely to non-linguistic Classical Studies.

During the academic year 1973–4, HMI carried out a major survey into the position of Classics in comprehensive schools. The report was said to be 'a tentative evaluation of the present position of Classics in comprehensive schools, both quantitative and to a smaller extent qualitative'.[58] Some reference will be made to this report in Chapter Eleven, together with the findings of other studies which were carried out during the mid-1970s. The general conclusions of the HMI survey were as follows:

> Classics teaching has moved a long way from the time when Classics courses were geared to the task of training potential scholars. Much remains to be done. The rationale of Classical Studies needs to be developed and clarified. The new type of Latin course must be shown to provide a basis for the training of the future scholar as well as offering a nourishing ingredient to the diet of the non-scholar. In a number of comprehensive schools Classics is making a substantial contribution to the general education of the

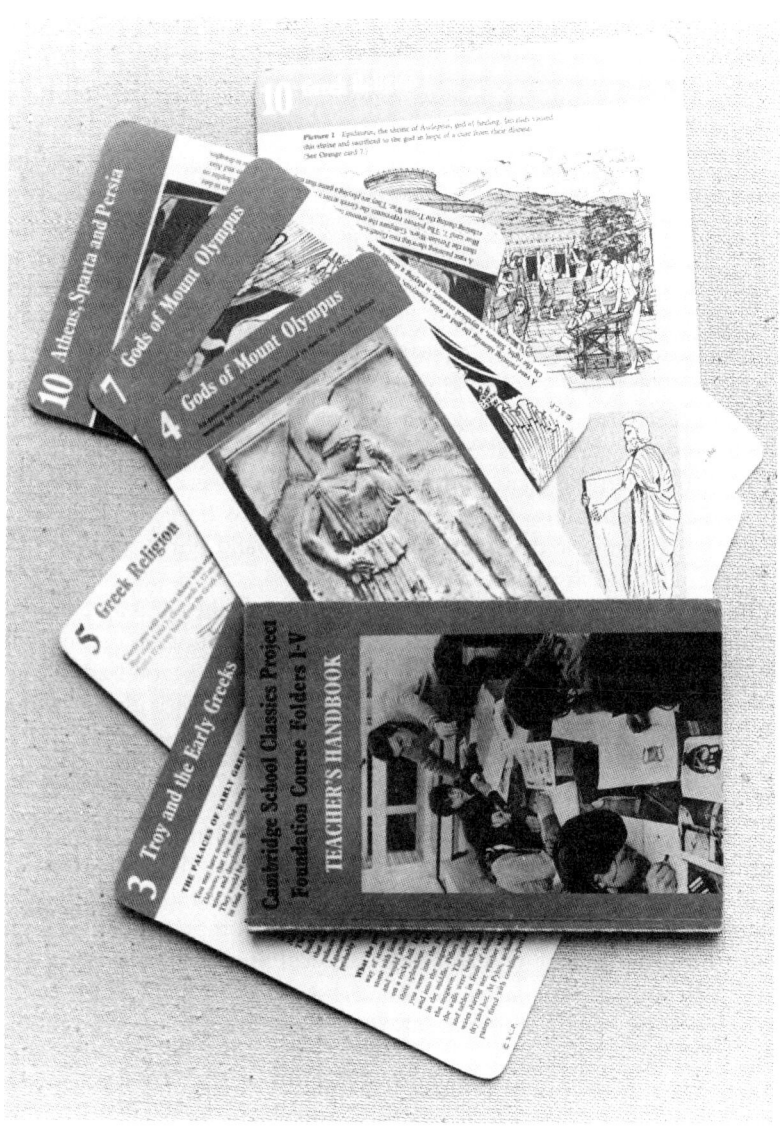

Figure 5. A selection of resource cards and teacher's handbook as used in the Greek Foundation course (1972).

majority of pupils in addition to fulfilling, though in new ways and for a wider clientele than in the past, its more traditional role of offering a more demanding educational experience to the more able.[59]

Developments north of the border

Ecce Romani, a Latin reading course prepared by the Scottish Teachers Group and revised in the light of school trials, was published hard on the heels of the CLC.[60] The twin aims of the course were to bring pupils quickly to the point where they can read Latin with confidence and to give some insight into life in the early Roman Empire. The course not only became widely adopted in Scotland, but also had widespread appeal to Classics teachers south of the border. *Ecce Romani* had in fact been influenced by the development of the CLC. Two visitors from the Scottish Teachers Group, Dr Miller of Perth Academy and a Scottish HMI, H.L. Philip, had visited the Project during the autumn of 1967 on a fact-finding mission. They had engaged in discussions with the Project team and had visited some trial schools. But though there were many similarities between the CLC and *Ecce Romani* there were also important differences. For example, no attempt was made to base the linguistic scheme on a systematic development of sentence and phrase patterns as had been attempted in the CLC.

In *Ecce*, traditional terms were used for the case names and an element of systematised grammar was introduced. To many who were committed to the CLC, *Ecce Romani* appeared nonetheless to be a good course in which an effort had been made to use some new ideas without losing sight of the formal nature of Latin.[61] To the more traditionally minded this appeared to be 'the kind of course on to which Latin prose composition could be built' in the early stages.[62]

The development of Classical Studies courses in Scottish schools was even more dramatic than in the rest of the United Kingdom. HMI noted that in September 1974 (before local government reorganisation in Scotland), Glasgow had forty-four of its fifty-four comprehensive schools teaching Latin, with forty-two teaching Classical Studies. The existence of foundation courses appeared to be assisting the survival of Latin following comprehensive reorganisation. There were also twelve schools teaching Greek.[63]

Here again the Scottish reformers of the teaching of Classics were more cautious than their counterparts south of the border. There had been some interest in the Project's Classical Studies materials and this interest continued through the 1970s. However, materials developed for publication in Scotland, unlike those of the Project, followed a conventional book format. Scottish teachers were also consistent in their

112

advocacy of introducing pupils to Latin and Greek words as well as derivatives in the context of a 'non-linguistic' course.

In Scotland, there were several areas where a strong commitment to Classics had resulted in the appointment of specialist advisory staff. A good example of the support which could be forthcoming in those authorities was to be found in the then county of Lanarkshire. Here Forrest, together with several experienced Classics teachers in the TAG, took part in an in-service programme immediately before the raising of the school leaving age. [64] All teachers of Classics in the county were required to attend and were encouraged, though not obliged, to adopt ideas and materials presented to them by the Cambridge Project.

The international dimension

As publication of the Project's materials in Britain loomed, steps were taken by the Cambridge University Press to explore the potential North American market. The visit to the United States originally proposed for David Morton during 1968 had been postponed because of the Project's internal difficulties. However, a hundred specimen copies of Unit I were that year sent to the CUP's New York office for distribution to selected teachers. [65]

Increased interest followed the publication of Unit I of the CLC in 1970 in both the United States and Canada. The early success of the CLC in North America has been ascribed to the 'widely appreciated visits of CLC officials and authors'.[66] In 1972, David Morton and Pat Story took part in a conference on innovative Latin textbooks for high school Latin teachers at the University of Massachusetts at Amherst. Two years later, David Morton also conducted a workshop for Latin teachers at McArthur College of Education, Queen's University, Kingston, Ontario. Interest in the Project in Canada had been aroused by the publication in 1970 of an article in the Classical Associates of Canada's periodical *Classical News and Views* by Mr G. (Garth) Lambert of Althouse College of Education, University of Western Ontario.

Garth Lambert had visited Cambridge and Bristol in 1970 and had spent some time interviewing members of the Project team about their courses and materials. His visit to Britain was followed by that of the Programme Consultant for Classics in the Ontario Ministry of Education, Mr V.J. Cunningham. The initial interest in the Project generated by these developments led to the adoption either formally or on an experimental basis by many schools and colleges and ultimately to the production of two North American editions of the CLC.

Interest in the Project's developmental work was stimulated in continental Europe by contributions made to international *colloquia* on the teaching of Classics held at Frankfurt in 1969 in which the CLC featured, and in Canterbury in 1971, in which both the CLC and the Project's Classical Studies developments formed part of the programme.[67]

In West Germany during this period, Classics teachers were facing the prospect of school reorganisation in which the *Gymnasia* would be transformed into comprehensive schools or *Gesamtschule*. A strategy for Classics in the new schools as outlined at the Canterbury Colloquium seemed attractive to several university teachers from West Germany who attended that gathering. William Thompson, Martin Forrest and John Muir, the last being equipped with video-recordings showing the CLC in operation, were invited to contribute to a programme of meetings organised for classical teachers at the University of Cologne in the autumn of 1971 by Dr Peter Wülfing.[68] Initial reaction to the proposal for a Classical Studies foundation course by Thompson and Forrest proved to be somewhat mixed. The suggestions for the transformation of Classics in contemporary schools were also greeted with some scepticism by a youthful audience of undergraduates assembled by Professor Harold Patzer in the highly political atmosphere of the University of Frankfurt. In contrast, a well-attended gathering of teachers and students at the University of Münster organised by Dr Kjeld Matthiesen showed polite appreciation of what their English colleagues were attempting to do.

The possibility of a German edition of the CLC was talked about but the idea was never fully developed. On the other hand, interest generated among some Dutch classicists resulted in negotiations with the Cambridge University Press for an edition of the CLC in Dutch. Although the first edition was very similar to the English edition, the course moved progressively away from its British counterpart and in its latest edition differs considerably both in approach and subject matter. It is more formal in its approach to the language and sections on the Roman Netherlands and Germany have replaced those on Roman Britain.

Classics and the schools in the early 1970s

The return of a Conservative government in June 1970 may have provided a reprieve from reorganisation for independent schools and for those grammar schools in local authorities which had been resisting comprehensive reorganisation, but for large numbers of grammar schools the move towards reorganisation continued unchecked.

The number of pupils attending comprehensive schools had in fact more than doubled within the four years of Conservative government; and by the early 1970s, the teaching of Classics could now be shown to have an important part to play in the curriculum of such schools. Not only had the middle school Classics been transformed into Classical Studies followed by a Latin reading course, but it was demonstrably a

114

subject that had something to offer across the whole ability range through the medium of English. The study of Latin could now be shown to be an enjoyable experience, intrinsically worthwhile in educational terms for a wider range of ability than the traditional grammar school Latin course had catered for. Limited surveys carried out by the Schools Council Classics Committee in 1969 and in 1971 by LACT came too early to assess the effects of reorganisation upon Classics in schools, but the HMI survey of 1973–4 provided abundant evidence that Classics was capable not only of survival under reorganisation but of prospering, especially in the larger 11–18 schools where staffing was not a problem.

The high profile consistently adopted by the Project, together with JACT's publicity drive from 1969 onwards for the new Classics and its place in comprehensive schools, had achieved significant success. Whilst there might be individual cases of schools where Classics was abolished or reduced to a token presence, despite a preparedness to undergo trans-formation, there was widespread (if not universal) recognition that Classics had some place within the new order of things.

Many Classics teachers took advantage of what was on offer and many set about transforming the teaching of Classics in their schools. John Sharwood Smith writing in the 1973 *JACT Bulletin* was greatly impressed: 'It is astonishing, when one considers that teaching is notoriously a conservative profession and Classics notoriously the most conservative of subjects, how many Classics teachers have radically altered their outlook and practices'.[69]

Within the independent sector the threat posed by Crisis Two of enforced integration into the comprehensive system had now retreated, although the impact of Crisis One was now beginning to have an indirect effect, at least in the preparatory schools. A number of independent day schools expressed interest in the CLC and, to some extent, in the Project's non-linguistic approaches and materials, although interest in the latter appeared to cool off during the early 1970s.

For Classics in the maintained sector, the period between 1970 and 1974 appears at first sight to resemble Gibbon's Indian summer of the Antonines.[70] This was a time when, it seemed, Classics as a school subject had been transformed into one which could survive and flourish in the comprehensive school, but as Walbank has demonstrated in the case of surface prosperity under the Antonine emperors, there is a need here also to 'penetrate behind the veil' and 'to isolate some of the tendencies which were developing within'.[71]

CHAPTER NINE

The Cambridge Latin Course Under Review

The political background

In the General Election of February 1974, following a bitter election campaign fought in the midst of the Conservative government's confrontation with the miners, no party gained an overall majority. A minority Labour administration was formed. Returning as Prime Minister after a four year period, Harold Wilson acted swiftly and decisively, determined that Labour would govern as if they had a majority. There would be no retreat from the election manifesto and no alliances with other parties.[1] Once again, comprehensive reorganisation was given an official shot in the arm. In April, Mr Reg Prentice, as Secretary for Education and Science, acted to speed the shift towards comprehensive reorganisation.[2] A government circular made it clear that LEAs which refused to put forward reorganisation plans would not be allocated cash for new schools. [3]

After the shortest parliament since 1681, the government chose to go to the country again in October. Despite widespread predictions of a comfortable Labour win, the result proved to be yet another cliff-hanger.[4] Prentice continued in office. The amount of grant paid to direct grant schools was frozen, and schools were given notice that from 1976 they would be given the option of becoming wholly independent or becoming part of the state system as comprehensive schools.[5] The majority of schools chose independence.[6] The commitment by central government to a comprehensive system of secondary education was once again confirmed. The direct grant schools generally had strong Classics departments, generously staffed compared with their state counterparts, with Latin and Greek continuing to play an important part in the school curriculum. Classics teachers in some of these schools, Manchester and Bristol Grammar Schools for example, had been closely associated with the Cambridge Latin Course since 1967 and they continued to recognise, though by no means uncritically, the achievements of the Project. These schools in the mid-1970s now became the exclusive preserve of fee-paying pupils. The possibility that they might become integrated into the state comprehensive system no longer existed. Classics in these schools continued largely to fulfil its traditional grammar school role.

The CSCP evaluation study

The Cambridge Project undertook an evaluation study in 1976, partly to provide information that would be helpful in revising the first edition of the CLC. It took the form of a detailed investigation into the use of the CLC in schools. A full report has never been published, although it does exist in draft form.[7] A summary of findings was included as an appendix to the supplementary handbook published as part of the first edition of the CLC.[8] The responses from schools were analysed at Cambridge with computer assistance and the findings were used by those responsible for creating the second edition of the CLC.[9]

In order to identify schools where the CLC was in use, a preliminary enquiry postcard was first sent out. Postcards were sent to (and mainly returned by) a random sample of 1,540 schools in both the maintained and independent sectors.[10] This sample represented 30 per cent of those schools in England, Wales and Northern Ireland which were listed at that date by the Statistics Branch of the DES. Of the schools that replied, 764 said that they taught Latin and of these 324 were using the CLC.[11]

The eventual sample of schools surveyed by the Project was drawn from those schools which said that they used the CLC and where the initial response had indicated a willingness to take part in the next stage of the evaluation. The evaluation study was based upon the returns of 377 teachers in 247 schools. Data were collected using school information questionnaires and the somewhat lengthier evaluation questionnaires which were to be completed by each teacher using the CLC. Supplementary data was also recorded on audio-tape at two specially convened conferences of teachers as part of the evaluation study.

The schools' information questionnaire asked for some basic information about the schools and the position of Classics teaching within them. The detailed evaluation questionnaire was also highly structured in its format, but ample space was provided for teachers' own comments on their perceptions of the course. Where more than one teacher in the same school was involved in using the course, each teacher was asked to complete a separate evaluation questionnaire. The information contained in the responses of teachers provides a detailed picture of Classics teaching in 1976, in those schools where the CLC was in use.

Table 1: The sample of schools approached, September 1976

	CLC	CLC + class std	Other CLC in past	Other Latin course	Other Latin course +class std	Class stds without Latin	Neither Latin nor class stds	Queries etc	No reply	Total
Comprehensive	70	86	30	108	52	25	316	1	84	772
Sixth-Form College	2	3	1	8	4	0	1	0	1	20
Middle	2	3	2	2	2	10	95	0	26	142
Maintained Grammar	39	31	4	37	26	0	11	1	7	156
Direct Grant Grammar	7	9	1	11	7	0	0	0	0	35
Independent Primary & Secondary	10	11	3	33	27	1	18	1	22	126
Independent Secondary	16	12	1	16	14	1	11	2	10	83
Independent Primary	9	14	6	43	50	0	45	3	36	206
Total	155	169	48	258	182	37	497	8	186	1,540

Questions on school information covered such items as status and size of the school, the distribution of pupils studying Classics within the school, the number of hours devoted to teaching the CLC in each year and the number of candidates entered for external examinations. Although the evaluation was primarily concerned with the Latin course, schools were also asked to indicate whether or not Latin was preceded by a Classical Studies foundation course and to say whether or not the Project's foundation course materials were used.

The detailed evaluation questionnaire included an invitation to teachers to indicate the degree of importance they attached to each of a number of skills which the Project sought to foster. They were also invited to identify any additional aims which they personally felt to be important in their own teaching, and to identify factors which they considered to be a serious hindrance to teaching Latin in their school. Separate sections dealt with the materials, teaching methodology and the further study of Latin at sixth-form level. In addition, teachers were asked to provide information about themselves and their training.

By far the largest group of schools in the sample was comprehensive, with 156 teachers responding from 119 schools. In addition there were 50 grammar schools (71 teacher responses); 19 direct grant grammar schools with 44 teachers (in a number of cases it was pointed out that the status of the school was now changing to independent); 34 independent schools with 57 teachers responding; and finally 11 preparatory schools with 17 teachers responding. The total number of schools in the group was 233 with 333 teachers responding.

It is important to note that this group consisted entirely of schools in which the CLC was used and where favourable consideration had been given towards cooperating with the Cambridge Project in its evaluation exercise. At this date these schools may still be assumed to be typical of schools in general. Since they all used the CLC, they may be assumed to represent those schools which were generally in touch with new thinking in Classics teaching.

The first point of interest is to ascertain the extent to which schools in the sample had or had not established a foundation course in Classical Studies, as both JACT and CSCP had been advocating during the previous ten years. All schools were asked whether Latin was preceded by a Classical Studies course of some kind. In the comprehensive schools where one would have expected there to be most evidence of change, out of 103 schools with the first year of entry at 11 or 12, 28 provided a course in Classical Studies prior to Latin and a further 10 a course in Humanities which included a Classical element. One school was in the process of discontinuing its Classical Studies foundation course.

Thus a total of 38 schools out of 103 (less than 40 per cent) had implemented the strategy which had been recommended by JACT and the CSCP, and which was now being supported by other official bodies, including the Schools Council Classics Committee and HMI.

A second point of interest is to establish the extent to which compulsory Latin still persisted. Again, the focus was upon comprehensive schools with other schools as a comparison. All schools were asked: is Latin compulsory? Some schools, it would appear, were still using an element of compulsion, despite the change to comprehensive status, at least in the early years. In two cases, even though 'free choice' was said to operate, Latin was said to be compulsory (presumably for the abler pupils). This caused resentment where pupils were made to do Latin rather than German or 'activities'.

Table 2: Comparative table based on an analysis of data

	n=schools	Foundation course	Compulsory Latin
Maintained sector			
COMP	121	38	32
GRAM	50	12	27
Independent sector			
DGT	19	5	15
IND SEC	34	14	23
IND PREP	11	4	9

A third area of interest is to establish the extent to which schools which had committed themselves to the CLC and adopted a foundation course in Classical Studies had also adopted the Project's Classical Studies materials. Responses from schools indicate that a total of 29 out of the 38 schools with a foundation course had adopted the Project's materials. It should be added that it is not clear from the returns whether schools were referring to their use of the later trial materials based on the Roman world, made available to schools on a limited basis or to the previously published materials based on ancient Greece (see below p. 127). Probably most schools were referring to the latter. A small number of schools claimed not to teach Classical Studies courses in their schools but ticked the box on the questionnaire which indicated they used the whole of the Project's foundation course materials. The likelihood is that in these cases the box was completed in error and there was some confusion with the CLC material. Of the 29 schools referred to above, 22 used the materials in part, and there were 7 schools where the material was fully used. From the Project's point of view, therefore, it was gratifying to note that three-quarters of those comprehensive schools which operated foundation courses as a precursor to the CLC had also committed themselves to using in whole or in part the Project's foundation materials. By contrast, only 3 of the 12 grammar schools which operated a Classical Studies foundation course claimed to be using the Project's foundation materials for this course.

There is evidence from the survey that some schools used the Project's materials for other purposes than foundation courses. A further 17 comprehensive schools used them either as part of a course offered as an alternative to Latin or in order to supplement linguistic studies. There is also evidence of similar use of this material by schools other than comprehensives.

If we return now to the full sample studied, a fourth point of interest is the extent to which teachers using the CLC had received formal training for the teaching of this radically new course. Table 3 summarises the responses received to questions on this subject.

Table 3: What training have you received in the use of the CLC materials?

	Yes	No
Part of pre-service training	18%	82%
In-service course run by the Project	34%	66%
In-service course run by others	12%	88%
Informal training only, e.g. discussion with teachers, observation of lessons, etc.	28%	72%
None	18%	82%

An analysis of teacher information supplied by those using the CLC suggested that teachers were generally well qualified, with 76 per cent having a degree which included Latin and 73 per cent with a teaching qualification. It is interesting to note, however, that as many as 46 per cent of the teachers had received no formal training for the new course. The number of teachers who admitted to rarely or never using the Teacher's Handbooks varied between 20 and 27 per cent according to the stage being studied.[12]

A fifth point of interest relates to course aims. As a preliminary, all teachers surveyed were reminded of the two central aims of the CLC: (1) to teach comprehension of the Latin language for reading purposes; (2) to develop an understanding of the content, style and values of Roman civilisation, with particular reference to the first century AD. They were then asked to say what degree of importance they attached to a number of skills which were felt to contribute to the fulfilment of these aims:

1 The ability to read, with help, selected passages from a prescribed group of Latin authors at 'O'/CSE level.
2 The ability to understand, without help, a piece of unseen Latin of an appropriate standard.
3 The ability to read Latin aloud.
4 The development of literary appreciation.
5 The development of some historical and some social understanding.

Teachers were asked to assign each skill to one of the four categories: very important, important, unimportant, very unimportant. In the whole sample of teachers, the first, second, fourth and fifth skills were rated as important or very important, by all but a tiny minority, whilst the ability to read Latin aloud was not regarded as important by 49 per cent of the sample.[13]

Teachers were also asked whether they thought these skills were practicable. More than 90 per cent thought that the first and fifth skills listed were practicable. A majority felt the same about the other three skills but there was a sizeable minority of doubters; for example, 21 per cent claimed that literary appreciation was 'barely practicable'.

Sixthly, teachers were asked: 'Do you personally have other intentions in teaching Latin, instead of or as well as those listed above? Indicate below briefly what they are and how you rate their importance to you.' Additional intentions commonly included transmission of the classical 'heritage' and development of 'language awareness'. The most frequently mentioned objective was that of giving children a grasp of the language, its structure, grammar and vocabulary. This was mentioned 100 times in the full sample and there were also 69 references to the help Latin could give in learning other foreign languages. In the smaller sample, 11 teachers also cited the 'transfer of training' argument (or variations on the same theme).[14]

Seventhly, the following question was posed: 'What factors in your school in your opinion are a serious hindrance to your teaching Latin?' There were many complaints, mainly from comprehensive schools, about inadequate time allowances, although this was not always consistent with the information about the school supplied in the previous questionnaire. There was in some cases a sense of feeling unwanted, or being without influence in their school, resulting sometimes in poor resource allocation. Other sources of difficulty, as perceived by comprehensive school teachers, were the qualities and attitudes of the pupils (and their parents), the effects of reorganisation (especially in urban areas) and the implications of mixed ability grouping for language learning. Some teachers undoubtedly felt that arrangements for teaching Latin compared unfavourably with what they were used to under selective schooling. These caused them difficulties which could only get worse. Here are some sample comments from the teachers' reports:

> many pupils do not choose to study or continue Latin in preference to other option subjects. Also Latin has had a 'bad press' recently, which influences parents without Classics experience against Latin.

> Parental pressure for German and modern languages, Latin being set against German.

> the universal erosion of all culture in a decaying civilisation.

> Home background of pupils, which does not favour literary or wider interests.

> The lack of grammatical background. Inattention to detail . . . The lack of real effort (memorisation and to grasp sufficiently) in pupils. They wish to be amused constantly.

> The inadequate staffing ratio of 11–16 comprehensives often results in language classes being larger than ideal or than in the old grammar school norm.

> Mixed ability grouping in most other subjects does not accustom even the best pupils to pace and intensity of most elementary language learning.

> The poor social catchment area with only about 7% of pupils with IQ's of more than 100—declining numbers in the inner city areas through demolition.

The major hindrance is the fact that children nowadays are given little or no training in the grammar and functioning of English, while they are at primary school.

Too many competing options—Latin is dying because of this, having barely got off the ground.

No tradition of teaching Latin in the school. Only the most able would benefit from a linguistic course.

Prejudice of parents against their children choosing a 'dead' language.

Older generation including many teachers remember their Latin experience in school.[15]

Although the above comments reflect the anxieties of teachers in comprehensive schools, it is worth noting that as many as 43 per cent of teachers in the full sample chose not to comment, when invited to do so, upon hindrance factors.

A central question concerned the use of complete 'sample' sentences as the means of introducing a new linguistic feature. It will be recalled that this 'whole sentence' approach lay at the heart of the Project's approach to Latin learning from the outset. Table 4 indicates responses to this question.

The presentation of the language in Units I and II was generally satisfactory in the sample as a whole, although there was some demand for more traditional treatment of vocabulary glossing from the outset. Unit III, especially the latter half, was strongly criticised by teachers for the steep gradient of linguistic input and for the sheer volume of reading matter. There was also felt to be a severe lack of consolidation in this unit and there was a demand for more manipulation exercises. There was also a demand for more summaries of grammar in the traditional tabular form.

Just under half the teachers consistently followed the Project's usage of 'A', 'B', 'C' forms etc., with many using these alternative labels alongside the traditional names. As many as a quarter of the teachers claimed never to use the Project's terminology.

Table 4: 'The whole sentence is used as the unit for introducing a new linguistic feature. Is this effective for the majority of pupils?'

	Usually	Sometimes	Rarely
Unit I	90%	9%	1%
Unit II	88%	10%	4%
Unit III	65%	31%	4%
Unit IV	58%	31%	11%

There was a small amount of evidence of English into Latin translation being undertaken as a means of consolidation. One third of the teachers subsequently taught prose composition skills to some or all of those pupils who moved from the CLC to 'A' level study in the sixth form.

Two conferences held at London and Manchester for a small number of very experienced teachers enabled the Project team to invite further discussion of the issues which had emerged from teachers' responses to the questionnaires. The general tenor of these two conferences was summed up by a Project research worker who studied the tape recordings as follows:

> The overall impression that I have gained . . . is that teachers are eager not to compromise the principles and the spirit of the Course—its emphasis on reading, on meeting grammar 'in situ', on the unity of the language, history and social culture—but that they are crying out for help with additional exercises for variety and consolidation, and have a desire to see some linguistic aspects of the Course clarified by a clearer indication of its grammatical content.[16]

Criticisms of a rather different kind were made by T.R.A. Reader some eight years after the first edition began to emerge. Writing in the first issue of the journal *Hesperiam*, published in 1978, Reader offered some thoughtful criticisms of the CLC and its original course design.[17] In his article, he raised doubts about the linguistic theories of Chomsky upon which the original linguistic scheme was said in part to be based. Difficulties with grammar were real and frequent, argued Reader, for users of the CLC. He advocated the incorporation of some of the insights of formal grammar into teaching the course. Teachers would thus be able to move away from a situation in which the pupil was left to infer the underlying rules of language by intuition, towards a situation where the language was still studied by reading at phrase and sentence level, but the teacher might express and explain 'deep structure insights' when it seemed necessary to do so. Reader claimed that he was not calling for a return to the teaching of formal grammar wholesale:

> for 'in this case, the rules of the formal grammar will underlie what we teach in the classroom, but the rules will not necessarily be overt in our teaching'
> —though they may be, on occasions, when the magical Chomskyan processes of intuition need some encouragement or reinforcement.[18]

Robin Griffin, who had been a member of the Project team during the later stages of the Project's full-time existence and who was to become

Revision Editor of the CLC, responded to Reader in the following issue of *Hesperiam*.[19] In so doing, Griffin drew upon evidence from the CSCP 1976 evaluation exercise and other sources:

> The experience of many teachers, reported at teachers' meetings and in their replies to the Cambridge Project's questionnaires, is that the CLC's subject-matter teaches the pupils something about Roman civilisation in a valuable and enjoyable way. There remains, however, much evidence of disappointing progress, especially in connection with the CLC's primary aim of developing a reading skill. The reports of O Level examiners, the comments of experienced teachers in articles such as Reader's, the results of the Project's evaluation exercise, views expressed at teachers' meetings—all these combine to give a gloomy picture, suggesting that though a reading skill does develop, in Units I and II, it stagnates or even diminishes thereafter.[20]

Griffin attacked Reader for his use of the phrase 'magical Chomskyan processes'. Other critics had referred to learning grammar through the pores of the skin. The fact of the matter was that the original design involving the rehearsal of significant patterns to the point where habits were formed in the learner had worked for Units I and II.[21] What was needed now was to examine in depth the problems pupils encountered in Unit III of the course:

> One possibility is that, for all the success of the early stages, the CLC's theory of language learning rests on a mistake: perhaps Latin's characteristic phrase and sentence patterns simply cannot be analysed to such a degree that they can be graded, sequenced and incorporated in a course-book in the way the CLC originally envisaged. Alternatively, it may be that the theory is sound but imperfectly executed.[22]

Griffin also commented that the CLC may have overstated its indebtedness to Chomsky in the first place; there are few references to Chomskyan concepts in the handbooks to Units III and IV. He then proceeded to identify four of the original CLC principles which had proved to be productive in Units I and II and which should be retained and further developed in the later stages of the course. These were:

1   The emphasis on content, whereby pupils are encouraged to ask themselves not 'what do these words mean?', but 'what information am I being given?' Interest is more likely to be aroused by a stress on subject-matter rather than by concentrating upon linguistic aspects.

2 The inductive approach whereby experience of linguistic features precedes discussion.

3 The emphasis on typical phrase and sentence patterns.

4 The gradual progression of linguistic features built into the reading material in a sequential and systematic way.[23]

Griffin went on to reject the idea that the CLC might simply be supplemented with extra language work, 'a process often described by metaphors involving the word 'grammar'. He did, however, suggest that the sharp distinction originally made by the Project between knowledge of a language and skill in using it had perhaps been exaggerated. The problem was that traditional courses tended to go too far in the opposite direction by ignoring the distinction altogether![24]

Pat Story, since December 1987 Director of the Project, reflects that the early teachers' handbooks were very good at telling teachers how to introduce things but very bad at going more deeply into them. This was particularly true of consolidation. To compound this problem there were fewer and fewer manipulation exercises in Unit III and by Unit IV there were none. The team had taken what may be seen with hindsight as the naive view that pupils would not need them by that stage because they would be reading authors fluently.[25] In commenting upon teachers' reactions to the Project's presentation of grammatical information, David Morton suggested that their reactions were partly due to a misunderstanding of the authors' intentions rather than disagreement. This, he suggested, was perhaps largely a result of some inadequacies and undue complications in the original teachers' handbooks.[26]

The difficulties of reconciling the need to research into the basis of a linguistic scheme with the urgent need to produce a new streamlined Latin course have already been discussed in Chapters Four and Five. It seems likely that Wilkins hoped his collaboration with the Project writing team would produce a new core linguistic scheme on an experimental basis which could form the basis not of one but of several Latin courses.[27] The terms of reference and the commitments which had been entered into with the trial schools, however, obliged the writing team to put all their energies into producing a one-off Latin course. Although the Project was continually referred to as a research and development project, it was the development rather than the research aspects that were always dominant; the dispute within the Project during the late 1960s could only have been resolved by attending to the needs of the former at the expense of the latter.

CHAPTER TEN

Classical Studies and Developments in Bristol

Some mention should at this point be made of further developments on the non-linguistic front. In the long run the approach adopted was to have important implications for the future of courses in Classical Civilisation.

With the continuing needs of comprehensive schools firmly in mind, the Cambridge School Classics Project Committee had obtained the support of the Schools Council for a two-year extension based in Bristol from September 1973, with a view to completing the production of Roman material for a Classical Studies foundation course aimed at all abilities in the 11–13 age range.[1]

This extension enabled the Project to appoint M.J. (Mike) Hughes, an experienced teacher from an independent secondary school, as full-time research assistant to work at the College of St Matthias under the general direction of Martin Forrest.[2] Although some useful preliminary work had been undertaken with the help of the Teachers' Advisory Group, the new full-time appointment provided the opportunity to start afresh. By October 1974, after an initial gestation period, a package of trial materials emerged. The package consisted almost entirely of primary source material translated by team members, accompanied by a teacher's handbook.[3] Feedback from schools at an earlier stage had favoured development of Roman-based materials for the second year of the foundation course, to complement the earlier Greek-based material.[4] The new package did not entirely abandon the story-centred approach followed by the Greek material (a booklet of translated stories from Ovid, Apuleius, and other writers was included in the pack); but there was a firm shift towards a study of the ancient world based upon handling evidence. One important innovation was the inclusion of a substantial body of epigraphic material. Particular use was made of the rich source of inscriptions from ancient Gaul to be found in *Corpus Inscriptionum Latinarum* (*CIL*) Volumes XII and XIII, especially those from Lugdunum (Roman Lyon), a major city of the Roman Empire during the first two centuries AD. Another important feature of the material was the wide range of Greek and Roman sources (all of which were translated by the Project team) that were selected for inclusion.

The trial material continued to emphasise group as well as individual investigation and response. Eusebius' account of the Christian martyrs of Lugdunum (AD 177), was used as a starting point for exploring city life in the Roman provinces; it led to the further study of literary sources, inscriptions and archaeological evidence. Three other areas were identified for future development: well known events and personalities, ancient technology and Roman Britain.[5]

Teachers of Classical Studies were encouraged to establish with their pupils the idea that in trying to recover the lives of men and women dead for 2,000 years, they were presented with a great detective problem, a jigsaw from which many pieces were missing. Each piece of evidence is unique and has survived by chance.

> What the teacher and the children will be doing all the time is using their ingenuity to establish the limits of the evidence, deciding what they do not know and what they would like to know. Answers to these questions will be sought by examining fresh evidence and reassessing the old. In short, they will be reconstructing models of the ancient world for themselves from the sources. The teacher's role will be to encourage the right sort of approach to evidence, to suggest the more fruitful sorts of questions to ask of it and to help keep the theorising within reasonable bounds.[6]

Each piece of evidence had been selected for its own intrinsic worth and could be used as a stimulus for drama, painting, model-making or written work. But also each item could be treated as part of a wider collection of evidence which had survived from antiquity. Items were said to

> contain possibilities of relationship with each other because they come from the same cultural context. One item lends significance to another. This serves both to define the content more clearly and make it more resonant, and to reveal details which would not otherwise have been apparent . . . its 'contextual interest'. . . makes it a 'building block' with which the ancient world can be recreated, and it is this process of recreating the ancient world which is central to classical studies.[7]

Techniques such as the 'occupations game' were developed as devices for analysing the available evidence for the ancient economy, listing the findings and making judgements on the basis of those findings. In the course of school trials a rationale based upon recreating the ancient world was formulated in which all source items were identified as having both intrinsic interest and contextual interest.

The Classical Studies materials were eventually published as *The Roman World* and were promoted for use with pupils aged 12–14, although there had always been a belief on the part of the team that this material could also contribute to a CSE programme of study.

Teachers were presented with two large packs of source material based on an extension of the original selection used in the 1974–5 school trials. Two handbooks were published, one providing an outline of the approach being advocated, the other a detailed compendium of practical advice on how the material might be used in a variety of situations. In developing this approach, the team had been influenced by recommendations of the Bullock Committee, especially Chapter Eight of their report, in which critical reading skills were emphasised and by other contemporary publications including the work of Christopher Walker which dealt with 'higher order' reading skills.[8]

Early in 1974, the Project Committee considered a request that the development work at Bristol be extended further. It was reported to the Project Committee that the situation in Bristol 'was working very well'.[9] Two areas suggested for further development were the dissemination and the development of materials for CSE courses.

Both these proposals followed naturally from the work being undertaken in Bristol. It was agreed by the Project Committee that a framework for a course and some additional materials should be prepared. It was further agreed to approach the Schools Council, whose representative was present at the meeting. Final approval for an extension costing £25,000, over three years, was granted by early December 1974.[10]

Although it was clear that not all members of the various Schools Council steering committees were initially happy to grant an extension to this particular project, impressive evidence was now available of Classical Studies materials already produced as the result of the Project's work, and a display of recently published Greek foundation course material had been mounted in the committee room for inspection by members of the Council's steering committees. This may have ensured success for the Project's application at a time when there was increasing unease in the Council about some other curriculum projects which had failed to deliver. The extension for a further three-year period meant that Mike Hughes' contract would be extended for the same period.[11] Provision was also made for further staffing to be made available during 1976–77. This particular academic year was the only period when the budget would enable two individuals to work full-time on the development of non-linguistic Classical Studies materials.

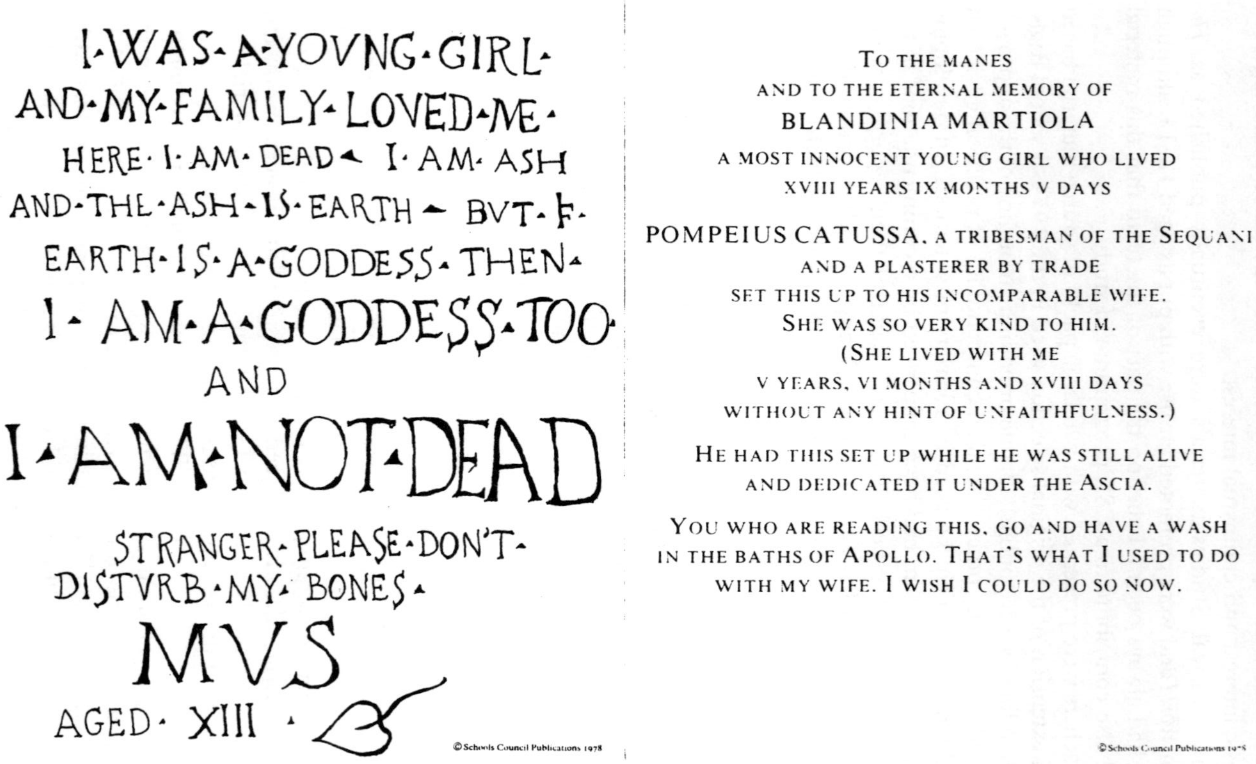

TO THE MANES
AND TO THE ETERNAL MEMORY OF
BLANDINIA MARTIOLA
A MOST INNOCENT YOUNG GIRL WHO LIVED
XVIII YEARS IX MONTHS V DAYS
POMPEIUS CATUSSA, A TRIBESMAN OF THE SEQUANI
AND A PLASTERER BY TRADE
SET THIS UP TO HIS INCOMPARABLE WIFE.
SHE WAS SO VERY KIND TO HIM.
(SHE LIVED WITH ME
V YEARS, VI MONTHS AND XVIII DAYS
WITHOUT ANY HINT OF UNFAITHFULNESS.)
HE HAD THIS SET UP WHILE HE WAS STILL ALIVE
AND DEDICATED IT UNDER THE ASCIA.
YOU WHO ARE READING THIS, GO AND HAVE A WASH
IN THE BATHS OF APOLLO. THAT'S WHAT I USED TO DO
WITH MY WIFE. I WISH I COULD DO SO NOW.

©Schools Council Publications 1978

I·WAS·A·YOVNG·GIRL·
AND·MY·FAMILY·LOVED·ME·
HERE· I· AM· DEAD I· AM· ASH
AND·THE·ASH·IS·EARTH – BVT·F·
EARTH·IS·A·GODDESS·THEN·
I· AM·A·GODDESS·TOO
AND
I·AM·NOT·DEAD
STRANGER·PLEASE·DON'T·
DISTVRB·MY·BONES·
MVS
AGED· XIII ·

©Schools Council Publications 1978

Figure 6. A pair of translated Roman inscriptions published in the Roman World materials (1978).

During the period of this further extension, video material was prepared based upon the Project's Roman World materials in action. An edited version of recordings made by the Mobile Recording Unit of King's College, London, was subsequently made available to interested schools as part of a dissemination programme.

Further development of the Classical Studies rationale for the 13–16 age range, involving a range of skills, took place during the latter part of the extended period; this development included school trials of three sample sets of material for use as part of a CSE/GCE programme.

The Project was able to link up with six LEA schools in the south west of England where there was interest in offering Classical Studies as a Mode III examination. The original Classical Studies syllabus had been developed by a working party and approved by the region's examination board, following the 1966 Bristol conference, at which David Morton first encouraged discussion of Classical Studies in the CSE. The Project link enabled all six schools to use the three units of trial 13–16 material in their provisional form. They had been foreshadowed in the 1974 Roman World handbook. The topics treated in the units were Roman Britain (the 'discovery' of Britain by the Romans and its subsequent conquest by the Roman army); ancient technology (the manufacture of textiles in the Graeco-Roman world including substantial practical work); and events and personalities (based upon stories of the late Roman Republic, but originally featuring an attempt to link biographical material about Pompey and Caesar with stories of early Rome).

In the years immediately following the completion of Mike Hughes' period as Project Research Officer, a working party was formed to consider further the development of a common examination at 16+; these years also saw the steady publication of the units of 13–16 material, including in each case a handbook for teachers.[12] The published handbooks included a refined version of a skills-based approach to Classical Studies which identified a full checklist of skills which had been hammered out with teachers in the trial schools and which eventually formed the basis of assessment objectives for the Project's own examination syllabus. A further development in 1980 was the production of Classical Studies foundation course materials in Holland which in part drew their inspiration and some of their content from the Project's materials centred on Roman Lugdunum.[13]

CHAPTER ELEVEN

The Realities of Curriculum Change

The Schools Council's 'Impact and Take-up' survey of secondary school teachers, published in 1980 and carried out two years previously, suggested that the influence of Schools Council curriculum development projects was varied, widespread but attenuated and that use of projects was 'generally partial and modified'.[1] In fact the CSCP achieved the highest rating of all projects in terms of making contact with teachers, although there may have been special factors at work in the case of Classics.[2] A closer study of the returns from 100 Classics teachers who wrote in some detail about the project they knew best provides a striking contrast between the educational values of many teachers and those held by members of the original Project team and embodied in the CLC materials. Comments made by teachers frequently echoed responses to the Project's own evaluation questionnaire which had been carried out in 1976.

As many as 55 per cent of the Classics teachers who responded were using Project materials and a further 16 per cent claimed to have been influenced by the Project's thinking. This percentage did include a small number of teachers who were using the Classical Studies materials, although the vast majority referred only to the CLC. Teachers from half the sample were critical of aspects of the CLC, and in almost every case their criticisms were directed at the perceived absence of grammatical structure in the course and the shortcomings which had become apparent in Unit III. Even among the critics, however, there were many complimentary statements made about the cultural aspects of the course and about the degree of motivation which the CLC was seen to have provided in the case of 'less able' pupils.

Some very positive views were in evidence:

> I have found the Project very acceptable to able pupils and of much
> greater value than the traditional type of course to those who have

little aptitude for languages. The social and cultural material is a great source of interest, and has enabled Latin to remain viable during the transition to comprehensive education as well as providing a sound basis for 'A' level Latin.[3]

By contrast, critical views came from another teacher of a more traditional frame of mind who had first met the CLC during his PGCE course, and who saw English into Latin as a vital course component for intending 'A' level candidates. In fact, the Project's survey had revealed that as many as a third of teachers who were using the CLC subsequently taught prose composition to some or all of their pupils who went on to study Latin in the sixth form.[4]

Traditionalist values are well summed up in the following comments written by one experienced teacher of Classics who wrote in her response to the Impact and Take-up Survey:

> The Head of Classics uses it . . . I teach grammar and syntax with the help of Ritchie's 1st and 2nd Steps and Kennedy's Latin Grammar . . . It is terrible . . . the books are useful as Latin readers and the background material is good. Otherwise, it is a good recipe for preventing boys from understanding Latin.[5]

Significant advances in the adoption by teachers of the 'new' Classics were also remarked upon by others. The HMI survey published in 1977 presented a picture which was broadly encouraging to those who had worked hard for change. John Sharwood Smith expressed astonishment at the way in which so many Classics teachers had 'radically altered their outlook and practices'.[6] During the early stages of school trials, all the Project's materials, both linguistic and non-linguistic, and also the experimental material produced by the Scottish teachers had been well, if not enthusiastically, received by teachers.[7]

However, there is another side to this story. Evidence from studies carried out during the mid-1970s suggests that the realities of curriculum change, both in comprehensive schools and in those maintained grammar schools which remained, differed considerably from the surface indic-ations that radical change had come about.

Firstly, it is true that the growth of non-linguistic Classical Studies to 1974 had certainly been remarkable and widespread and was over-whelmingly to be located in the first two years of secondary schools, where it was taught to a substantial proportion of the pupils, mainly in mixed ability groups.[8] Where these courses were in operation, it is clear that the Project's folders of material which had been designed for use with non-streamed classes were contributing to the process of implementation. The HMI survey as a whole shows, however, that non-linguistic Classical

Studies was taught in less than a quarter of comprehensive schools.[9] Classical Studies was defined for the purpose of the survey as including foundation courses, courses in classical literature in translation, ancient history etc. Schools were asked to indicate also if any of these forms existed either as a separate subject or as a substantial part of an English, History or 'integrated' Humanities course.[10] It is clear that in many of the comprehensive schools surveyed, Classical Studies had not become established as a precursor to Latin, but was provided as an option further up the school, sometimes as a lower status alternative to Latin.

A detailed survey carried out by a classical researcher in the mid-1970s, E.C. Milleounis, showed that less than half the teachers (44 per cent) in his sample believed that Classical Studies should be compulsory for all pupils.[11] No breakdown is available to indicate the percentage of teachers in comprehensive schools who took this view. The CSCP's 1976 survey indicated that less than 40 per cent of the comprehensive schools surveyed had foundation courses. In the CSCP survey also, only 12 of the 50 selective state schools offered foundation courses. Yet for as long as the government pursued its policy of comprehensive reorganisation, these were the very schools that were due to undergo change and they would have done well to prepare themselves in advance for receiving a broad ability range.

A survey carried out by the London Association of Classical Teachers in 1971 had shown that the proportion of London area schools which had adopted foundation courses was also in the region of 40 per cent.[12] There can be no doubt that in the late 1960s and early 1970s, there was a rapid increase in the number of classical foundation courses introduced in one form or another. During the Project's 1973–1978 extension, furthermore, some evidence emerged that this movement had slowed right down. The new Classical Studies materials, based on the Roman world, probably came too late to assist with the growth and expansion of Classical Studies in schools in a way that the Greek foundation course folders had done in the late 1960s and early 1970s.

Secondly, there is evidence that in more than a quarter of comprehensive schools in the 1976 CSCP survey, Latin remained compulsory for some pupils, at least in the early stages. In contrast, Milleounis' survey of teachers in Scotland and the North of England showed general agreement that Latin should not be compulsory (there were only four dissenters from this view).[13] A.H. Jennings, a classicist and Head of a Sheffield comprehensive school, speaking at the AGM of the Classical Association in 1975, welcomed the removal of compulsory Latin and acknowledged the reason why Latin in some cases remained compulsory after reorganisation: 'It is good that headteachers are no longer so ready to decree whole forms "must" do Latin, as a means of justifying the Classics teacher's time.'[14]

The policy of JACT in response to comprehensive reorganisation from 1964 onwards had been to argue for Classical Studies for all pupils followed by optional Latin for those who were able to benefit from it. The Cambridge Project had consistently advocated this pattern for reorganised schools. There is evidence that a critical review of the traditional role of Classics teaching had been undertaken and new courses widely adopted. It is also clear, however, that there was considerable reluctance in some schools to abandon compulsory Latin in favour of a Classical Studies foundation course for all until forced to do so. Moves to establish some Classics for all through the medium of English throughout the country during the 1960s and 1970s may be regarded as having been only partially successful.

One LEA which took steps to centralise the reform of Classics teaching in all its secondary schools was Swansea. As part of its plans for comprehensive reorganisation in 1970, the LEA drew up a Classics charter which made provision for the continuance of Classics in the curriculum of reorganised schools. Christopher Stray's study of Swansea and West Glamorgan Classics teachers, undertaken in the mid-1970s, involved face to face interviews with many teachers who were at the time attempting to come to terms with curriculum change.[15] Stray's analysis provides some interesting insights into what can happen under a centralised curriculum.[16]

Swansea LEA drew up a Classics charter which guaranteed the survival of some Classics in the secondary curriculum of all reorganised Swansea schools, something that appears to have been unusual in Welsh and English authorities. Classics teachers in Swansea had the blessing of their LEA, and were strongly supported both by a local adviser and by their regional Classics HMI. But there are two aspects of this centralised policy decision that require closer examination in the light of Stray's work.

Firstly, although the inclusion of Classics was guaranteed, the charter left open the nature of this inclusion. In fact, the position of Classics in the allocation system of each school was not guaranteed but subject to negotiation. The terms of the charter were that non-linguistic Classical Studies would and Latin might be taught in the four junior high schools which took pupils aged 11–13. In practice, most pupils in these schools were taught one or two periods of Classical Studies per week and a small group of second year pupils was taught Latin (as one of several options available to the top stream). All these junior high schools were former secondary modern schools and most of their heads were former secondary modern heads. The reality was, however, that little support was given to Latin as far as timetabling was concerned.[17] Even non-linguistic Classical Studies, which was compulsory, was subject to variation at whim. In one school the teaching of Classical Studies was farmed out to five different teachers, who each taught one Classical Studies period per week. Two of these teachers were Needlework specialists. Other teachers brought in were Modern Language teachers who had also been give peripheral responsibility for Classics. Stray concluded that in the 11–13 schools, a wide range of interpretation had been given to the meaning of 'provision', the distributors of Classics were relatively uncommitted to it and its disappearance would leave them 'regretful but not alarmed'.[18]

A second interesting feature in Stray's study is Swansea's guarantee to furnish all schools with teaching materials published by the Cambridge Project.[19] These were the CLC and the Classical Studies foundation course materials based in ancient Greece. The agreement with schools not only offered protection against current challenges to the subject, it also provided the materials to enable both Classical Studies and Latin to be taught in the reorganised schools using appropriate materials.

The case of Swansea is interesting in that it illustrates some of the negative as well as the positive results of introducing a compulsory curriculum. Stray also put the spotlight on the dilemmas facing Classics teachers as they struggled to come to terms with a comprehensive system. He concluded that the new rules of economic viability, organisational efficiency and 'relevance to the comprehensive ideal' were alien and separate from the old rules which Classics teachers understood in the academic market of the grammar school. The more stable world in which Latin was once centrally located had now come to an end. The hopes of Classics teachers must henceforth be pinned on recruitment in the curriculum market place. Stray commented: 'Classics thus seems to have a future; whether this is a future—or a "classics"—to which they can feel any commitment, is another matter.'[20]

Christopher Stray identified the problems posed for Classics teachers by the changed role of Classics from compulsory status to one which was now subject to market forces. A temporary stay of execution for compulsory Latin during the transition from selective to comprehensive schooling might have had its attractions, in that it provided protection at least for the time being. On the other hand, the move to the marketplace made Classics teachers reconsider their aims and attitudes. As long as the traditional pattern of organisation survived, the Classics teacher was protected from the reality of market forces within the school and ill-prepared for meeting the challenge of offering his/her subject to the wider comprehensive clientele.

One teacher who responded to the CSCP evaluation questionnaire illustrated a contrasting approach which is in line with the progressive tradition:

Size of school only supports one full-time Classics teacher and I feel that Classical Studies makes a far greater contribution to the curriculum as a whole than Latin. Therefore there is no room in my timetable or in the option scheme for Latin.[21]

Many Classics teachers, however, saw themselves primarily as linguists and felt less at ease cast in the role of Humanities teacher. Classical Studies courses, if they were to be established, were frequently not taught by the Classics specialist, although the classicist on the staff might take on a coordinating role.[22] In schools where it was possible to teach a classical language, Classical Studies was sometimes seen by the Classics specialist as a form of 'background', regarding the latter as a low status alternative.

The period 1974–8 is notable for some changes in reaction amongst teachers of Classics to the new approaches which had generally been welcomed so warmly during the previous decade. By 1974, both the CLC and *Ecce Romani*, having enjoyed a generally favourable period in trial schools, were made available in their first editions. Something of a backlash followed, particularly directed at the CLC, with numerous specific criticisms being made very often by teachers who at a general level were favourably disposed to the course. The resurgence of traditional attitudes among Classics teachers was very marked and widespread.[23]

The changing educational climate, the publication since early 1969 of the Black Papers and the dissemination of ideas contained in them, began to have an impact on many teachers including classicists.[24] They recognised some of the criticisms directed towards the curriculum reform movement of the 1960s could be felt to apply to developments in Classics. Evidence from the Project's evaluation study of the CLC suggests that some of the Cambridge Project's more adventurous ideas about language teaching were now viewed by an increasing number of teachers as too extreme (including by this stage members of the Project team). This also applied in some respects to the non-linguistic developments, although there is an absence here of any systematic attempt to gather the reactions of teachers on a large scale.

CHAPTER TWELVE

Classics in the 1980s

The year 1976 is now widely seen as a turning point for education in Britain. In October of that year, the Labour Prime Minister, James Callaghan, delivered a speech at Ruskin College, Oxford in which he called for a 'Great Debate' on education. His speech was designed to capture the public mood of the time. The Prime Minister's call for more vigorous educational standards, for greater monitoring and accountability of teachers, for greater concentration on basic skills and literacy and numeracy, and for giving priority to technical, vocational and practical education set the agenda for all subsequent education ministers. Since 1979, there has been a succession of far-reaching legislative and fiscal measures, all the product of Conservative governments, which have transformed the educational scene beyond recognition.

Classics in maintained schools and the arrival of a third crisis

In the years since James Callaghan's Ruskin speech, four major factors have emerged which have operated, frequently in combination, to impose severe limitations on the teaching of classical languages in maintained schools. These factors taken together may be regarded as constituting for Classics teachers a third crisis. This has been even more devastating than either of the two previous crises. Two of these factors are concerned with the curtailment of resources; the other two are major national developments that have taken place with regard to the school curriculum.

Financial constraints imposed by central government in the later 1970s were deeply felt by schools and teachers at local level in 1978 and 1979 and their impact was to have lasting effects. This caused every secondary school head to scrutinise even more critically than before small subject option groups. The word 'non-viable' came into widespread usage in connection with minority subjects. A large fall in the birth-rate had, by the early 1980s, caused secondary schools to agonise over their ability to

138

deliver a 'balanced' curriculum. Classics was seen as a subject to be squeezed with the resulting loss of Classics teaching posts. Thinner budgets have ensured continuing pressure ever since. Long before the introduction of the ill-starred community charge and its more recent successor the council tax, there had been a progressive erosion of the rate support grant received by local authorities from central government. During the 1980s, this financial stringency was rendered even more unpalatable to local authorities by a government decision to 'cap' authorities deemed to be overspending.

Even more serious for school Classics in the longer term has been the crisis in the training provision for specialist Classics teachers in university departments of Education. The crisis was provoked by the decision of a number of universities for financial reasons not to replace on retirement their specialist lecturers in Classics teaching method. Education departments which have ceased to offer a specialist training in Classics as a main subject since 1978 include the Universities of Leeds, Exeter, Bristol, Hull, Birmingham and Wales. In Scotland, teacher training is now confined to a single institution, Jordanhill College (now part of the University of Strathclyde). By 1994 in England and Wales, Classics was available as a specialist subject only at Cambridge and in London (King's College and St Mary's College, Twickenham).

Two other factors that by the late 1980s had come to dominate the school curriculum were both foreshadowed by the Callaghan Speech in 1976. Firstly, there was the concern for greater accountability of teachers and schools. A series of exercises in intervention by successive secretaries of state and their officials in the curriculum of state secondary schools culminated in the imposition of a National Curriculum as a provision of the 1988 Education Reform Act. Classical languages did not feature as a subject requirement. As will be seen in the next chapter, this has tended to hasten the demise or reduction of Classics in many schools, especially at a time of financial stringency. Teachers have not been replaced, time allowances have been cut and such teaching as remains in the maintained sector is often relegated to 'twilight time' outside the curriculum. Subjects which lie outside the National Curriculum, including classical languages, must inevitably be at risk even where they still hang by a slender thread.

Secondly, recent years have seen the progressive development of pre-vocational education inside the school curriculum. The concern about preparing youngsters for the world of work was again one of the issues raised in the Ruskin speech. The major impetus for this initiative, accompanied by, in the first instance, a massive injection of public money, came not from the Secretary of State for Education and Science but from the Department of Employment, through the Manpower Services Commission. The creation of the Technical and Vocational Educational

Initiative (TVEI) in the early 1980s, at first on a selective geographical basis, but subsequently adopted by schools all over the country, has provided a new and attractive range of curriculum options, against which the traditional Humanities subjects, including Classics, have had to compete.

The position of Classics in independent schools

Classics HMI carried out their last major study of independent schools in 1981–2. This was published as *Classics in Independent Schools: a Survey by HMI* (London: HMSO 1984). During that academic year, thirty-three schools with a known commitment to Classics, including two in Wales, were visited. The schools included ten former direct grant schools. The conclusion reached on the basis of evidence from this survey were that there had been a 'perceptible, and desirable, move away from some of the values and methods traditionally associated with classical language teaching'.[1] Most schools were said to be using at least some modern materials for teaching the languages below sixth-form level.

However, some of the criticisms traditionally levelled at classics teaching can be discovered in the text of this report: schools still saw Classics in terms of language teaching only and showed a continuing reluctance to see the place of Classics in the curriculum in terms of an educational experience for *all* pupils. Only nine schools made any provision for classical courses below sixth form level which did not include a classical language. The report concluded:

> Classical myth, legend and history are part of general education. Appropriate courses in these aspects of classics can be made available in the early years, at the various levels of external examination and as an element in sixth form general studies.[2]

The problem of 'drop-outs' who failed to make progress at Latin, or who abandoned the language in favour of other subjects, continued to be widespread and there was a need to 'devise realistic intermediate objectives' for an abbreviated course. It appears that some of the key issues which long needed to be addressed in the maintained sector and which the prospect of comprehensive reorganisation had helped to change, had yet to be considered in many independent schools by the early 1980s. The position of classical languages in these independent schools was generally at this date still strong. All the secondary schools in the study had 'main-school' Latin courses culminating in a GCE 'O' level examination. Of the twenty-eight secondary schools, eleven schools offered five-year courses and fifteen offered four-year courses. Of these schools, nineteen also offered main-school Greek.[3]

The North American Cambridge Classics Project

In summer 1980, David Morton and Pat Story made a return visit to the United States accompanied this time by Rosemary Davidson of the Cambridge University Press. They met North American teachers at the Institute of the American Classical League in Durham, New Hampshire, and at the New England Classical Institute and Workshop at Tufts University, Medford, Massachusetts. A transcript of the proceedings was subsequently published in *Classical Outlook*.[4]

As a result of these meetings, the Cambridge University Press invited Professor Ed Phinney, Chair of the Department of Classics, University of Massachusetts at Amherst, to rewrite the pamphlets containing information about the language and the teacher's handbooks specifically to meet the needs of North American students and teachers, in particular, by using the American case order in paradigms of nouns, and by describing classroom procedure in terms used by North American teachers.

Phinney corresponded initially with all those North American teachers of the CLC who were known to him personally and subsequently with an ever-expanding network of teachers throughout the continent. In March 1982, the New York office of the CUP inaugurated a CLC Newsletter. By this time interest among North American teachers was said to be reaching fever pitch.[5]

Phinney himself was fully committed to what he refers to as the 'Cambridge cultural and inductive approach'. He set about adapting the CLC approach: on the one hand, the interests, varying abilities and different ages of students in American schools and, on the other, seeking to reconcile the demands of administrations and parents who saw Latin as a preparation for the achievement test in Latin or as an aid to English vocabulary building with a culturally oriented course. By this time the North American public had become particularly concerned about what they saw as a decline in verbal skills among young people. As Phinney noted in his preface to the second edition:

> The Latin teacher, while accommodating himself or herself to the demands of parents who want Latin taught as a vehicle primarily for improving English, has been forced to respond to the equally strong demands of parents who are eager for their children, in an international age, to become less insular and more 'globally aware' than heretofore in our national history.[6]

The North American second edition was identical to the British second edition, though the handbooks and grammar prepared by Phinney were distinctively different. These materials, published in 1982, came to be adopted by far more schools in the United States and Canada at both secondary and college level than the first British edition had done in that continent. A third edition of the North American course was published in 1988. This time changes were also made to the pupils' books, including the addition of further visual material and exercises based upon the derivations of words.

CHAPTER THIRTEEN

The Education Reform Act 1988

Kenneth Baker's Education Reform Act contained a number of far-reaching changes to the British education system. Included in these changes was the conferring of unprecedented powers upon the Secretary of State and the establishment for the first time of a compulsory National Curriculum. Following the passage of the Act, machinery was set in place to implement a centrally directed curriculum comprising 'core' and 'foundation' subjects. There were to be nine National Curriculum subjects. Classical languages were excluded from the compulsory subjects. Despite the initially optimistic statements of ministers and HMI, there was widespread recognition that the National Curriculum subjects, together with Religious Education (compulsory since 1944), would leave little room for optional subjects.

Although the Cambridge Project's choice of the Pompeian entrepreneur Caecilius as a central figure in the CLC is believed to have attracted approving comment from a minister in a strongly market-orientated government, the inclusion of Latin as part of the National Curriculum requirements was never a realistic possibility. A late night adjournment debate held towards the end of the previous parliament, had elicited the government response that priority must be given to the acquisition in schools of a modern foreign language.

Replying to the debate, the Minister of State at the Department of Education and Science, Mrs Angela Rumbold, firmly took issue with a suggestion that Latin or Greek might be substituted for a modern foreign language in the list of foundation subjects: 'Knowledge of a potential customer's language can be a deciding factor in securing and maintaining exports'.[1]

It is not difficult to imagine the initial impact of a central decision not to include Classical languages in the National Curiculum. As was noted in Chapter Twelve, priority will clearly be given to staffing and resourcing those areas of the curriculum which are legally required to be taught.

A survey of Classics teachers in 1993

No major surveys on the scale of the Cambridge School Classics Project's 1976 evaluation or of the HMI 1973–4 survey have been undertaken in recent years. The most up to date indication of the state of Classics in maintained schools following the passing of the 1988 Act comes from responses to a questionnaire distributed to JACT members in 1993. The results of the survey, published by JACT, showed that whilst 21 per cent of respondents expected an improvement in the position of Classics in their schools over the next five years, as many as 37.5 per cent believed that there would be less Classics. A further 6 per cent feared that this would be the case, whilst 35.5 per cent hoped that the *status quo* would be maintained. Respondents in sixth-form colleges were reasonably optimistic, although the prospect of 'incorporation' as autonomous institutions, independent of local authorities, was causing some anxiety. Nearly half of all the respondents and almost all those who expected their Classics to be reduced mentioned the National Curriculum as a damaging factor in the fight to retain Classics on the timetable. Interestingly enough, of the small number of responses from Scottish teachers in maintained schools, all except one expected the amount of Classics to increase. It is worth noting here that the curriculum provision under new centralised arrangements takes a different form from that in England and Wales and it is one which is potentially more favourable to Classics.

The Executive Secretary of JACT, Mrs Jeannie Cohen, in her analysis of the completed questionnaires, commented: 'Many respondents write passionately about the esteem with which their subject is held in their school by pupils and staff alike . . . but the National Curriculum is inexorable, and Classics gradually loses its place'.[2] On a more optimistic note, however, it is important to note one positive development for Classics which has taken place in the setting up of the National Curriculum. The decision was made at the outset to include in the History programmes of study for English schools core units on ancient Greece (Key Stage 2) and the Roman Empire (Key Stage 3). Such a selection of content has ensured for the first time that all pupils in English maintained schools have some acquaintance with the classical world through the medium of English during their primary and secondary schooling. In Wales, the study of ancient Greece at Key Stage 2 and of the Roman Empire at Key Stage 3 were both made optional. However, by 1994 in England at least, the Greek and Roman world are seen as making a contribution to the curriculum of all pupils along the lines originally argued for by JACT and the Cambridge Project. It is clear from responses to the 1993 JACT questionnaire and from other sources that some Classics specialists have taken the opportunity to contribute to these core

144

National Curriculum units as well as to language awareness elements in the English curriculum.

A whole new generation of teaching materials has been created for primary and secondary schools, which aims to meet the needs of schools undertaking the History programmes of study. These materials have been structured around the prescribed details of the relevant History study units and the three attainment targets as defined in the original statutory History orders.

How far have independent schools suffered from the impact of a National Curriculum which was principally conceived with the maintained sector in mind? Ten years or more after the HMI survey of Classics in independent schools referred to in Chapter Twelve, it is clear that the independent sector has by no means been insulated from those major developments which have made their impact on maintained schools. Even when the 1988 Education Act was fresh on the Statute books, there were predictions that independent schools would come under the influence of the National Curriculum requirements. It was also becoming clear that some heads of independent schools were increasingly prepared to expose their classical colleagues to competition in the curriculum marketplace by, for the first time, removing compulsory Latin.

The 1993 JACT questionnaires suggested that the position of Classics in fee-paying schools was rather better than in maintained schools, but even here there were some causes for concern. Of the small sample of teachers from preparatory schools, nearly half were not optimistic about the possibility of an increase in Classics. The National Curriculum was seen to be responsible for a significant decrease and only one teacher thought there was any possibility of an increase. Of the fee-paying secondary schools represented, as many as 19 per cent expected to have less Classics within five years and a further 5 per cent feared that this might be the case. However, 37 per cent were confident or hopeful of more and 39 per cent expected to maintain the *status quo*.

The Cambridge School Classics Project's more recent responses to change

Since the 1950s, buffeted by the succession of the three crises identified and described in this book, the teaching of classical languages in the maintained sector has moved from being a 'high status' subject and for many a regular road to sound career prospects, to, at best, a minority subject option lying outside the requirements of a compulsory National Curriculum. In the majority of maintained schools, opportunities no longer exist for studying the two ancient classical languages. Where opportunities do exist, time is likely to be very limited and the subject must compete in the curriculum marketplace with a number of attractive alternative options. In the independent sector too, a process of attrition has placed the teaching of Classics in a much more vulnerable position, where Classics teachers must make their subject more attractive or perish.

It is ironic that the same period of the twentieth century has witnessed the transformation of Latin teaching into an attractive subject for which school pupils will opt not merely for reasons of career or university entry requirements. Furthermore it is a subject that youngsters will almost universally enjoy. The Cambridge School Classics Project has played a central role in this transformation. It is a pleasure to meet young students who have experienced the CLC and who freely admit to having enjoyed the experience of learning Latin at school.

The changed circumstances have led to some further developments on the part of the Project. Whilst it is true that supportive heads and governing bodies are prepared to see the continuation of Latin in their schools even when faced with the imminent retirement of a Latin specialist, the available time allowance is under constant pressure. The situation has changed dramatically since 1966 when the Project tested its first pilot material.

By summer 1993 the numbers entered for GCSE Latin in England and Wales had dropped to 12,574, and of these candidates over a third were entered for the CLC examination offered either by Northern Examinations and Assessment Board (NEAB) or by Midland Examining Group (MEG). For many pupils, however, a shortened Latin course may mean that pupils will have difficulty in reaching a GCSE goal.

The Project in its recent initiatives has been mindful of the many schools where no opportunities to learn Latin exist within the formal curriculum. Where Latin specialists or language teachers who have some Latin do exist in schools, there may be opportunities for twilight teaching or independent learning. The challenge here has been to build on the published CLC in order to facilitate effective learning in these situations.

The Project first introduced its graded objective tests scheme in 1985. The setting up of this scheme involved the identification of a number of clearly defined, medium-term goals that would be within reach of most students using the CLC. The scheme parallels similar developments in Modern Language teaching. Pupils are tested at the end of each unit and are awarded a certificate to show that they have 'passed' that particular section of the course. The scheme proved from the start to be popular and by 1991 more than 38,000 pupils had received certification relating to individual tests. By mid-1994 that figure had reached 87,600. The CLC was felt to be particularly suitable for a system of graded tests in view of its clearly defined twin objectives to develop the ability to read Latin and to develop understanding of the Roman world. The intention in developing the graded tests scheme has been that pupils reaching a pass standard in a particular unit will be motivated to continue with the subject, or, at least, if their study of this subject came to an end for whatever reason they will feel some sense of achievement.

A more recent Project development has been the piloting and publication of independent learning materials to accompany the CLC. The *Cambridge Latin Course Independent Learning Manual Unit 1* contains photocopiable material and is designed together with its accompanying *Answer Book* for use in conjunction with the published multi-media materials comprising pupil's text, tape recording and film strips. (The last now replace the original sets of slides.)

The manual is addressed to the student whether working as an individual or in a larger group. The materials are seen as providing for a variety of situations, including schools where Latin is regularly taught, but where the teacher is absent or where pupils need to catch up after illness or where they transfer from another school. The materials may also be helpful in classes where groups of pupils are working at very different levels. The principal motivation for producing these materials, however, has been the need to help pupils learning Latin on their own to do much of this work by themselves for the straightforward reason that specialist tuition is not available. Another significant publication has been the series of photo-master exercises, designed to supplement the exercises in the pupils' texts.

With regard to the Project's response on the classical civilisation front, it is worth noting that the original folders of material based on the ancient Greeks and aimed at the 11–13 age range have now long since gone out of print. In the later 1960s and early 1970s these materials played a crucial part in the dissemination of the Project's thinking and in helping Classics teachers to develop civilisation courses for a broad range of ability in the new situation in which they found themselves. At the time these materials were much sought after. They offered a basis for teaching about the ancient Greeks to mixed ability classes and provided food for thought for teachers of other subjects who faced similar problems. The resource packs, consisting entirely of cards, had been designed for this purpose, and the duplicator masters for individual worksheets based on items in the folders were also a new concept. These materials are still to be found in use in lower school Humanities courses.

However, the materials fell a little short of the mark when it came to providing for this full range of ability in a mixed ability class within mainstream comprehensive schools, since they did not always cater for the least able pupils.

Following an analysis of language levels by Keith Gardner of the University of Nottingham, of the first two Greek folders which had originally been published, some supplementary material was written and published as part of a second edition in the early 1980s. These two folders had been the first to be published almost ten years previously in 1972 and had run out of print. The remaining folders in the original series did not follow suit in a second edition. By the early 1990s the Roman World packs were no longer available in their original format. A limited second printing, whilst not retaining the precise format of the original materials, did enable schools to have access to the content. Resource packs consisting of individual cards and booklets were no longer in fashion and the National Curriculum requirements necessitated the provision of new materials. Individual textbooks, rather than resource packs, had by the 1990s become the norm in secondary schools.

Reference has already been made above to recent encouraging developments regarding the National Curriculum History programmes of study. Classicists could at least take heart that core units on ancient Greece and on the Roman Empire were written into Key Stages 2 and 3 respectively. Moreover the approach advocated by the History Working Group and reflected in the three History attainment targets is by no means inconsistent with the Project's original thinking. The Project's contribution to these developments can be traced back to those early days in 1965 and 1966 when the provision of courses through the medium of English was seen as crucial to the survival of Classics. The Project's brief, however, related only to the traditional secondary school age range.

Earlier chapters have shown how the Cambridge Project explored the possible contribution of Classics through the medium of English, particularly at the younger end of the secondary school, and was keen to encourage the study of myth, legend, history, art and archaeology as part of a general Humanities curriculum. The approach advocated encouraged teachers to develop both creative and investigative approaches for young pupils. The extension based in Bristol (see Chapter Ten) concentrated largely on an investigative approach to the Roman world, making available sizeable quantities of primary source material, much of it not previously accessible to classroom teachers. The Schools Council History Project team (SHP), working full-time during the 1970s, gave central emphasis to the handling of first-hand evidence and its interpretation in the study of history.[3] The Cambridge University Press, in briefing their sales staff in the late 1970s, were keen to show that the Project's approach to the Roman world, as advocated for 12–14 year olds, had some similarities with the SHP's approaches, which were becoming widely disseminated among secondary teachers of History. Although never likely to attract a large clientele, the Project's own approach was extended to the 14–16 age range in the form of a GCSE syllabus offered by MEG which contrasted with some of the more traditional classical civilisation approaches at 16+.

Whilst the main thrust of the Project's curriculum development work was aimed at 11–16 year olds, a small amount of interest in the Project's work has been created among primary and (in the independent sector) preparatory school teachers. However, Roman (and to a lesser extent) Greek topics have always featured in primary schools. The decline in opportunities to study classical subjects in secondary schools, and fears that a high percentage of pupils might never encounter the classical world during their secondary schooling, led to some 'official' recognition that classicists should lend support to primary school teachers wishing to include Graeco-Roman topics in their curriculum. In 1985, JACT responded to the Select Parliamentary Committee enquiry into the curriculum of primary schools in a positive and realistic way. During the late 1980s, the possibility that Classics might feature in the curriculum of primary schools also began to figure in HMI thinking. The Project's own developing support for primary school teachers is reflected in two short monographs published by the Cambridge Project in 1989 and 1992.

The author of this book, Martin Forrest, together with an experienced primary schoolteacher, Jean Farrall, explored a number of approaches to Greek and Roman topics with pupils aged 7–8 at St Anne's C of E School at Oldland near Bristol. The Head of this school, Michael Turner, a keen student of ancient history, wished to see the Graeco-Roman world making a contribution to the Humanities curriculum in his school. Many of the ideas which were tried out with Jean Farrall's classes over a two to three-year period, including a very brief acquaintance with the CLC, were disseminated, through the Project's first monograph and through other sources, to interested primary school teachers.[4] The second monograph on the ancient Greeks, written by Robin Cowen, an experienced Deputy Head from a primary school near Bristol, was based on his own practical experience of undertaking a project on the ancient Greeks.[5] Information on the work undertaken at St Anne's School was also sent to the History Working Group as they deliberated on the possible content of History programme for Key Stage 2.

In May 1988, JACT staged a one-day conference at St Mary's College, Twickenham, to consider ways of assisting primary schools to draw on classical material in their work with pupils aged 7 upwards. This conference led to the publication of six pamphlets in the JACT 'Themes' series. The series drew upon the experiences of teachers who had used or were currently using Greek and Roman topics in their classrooms and included some of the work undertaken at St Anne's School.[6]

During the time that these pamphlets were in preparation, the National Curriculum History Working Group was deliberating on the content and structure of its proposals for England. Advice was taken from classicists on the content. The consultative phase which followed led to the establishment of the History programmes of study and attainment targets, as we came to know know them, with requirements to include at Key Stage 2 a small, but necessary, element on the Roman invasion of Britain (Core Study Unit 1) and a whole core unit (Core Study Unit 5) devoted to ancient Greece. Since 1990 opportunities have arisen for the author to contribute to the Ginn History Scheme for Primary Schools and to trial some Greek language awareness materials for Open School as an extension of the opportunities offered by the compulsory study unit on the ancient Greeks.[7]

The Project was not in a position to publish any materials explicitly geared to the needs of those undertaking Key Stage 3 History and embarking on the original Core Study Unit 1: The Roman Empire. A number of textbooks have been specifically produced for the new National Curriculum market. The published materials are all dovetailed with the requirements set out in the National Curriculum document-ation. The Roman World materials published in late 1970s are still to be found in the history stock cupboards of some secondary schools. These materials, even in their present format, have been playing a useful role in the delivery of the Roman Empire Study Unit. The advent of new forms of information technology, notably the CD-Rom and other ways of exploring multi-media materials, make these materials a prime candidate for conversion to a new format.

The future prospects for Classics in Britain

The original twin intentions of the Cambridge School Classics Project have now been fulfilled, namely that there should be opportunities for all pupils to study the classical world and that there should also be available a Latin reading course for all who wish to study it. The arrival of a National Curriculum which excludes Latin, but which at least initially required all pupils in England to study some Greek and Roman civilisation as part of their history studies, has proved to be something of a bitter-sweet experience. Although HMI, before their reorganisation in 1992, remained optimistic that there was still room for classical language learning in that part of the curriculum which remains outside the core and foundation subjects, the 1993 JACT survey painted a rather different picture.

The importance of having classical elements within the History programmes of study cannot be underestimated. Much will depend upon the quality of learning that takes place at Key Stages 2 and 3. There can be no doubt that well-taught Greek and Roman topics which succeed in firing the interest and enthusiasm of young pupils before they are required to specialise may bear fruit in later years.

In some maintained schools the provision of Latin is still in place and it is to be hoped that as many schools as possible will be able to hold on to their existing staffing. The vast majority of state school pupils are in schools where there is no Latin specialist or where Latin cannot be given official timetable space, although some opportunities are now opening up for independent learning, using the CLC, as described earlier. Interest in the classical world among the general public remains high. Summer schools sponsored by JACT, which offer language learning opportunities to young people who have missed the chance to study Latin at school, continue to flourish. The demand for *ab initio* Latin and Greek language courses from the general public is considerable.

Among the key questions posed at an invitation conference called by JACT in July 1993 on the future of Classics, was the question 'How can we get people to study Classics at university if all the Classics they meet at school is Greeks in Key Stage 2 and Romans in Key Stage 3?' The conference was called because of anxieties about an excessively restrictive curriculum especially from the age of 14 onwards, which it was feared could squeeze out Latin from schools altogether. Following this conference and in its subsequent communications with its membership, JACT committed itself to doing everything in its power to 'roll back the constraints of the National Curriculum'. When the government in 1993 announced a major review of the National Curriculum, JACT members were urged to respond.[8]

The Dearing Review

The final recommendations arising from the first major review of the National Curriculum by the restructured curriculum and assessment body, SCAA, under Sir Ron Dearing were published in January 1994. The Secretary of State, John Patten, immediately accepted these recommendations and subject-specific working parties were immediately reconstituted and put to work, charged with the task of 'slimming down' the National Curriculum requirements.

The modified programmes of study which came into force in September 1995 continue to include a core study unit on Greece (at Key Stage 2) and maintain an opportunity for a brief encounter with Roman Britain at primary school level, although there is some disappointment that the Roman Empire (at Key Stage 3) has now become optional.[9] An important principle adopted by Dearing was that changes to content prescription should be kept to a minimum and it seems likely that many schools will continue to teach the Roman Empire now that they have equipped themselves with the relevant resources. It is also very clear that pupils aged 11, by and large, enjoy studying the Romans. However, for classicists, the decision to rein back the number of required National Curriculum subjects which pupils study from the age of 14 onwards will be seen as a major victory for common sense and as a reprieve for Latin and classical subjects for pupils aged 14–16. Those schools where opportunities still exist for studying a classical language will now have every chance of continuing to offer classical subjects, although fierce competition between the traditional humanities and the pre-vocational curriculum is now here to stay. Competition both from more traditional subjects and from the pre-vocational curriculum will nevertheless continue to be an important factor and Classics teachers will have to continue to market their subject effectively. With regard to Key Stage 2, Dr Nicholas Tate, the Chief Executive of SCAA, was recently reported as advocating that primary schools should use time freed up by the Dearing Review to teach Latin and Greek.[10] It remains to be seen how far schools will rise to the challenge.

Another factor which is likely to play an increasingly important part in determining the curriculum of schools is an increasing diversity of school provision. The relentless moves by central government to reduce the power of local education authorities in relation to schools seems likely to be accelerated. Encouragement given to schools to opt out from local authority control and to become 'grant maintained' has recently been given greater prominence by the British government. The arrival, too, of city technology colleges and the 'incorporation' of further education and sixth-form colleges as autonomous institutions all point to a greater diversity of provision in the future. As has been demonstrated, the response of LEAs towards Classics has always been, at best, patchy. The increased diversity of school provision which lies outside of LEA control suggests that much will depend upon how particular schools develop or build on particular curriculum strengths and specialisms in the years ahead. The term 'magnet school' has been used to describe schools which design their curricula to attract particular parental and student interests. Even within the maintained sector there are still in most counties schools which are well placed to offer a curriculum strength in Classics.

Most important of all will be the attitudes of parents towards the learning of classical languages. During the mid-1980s there was a episode in a meeting of the governing body at Queen Elizabeth's School, Crediton, publicly witnessed by television viewers, when a parent governor whose daughter had studied the CLC persuaded his fellow governors to resist a cut-back in Latin provision within the school. The time is fast approaching when a whole new generation of parents who themselves had the opportunity of using the CLC at school, have children of their own at the age when they themselves began to learn Latin. If these parents enjoyed their Latin and, above all, are convinced that learning the language using the CLC had some value for them, they will surely want the same opportunity to be available for their own offspring.

Such parental pressure, if it materialises, will not only provide support for the continuance of Latin in those schools where it already exists, but may even lead to demands for Latin to be taught in schools where it has not previously been taught.

CHAPTER FOURTEEN

The Achievement of the Cambridge School Classics Project

It will be useful to conclude with a short chapter devoted to attempting an assessment of the Cambridge School Classics Project. In this book, an attempt has been made to trace the origins of the Cambridge Project and to provide an historical account of the Project's early years. The output of publications by the Project, almost all of them published in their revised edition by the Cambridge University Press, has been prodigious. The visual impact of this enormous total output was witnessed by all who attended the Project's silver jubilee celebrations in 1991 when all these publications were for the first time assembled in one huge public display. A full list of publications is provided in Appendix 1. By far the largest number of published items relate to the CLC which, together with many items of trial material, published by the Project itself from 1966 onwards, helped to sustain beleaguered Classics teachers as they struggled to keep their subject alive in difficult times.

It was to the development of its Latin reading course that the Project from the outset always gave the greater priority and the reasons for this emphasis will have become clear in the course of this book. However, the output of Classical Studies materials, including the trial materials published by the Project itself, has also been substantial. The Greek foundation course materials, which helped significantly in the development of a Classical Studies course for a broad ability range in early years of secondary schooling, were later complemented by the Roman World materials and (eventually) by four volumes in the Classical Studies 13–16 series. Some of these later materials still continue to form part of prescription for the MEG Classical Civilisation Syllabus (1408). Although the foundation course materials, both Greek and Roman, have been allowed to run out of print, the underlying principle of Classical Studies for all pupils through English has been accepted, at least for the time being, as part of the History programmes of study.

The original materials, whilst they are still to be found in use in some schools, are now seen as having fulfilled their intended initial purpose and have now been replaced by other material deemed to be more directly geared to the requirements of the National Curriculum. The spirit of the original approach lives on in the existing work often to be found in primary school classes where the Core Study Unit 'Ancient Greece' is being studied and also in the work based on primary sources now being undertaken as part of the Roman Empire in secondary schools.

This study has sought to demonstrate that the Cambridge Project, despite experiencing some major difficulties of its own during the period of its full-time existence, which originated from the way the Project was set up and which had long-lasting repercussions, nevertheless enjoyed a high level of take-up by Classics teachers, especially in those situations where the teaching of Latin was under the greatest pressure as the result of Crisis One and Crisis Two.

An analysis of available statistical data shows that by 1977 the number of candidates being entered for the Cambridge Project's 'O' level examination offered by SUJB had reached almost one-third of the total. The peak year for the number of candidates entered for this examination was 1979 when more than 10,000 were entered. That more than 10,000 pupils took the Project's Latin course in 1979 is in itself a remarkable achievement, given that the revised course had only begun to be published in 1970. In recent years, candidates taking the MEG and NEAB Project exams have accounted for over a third of the total entry. However the influence of the Cambridge School Classics Project goes much further than this.

Far from being killed off by the onset of comprehensive reorganisation documented in this book, as many leading classicists in the 1960s had feared, Latin had been given a new lease of life in many comprehensive schools. As has been seen, this was particularly true in reorganised schools which incorporated a former grammar school in which Classics as a subject had been flourishing at the time of reorganisation. In such schools, the teaching of Classics could be found to be apparently alive and well with two or more specialists teaching Latin and with non-specialists contributing especially to the teaching of Classical Civilisation courses on a part-time basis. What had been crucial to this development was the availability of new teaching material which could support both the teaching of Latin in the changed situation and the implementation of effective Classical Studies courses for a wide range of comprehensive school pupils. The steadying in the number of Latin entries at GCE, albeit for a short period, must be accounted for by the surge of optimism as well as in the maintained numbers of pupils that the arrival of the new approaches to Classics teaching heralded.

Some of the underlying problems within reorganised schools have been referred to in Chapter Nine. It is also clear that there were many reorganised schools where Classics teaching either suffered an early demise or was allowed to continue under sufferance, before being quietly extinguished.

It was the arrival of what has been referred to as Crisis Three in the late 1970s which was to place new sets of obstacles in the paths of Classics teachers, even in some of those schools where Classics had continued to flourish after reorganisation.

Why was the CSCP so successful?

A number of reasons can be put forward to explain the success which the Cambridge Project achieved by the late 1970s in offering a widespread take-up and in transforming the teaching of Classics, especially in the maintained sector. Firstly, and most importantly, there were the two crises, the impact of which has been described in some detail during the earlier chapters of this book. The removal of the Latin requirement for entry to Oxford and Cambridge together with comprehensive reorganisation combined to ensure that the traditional form of Classics teaching available in the grammar schools of the 1950s *had* to change. Only a curriculum development project could provide appropriate course materials to meet the needs of reorganised schools. When the Cambridge Project came into being with its combined offerings of a Latin reading course and materials to support schools undergoing reorganisation, the response from schools was generally enthusiastic. Although there were doubters, schools faced with the prospect of reorganisation were well-advised to look to the Project for support and the Project thus had a ready market for its ideas and its materials.

A second reason was to do with dissemination and in-service support for teachers. From 1967 onwards, the Project made widely available sample materials, both for the Latin course trials and from its civilisation courses, and also information bulletins. A willingness to send speakers to any organisation, whether the sponsor was a local branch of JACT or the CA, a university department, or an LEA, was an important feature of the Project's approach from 1966 onwards. This ensured that the Project's developing thinking was widely disseminated and thus teachers under internal and external pressure were then offered some hope for the future.

More important still were two other features of the Project's work, which ensured effective and soundly based support for teachers who were adopting the new materials and approaches. The earlier Schools Council Projects which followed the Research, Development and Diffusion model were given no budget either for in-service training or for 'after-care' once the full-time life of the Project had ceased. In fact, in-service training did not even come within the remit of the Schools Council. The Cambridge

Project launched its major trial programmes for the new Latin reading course in the summer of 1967 at a self-financing training course at which it was expected all teachers taking part in the trial programme would attend. An in-service course which was self-financing was also arranged for teachers who were developing or considering the development of classical foundation courses early in 1968.

The Project continued to mount its own CLC in-service course on an annual basis, whilst at the same time responding to requests from other sponsors to provide or participate in training courses in many parts of the United Kingdom (or further afield). Major training and dissemination conferences were also organised for Classical Civilization courses in Bristol from 1972 onwards and requests from other sponsors were similarly taken up, whenever they arose.

Most important of all to the sustained development of the Project's courses were the continuing after-care arrangements which the Project was able to provide after 1970. The appointment of Pat Story as a lecturer in the Education Department of Cambridge University allowed her to continue to work on a part-time basis as the Project's Deputy Director. This meant that the Project had a continuing authoritative presence at Cambridge in the years after the full-time life of the Project had come to an end. The provision of an office in premises owned by the University (by this time at 17 Panton Street) and the continued employment of the Project's energetic secretary, Mrs Maire Collins, together with a number of part-time administrative and academic assistants, was made possible as the result of income received from the Project's own publications. These after-care arrangements provided a secure basis from which the Project's work could be continued over a number of years and these arrangements are still in place in the mid-1990s, though the nature of the task in hand has changed. There was thus a ready-made structure when the time came to carry out the major evaluation study of 1976 and to undertake the subsequent revision which led to the second edition of the CLC. The Project has also been in a position to respond to external pressures by developing new initiatives such as the independent learning materials, the graded tests and the primary school publications. Advice continues to be made available for teachers on GCSE course work and on teaching the Project's materials.

In this respect, the Cambridge Project differed from many other curriculum projects of the 1960s and 1970s. Teachers did not feel left 'high and dry' once the Project's full-time existence had come to an end and the team members had dispersed. Instead there was always someone on the end of a telephone line to whom they could turn for help. The Project was therefore able to provide friendly support to all those Classics teachers who put faith in its ideas and in its products. This must be seen as a major factor in the Project's successful dissemination of its thinking.

Schedule of Project Publications

A   CAMBRIDGE LATIN COURSE

First Edition

Unit I

Stages 1–12 (twelve pamphlets) and Words and Phrases	1970
Slides	1970
Tape	1970
Cassette	1970
Teacher's Handbook	1971

Unit II

Stages 13–20 (eight pamphlets) Words and Phrases and Information about the Language	1972
Slides	1971
Tape	1971
Cassette	1971
Teacher's Handbook	1971

Unit III

Stages 21–31 (eleven pamphlets) Words and Phrases and Information about the Language	1972
Slides	1973
Tape	1972
Cassette	1972
Teacher's Handbook	1973

Unit IV

Pliny, Tacitus, Catullus and Ovid (in seven pamphlets) and Words and Phrases	1973
Slides	Set 1: 1976; Set 2: 1977
Tape	1974
Cassette	1974
Teacher's Handbook	1976

Unit V

Dido et Aeneas, Nero et Agrippina and Words and Phrases	1974
Slides	Dido et Aeneas 1978 Nero et Agrippina 1979

Tape	1974
Cassette	1974
Teacher's Handbook	1977

Units IV and V

Information about the Language	1975
Supplementary Handbook	1980

Second Edition

Unit I

Pupils' Pack, Stages 1–12 (twelve pamphlets available in set and individually	1982
Pupils' Book, Stages 1–12 (same material as Pupils' Pack, in single book,	
mainly for North American market)	1982
Language Information Pamphlet	1982
Teacher's Handbook	1982
Filmstrip 1: Pompeii	1983

Unit II

Unit IIA: Pupils' Book	1982
Unit IIA: Language Information Pamphlet	1982
Unit IIB: Pupils' Book	1983
Unit IIB: Language Information pamphlet	1983
Unit IIA and IIB: Teacher's Handbook	1983
Filmstrip 2: Roman Britain	1984

Unit III

Unit IIIA: Pupils' Book	1983
Unit IIIA: Language Information Pamphlet	1983
Unit IIIB: Pupils' Book	1984
Unit IIIB: Language Information Pamphlet	1984
Units IIIA and IIIB: Teacher's Handbook	1985
Filmstrip 3: Rome	1986

Units I, II and III

Filmstrip 4: Additional material for Cambridge Latin Course	1990
Cassette to accompany Units I, IIA and IIB	1986
Cassette to accompany Units IIIA and IIIB	1986

Unit IVA

Pupils' Book	1986
Teacher's Handbook	1987

Unit IVB

Pupils' Book	1988
Teacher's Handbook	1990

B   NORTH AMERICAN VERSION OF SECOND EDITION
OF CAMBRIDGE LATIN COURSE

(In each Unit, pupils' texts, filmstrips and cassettes are the
same as the UK edition)

Unit I

Language Information Pamphlet	1982
Teacher's Manual	1983

Workbook for North American students (available in book form and in first printing only as Mazer masters)	1983

Unit II

Unit IIA: Language Information Pamphlet	1982
Unit IIB: Language Information Pamphlet	1983
Units IIA and IIB: Teacher's Manual	1983

Unit III

Unit IIIA: Language Information Pamphlet	1983
Unit IIIB: Language Information Pamphlet	1984
Units IIIA and IIIB: Teacher's Manual	1986

Unit IVA

Teacher's Manual	1988

C GREEK WORLD FOUNDATION COURSE

Folder 1: Troy and the Early Greeks	1972
Folder 1: Duplicator Masters	
Folder 2: The Gods of Mount Olympus	1972
Folder 2: Duplicator Masters	
Folder 3: Greek Religion	1974
Folder 3: Duplicator Masters	
Folder 4: Athens, Sparta and Persia	1974
Folder 4: Duplicator Masters	
Folder 5: Greek Festivals	1975
Folder 5: Duplicator Masters	
Teacher's Handbook	1972

Revised edition

Pack 1: Troy and the Early Greeks	1980
Pack 2: The Gods of Mount Olympus	1981

D THE ROMAN WORLD FOUNDATION COURSE

Unit I (Four books: Lugdunum, The Gauls, Two Journeys, The Witches of Thessaly and other stories), Resource cards	1978
Unit 2 (Three books: Baucis and Philemon and other stories, Three Letters from Pliny, The Villa), Resource cards	1979
Teacher's Handbook 1: Introductory Guide	1978
Teacher's Handbook 2: Resources and Commentaries	1980

E CLASSICAL STUDIES 13–16

Book 1: The Romans Discover Britain	1981
Book 1: Teacher's Handbook	1981
Book 2: How the Greeks and Romans made Cloth	1984
Book 2: Teacher's Handbook	1984
Book 3: Pompey and Caesar	1986
Book 3: Teacher's Handbook	1986
Book 4: Athens: City and Empire	1989
Book 4: Teacher's Handbook	1989

F NORTH AMERICAN: CAMBRIDGE LATIN COURSE

3rd edition

Unit 1: Students' Book	1988
Unit 1: Teacher's Manual	1988
Unit 1: Workbook	1988
Unit 2: Students' Book	1988
Unit 2: Teacher's Manual	1988
Unit 2: Workbook	1988
Unit 3: Students' Book	1989
Unit 3: Teacher's Manual	1989
Unit 3: Workbook	1989
Unit 4: Students' Book	1991
Unit 4: Teacher's Manual	1992
Unit 4: Workbook	1992

G NORTH AMERICAN: A STUDENT'S LATIN GRAMMAR   1992

H CAMBRIDGE LATIN GRAMMAR   1991

I CAMBRIDGE LATIN COURSE (continued)

Integrated edition

Unit I: Pupils' Book	1990
Unit IIA: Pupils' Book	1990
Unit IIB: Pupils' Book	1990
Unit IIIA: Pupils' Book	1990
Unit IIIB: Pupils' Book	1990
Unit IVA: Pupils' Book	1991
Unit IVB: Pupils' Book	1991
Unit I: Computer programs	1991
Unit I: Worksheet Masters	1993
Units IIA and IIB: Worksheet Masters	

Key Events Relevant to the Origins and Early History of the Cambridge School Classics Project

1960	April	Classical Association AGM held at Southampton: Professor C.O. Brink urges reconsideration of the goals of 'O' level Latin.
	May	Removal of the classical language admission requirement by Oxford and Cambridge Universities.
1962	January	Decision to establish the Joint Association of Classical Teachers.
1964	March	JACT offers advice to Classics teachers facing comprehensive reorganisation.
	June	Leicestershire Plan conference held at Cambridge.
	July	First meeting of C.W. Baty and K.G. Todd with R.W. Morris and R.A. Becher at Nuffield Lodge.
	October	Election of a Labour government pledged to end selection at 11.
	November	First Nuffield Lodge Conference.
	December	Second Nuffield Lodge Conference.
1965	January	Nuffield Trustees consider proposals for a curriculum development project in Classics. Detailed proposals for a Cambridge School Classics Programme submitted to Nuffield.
	April	Nuffield Foundation announces the establishment of a three-year project on the teaching of Classics in schools to be based at Cambridge University.
	May	First meeting of Cambridge School Classics Project Committee.
	September	CSCP Committee agrees to part–time consultancy link with Queen Mary College, London.
	December	First meeting of the CSCP Advisory Panel.

1966	January	The Project begins work at Silver Street, Cambridge on a Latin reading course.
	September	Small–scale pilot testing of Latin course materials begins.
1967	January	Work on non–linguistic Classical Studies materials begins.
	September	Large–scale trials of the Latin reading course begin. Small–scale trials of non–linguistic materials begin.
1968	January	Crisis deepens within the Project team.
	April	Further funding agreed with Nuffield Foundation and the Schools Council.
	September	Large–scale trials of the non–linguistic materials begins.
	November	Resignation of Project's first Linguistic Consultant accepted.
1969	May	Project moves to new premises at Panton Street, Cambridge.
1970	September	First schools begin using the published Cambridge Latin Course.
1972	September	First schools begin using the published foundation course materials.
1973	September	Extension based at Bristol begins: work on further Classical Civilisation materials begins.
1976	September	Evaluation of the CLC begins.

APPENDIX 3

Dramatis Personae

W.S. Allen	Formerly Professor of Comparative Philology in the University of Cambridge. Founder member of the CSCP Committee who sometimes deputised for the Chairman during the first years of the Project.
D.M. Balme	Formerly Professor of Classics at Queen Mary College, London. A contender for establishing a Classics project in London. Founder member and Chairman of the CSCP Advisory Committee. Head of Department of the Project's first linguistic consultant, J.B. Wilkins (q.v.).
C.W. Baty	Formerly HMI and Staff Inspector for Classics. Became the first Honorary Secretary General of JACT. Played a leading role establishing the Project and remained a key member of the CSCP Advisory Committee throughout the Project's full–time existence.
R.A. Becher	Formerly a senior officer employed by the Nuffield Foundation. Played a central role in negotiating funding for the Project and was a member of the CSCP Advisory Committee.
C.O. Brink	Formerly Kennedy Professor of Latin in the University of Cambridge. Played a seminal role in challenging the traditional 'O' level Latin course. Member of the CSCP Advisory Panel.
D.C. Chandler	Formerly full–time member of the Project team.
R.G.G. Coleman	Member of the Classical Faculty in the University of Cambridge. Former member of the CSCP Committee.
J.C. Dancy	Formerly Head of Marlborough College, Wiltshire and Chairman of the Schools Council's Classics Committee.
M.St.J. Forrest	(The author) Formerly full–time member of the Project team.
C. Greig	Formerly full–time member of the Project team.
R.M. Griffin	Formerly full–time member of the Project team and subsequently Revision Editor of the Cambridge Latin Course.
M.J. Hughes	Formerly full–time member of the Project during the extension based in Bristol (1973–8).
A.G. Hunt	Formerly member of the Faculty of Education and founder member of the CSCP Committee.
J.A. Jones	Formerly full–time member of the Project team.
W.A. Lloyd	Formerly Professor of Education in the University of Cambridge. Founder member of the CSCP Committee and first Chairman.

163

E.J. Kenney	Member of the Classical Faculty and founder member of the CSCP Committee.
T.W. Melluish	Formerly Head of Classics at the Bec School, Tooting. Held high office in the Classical Association, the Association for the Reform of Latin Teaching and Orbilian Society. Stout defender of traditional Classical teaching and fierce opponent of comprehensive reorganisation.
R.W. Morris	Formerly a senior HMI assigned to work in collaboration with the Nuffield Foundation to establish curriculum development projects.
D.J. Morton	Formerly a member of the Department of Education in the University of Nottingham. He was seconded from his post to be full–time Director of the Project for three years. Continued in a part–time capacity from September 1969.
C.W.E. Peckett	Formerly Head of the Priory School, Shrewsbury. Leading proponent of teaching Latin and Greek by 'direct' or 'oral' method. Leading member of ARLT and joint author of the Latin course Principia and the Greek course Thrasymachus. Also an early advocate of Classics taught through the medium of English to a broad ability range. Member of the CSCP Advisory Panel.
P.A.M. Seuren	Succeeded J.B. Wilkins (q.v.) as Linguistic Consultant to the Project.
J.E. Sharwood Smith	Formerly member of the Institute of Education in the University of London. Played the central role in the formation of JACT and in the formulation of a strategy to reform the teaching of Classics in the light of comprehensive reorganisation. Was involved in an early bid to locate a Classics project in London.
E.P. Story	Formerly member of the Department of Education in the University of Oxford. Joined the Project team as full–time Evaluation Officer, but went on to play a leading part in the production of both the trial materials and the published materials. Is currently Honorary Director of the Project.
W.B. Thompson	Formerly member of the Department of Education in the University of Leeds. An early advocate of Classics through the medium of English. Member of the CSCP Advisory Panel.
K.G. Todd	Formerly an HMI and Staff Inspector for Classics. Played an important part along with C.W. Baty (q.v.) in the early discussions which led to the establishment of the Project. Member of the CSCP Advisory Panel.
J.B. Wilkins	Formerly a member of the Classics Department of University College Cardiff. Moved thence to a post at Queen Mary College, London, under D.M. Balme (q.v), to develop research into the teaching of the Latin language. Was associated with an earlier London–based initiative to develop a school Latin course. Subsequently became part–time Linguistic Consultant to the Project throughout the early years of its full–time existence.
B.M.W. Young	A classicist and former Head of Charterhouse School who became Director of the Nuffield Foundation in time to be involved in early discussions about the creation of a Classics project.

Notes

Unauthored citations have been taken from a number of serial publications which are listed in the bibliography. Other citations from articles in serial publications are also referred to by author in the bibliography. Archival sources are listed in the bibliography on pp. 181–183.

A comprehensive list of Cambridge School Classics Project publications appears as Appendix 1. This list does not include the very large number of items which have emerged from the Project over the years as part of its school trial programmes. Reference is made in the text and in the notes to some of these early Project publications which were issued by the Project itself and which generally formed part of one or another trial programme from 1966 onwards. Only those specific items of trial material which are referred to in the text have been referenced.

Chapter One

1. M.L. Clarke, *Classical Education in Britain 1500–1900* (Cambridge: Cambridge University Press, 1959) pp. 174–75.
2. R.R. Bolgar, *Classical Influences on Western Thought AD 1650–1870: Proceedings of an International Conference held at King's College, Cambridge, March 1977* (Cambridge: Cambridge University Press, 1979) pp. 337–38.
3. Clarke, op. cit., p. 77.
4. U. von Wilamowitz–Moellendorff, *History of Classical Scholarship*, translated by A. Harris (London: Duckworth, 1982) p. 1.
5. Board of Education, *Report of the Consultative Committee on Secondary Education with Special Reference to Grammar Schools and Technical high Schools*, The Spens Report (London: HMSO, 1938). Recommendation 70: p. 364.
6. Ibid., Recommendation 77: p. 365.
7. Ibid., p. 176.
8. Ibid., p. 232.
9. Ibid., p. 231.
10. Ibid.
11. *Classical Association (CA) Proceedings* (1939) pp. 46–49.
12. *Latin for Today* embodied the 'word order method' developed by Mason Gray. It promoted the reading of continuous Latin from the outset and included material which dealt with the Roman inheritance. *Latin for Today* represented a more streamlined approach to the learning of Latin and one which in some ways anticipated the

later development of Latin reading courses such as the Cambridge Latin Course. However, translation from English into Latin was introduced very early in the course.

13. Board of Education, *Curricula and Examinations in Secondary Schools, Secondary Schools Examination Council Chaired by Sir C. Norwood* (London: HMSO, 1943).
14. T.W. Melluish, 'Why Latin?' *Greece and Rome* XIII (38–9) (1944) p. 59.
15. Ibid., p. 66.
16. D.G. Bentliff, 'Why no more Latin?' *Greece and Rome* XV (45) (1946) pp. 114–15.
17. *CA Proceedings* (1944), p. 15.
18. Melluish, op. cit., p. 60.
19. Horace, *Epistles* 2.1.70–1.
20. *Acta Diurna.* The title may be translated as 'The Daily News'. The newspaper included main news stories based on events in Roman history, as well as many items that one might expect to find in a modern day newspaper: feature articles, crosswords, cartoons.
21. A classical catalogue of visual aids was first published by the Orbilian Society in 1951. A later version was published by Centaur Books as: *A Classical Catalogue of Audio–visual Aids* compiled by P.M. Jennings.
22. Incorporated Association of Assistant Masters (IAAM), *The Teaching of Classics* (Cambridge: Cambridge University Press, 1954) p. 233.
23. Ibid., pp. 72–73.
24. Ibid., p. ix.
25. CA Council Minutes/Education Sub–committee Reports, 2/7/49 and 6/1/50.
26. Dora Pym Papers/Memorandum from Mrs D. Pym to Professor Fletcher dated 21/4/54.
27. Dora Pym Papers/Notice for Classical Conference to be held at University of Bristol 7/5/55.
28. Ibid.
29. *Latin Teaching* XXIX (1) (1955) p. 4.
30. Ibid., pp. 10–13.
31. *Latin Teaching* XXIX (2) (1955) pp. 48–58.
32. Ibid., p. 54.
33. C.W.E. Peckett and H. Loehry, *Heritage of the West* (Shrewsbury: Wilding, 1958).
34. *Latin Teaching* XXIX (2) (1955) p. 58.
35. W.S. Fowler, 'Common Core Classics', *Latin Teaching* XXX (4) (1958) pp. 121–25.
36. A.D.C. Peterson, 'The Examination Syllabus', *Latin Teaching* XXX (4) (1958) p. 118.
37. Thompson Collection/W.B. Thompson's lecture notes.
38. Ibid.
39. *Latin Teaching* XXX (5) (1959) p. 156.
40. *Times Educational Supplement* 24/10/58, p. 1563.

Chapter Two

1. Oxford: *Times Educational Supplement* 20/5/60, p. 1043; Cambridge: *Times Educational Supplement* 13/5/60, p. 978.
2. The main sources for this meeting are to be found in *CA Proceedings* (1960) pp. 22–23 and in *Times Educational Supplement* 15/4/60, p. 768. Reference is also made to the Southampton meeting in C.O. Brink, 'Small Latin and the Classics', in T.W. Melluish (ed.), *Reappraisal*, Supplement to *Greece and Rome* IX (1) (1962) p. 8.
3. *Times Educational Supplement* 15/4/60, loc. cit.
4. C.O. Brink, 'Small Latin and the University' *Latin Teaching* XXX (7) 1960 p. 201.
5. A survey of teacher opinion was carried out by the CA's Education Sub–committee. A list of questions was circulated to regional branches for discussion. The results were incorporated into an 'Interim Report' presented by T.W. Melluish to the Annual

Meeting in 1961 pp. 28–31. The Report was based on a summary of replies undertaken on behalf of the Sub–committee by D.G. Bentliff. An entertaining account of teachers' responses is to be found in *Reappraisal* pp. 42–47. This survey was regarded by some as an attempt to slow down the moves towards radical change. ARLT members were separately surveyed using a 'tear out' questionnaire published in *Latin Teaching* XXX (8) 1960 pp. 237–42, and the responses were summarised in *Latin Teaching* XXX (9) 1961 pp. 253–60. For a fuller account and discussion see M.St.J. Forrest 'Classics teachers, comprehensive reorganisation and curriculum change' (unpublished doctoral thesis, University of Exeter, 1989) pp. 109–120 and 154–55.

6. CA Council Minutes/ CA proposals to Examining Boards: The 'O' level examination in Latin, April 1961.
7. C.W. Baty, 'Classics in the Schools', in T.W. Melluish (ed.), *Reappraisal*, p. 12.
8. C.O. Brink, 'Small Latin and the Classics', in T.W. Melluish (ed.), *Reappraisal*, p. 9.
9. Interview (12/8/86) with K.G. Todd who was Baty's successor as HM Staff Inspector for Classics.
10. CA Council Minutes, 18/10/58, 11/7/59, 31/10/59 and 9/7/60. W.B. Thompson's personal notes for the meeting held on 31/10/59 provide some insight into what he had in mind. These proposals, however, are not fully reflected in the minutes of that meeting.
11. Thompson Collection/Letter from J.E. Sharwood Smith to W.B. Thompson dated 26/5/61.
12. Extispex, 'The First Decade: A Scrutiny of JACT' *Didaskalos* 4 (2) (1973) pp. 259–75, provides a brief published account of JACT's inauguration. M.St.J. Forrest, op. cit., pp. 129–53 provides a detailed account of the origins of JACT including the two conferences and of the strenuous efforts that were made to counter the opposition.
13. Sharwood Smith Papers/Documents relevant to the founding of JACT.
14. R. Pedley, *The Comprehensive School* (Harmondsworth: Penguin, 1963), p. 201.
15. Ibid., p. 45.
16. A.N. Fairbairn (ed.), *The Leicestershire Plan* (London: Heinemann Educational, 1980) pp. 1–2.
17. Leicestershire: S.C. Mason, *The Leicestershire Experiment and Plan*, revised edition (London: Councils and Education Press, 1963) p. 29. Bristol: Vyvyan Jones Papers/Numbers of pupils entered for Latin and Greek 'A' level examinations, summer 1965, 1966 and 1967.
18. *Joint Association of Classical Teachers (JACT) Bulletin* 4 (1964) p. 4.
19. JACT Papers/Leicestershire Plan file/Internal Memorandum 26/3/64.
The Leicestershire Plan and other reorganisation schemes which involved transfer of schools at 14 rather than 11, posed special difficulties for subjects like Latin.
20. JACT Committee Minutes, 25/4/64.
21. Thompson Collection/JACT file/W.B. Thompson's notes for JACT Committee, 25/4/64.
22. Ibid.
23. B.A. Knott Papers/Lecture handout 1964.
24. JACT Committee Minutes, loc. cit.
25. The pamphlet already published was *Robbins and the Classics*, JACT Pamphlet 1, edited by C.W. Baty and J.E. Sharwood Smith (London: JACT, 1964).
26. *Report of the JACT Conference held at Hughes Hall, Cambridge on 27–28 June 1964, on the 'Leicestershire Plan' and its Effect on Classics Teaching*, Mimeo (London: JACT, 1964) and JACT/Leicestershire Plan File/Letter from C.W. Baty dated 3/7/64 to an HMI colleague.
27. *Secondary Reorganisation and the Classics*, JACT Pamphlet 2, edited by D.J. Morton (London: JACT, 1965).

28. CA Council Minutes, 4/7/64.
29. Two UDE lecturers wrote to complain to the other Hon. Secretary, Professor B.R. Rees. JACT Papers/CA File/Letter from B.R. Rees to C.W. Baty dated 26/7/64.

Chapter Three

1. Sharwood Smith Papers/Documents relevant to the founding of JACT/Appendix to conference agenda, 30/9/61.
2. JACT/Committee Minutes, 5/10/63.
3. JACT/Research in the teaching of Classics file/Letters from C.W. Baty to L.A. Moritz 24/9/63 and from S. Morris to C.W. Baty 9/5/63. For a fuller discussion see M.St.J. Forrest, 'Classics teachers, comprehensive reorganisation and curriculum change' (unpublished doctoral thesis, University of Exeter, 1989) pp. 196–97. Baty finally confirmed that he was stalling on the question of a research panel in October (Nuffield Foundation/EDU 121/Letter from C.W. Baty to R.A. Becher dated 21/10/64). From November, the whole JACT Committee consitituted itself as a research panel. Meetings took place on the mornings of committee days. The main function of this group appears to have been to receive reports on research and curriculum development initiatives rather than to undertake research itself. Sidney Morris of the University of Birmingham Department of Education who was keen to play a leading role in any JACT research panel, decided to develop and publish his own curriculum development proposals. These appeared as *Viae Novae*, a book of new techniques in Latin teaching published by Hulton Educational Press 1966; this publication was soon followed by a programmed Latin course.
4. The inauguration of this group by the Education Minister provoked the suspicion of the teacher unions who feared that this was the thin end of the wedge and the first beginnings of central control over the curriculum.
5. Interview with R.W. Morris 16/12/86. Correspondence between the author and R.W. Morris during 1995.
6. Ibid.
7. JACT/Gulbenkian File/Letter from C.W. Baty to J. Thornton dated 22/1/65.
8. JACT/Nuffield File/Letter from K.G. Todd to C.W. Baty dated 7/6/64.
9. Nuffield Foundation/EDU 121/Letter from B.M.W. Young to R.A. Becher dated 11/6/64.
10. JACT/Nuffield File/Letter from C.W. Baty to R.A. Becher dated 19/7/64.
11. JACT/Nuffield File/Fact and Opinion in the teaching of Classics: the case for an inquiry.
12. JACT/Nuffield File/Letter from R.A. Becher to C.W. Baty dated 24/7/64.
13. Ibid./Letter from C.W. Baty to R.A. Becher dated 28/7/64.
14. Ibid./Letter from R.W. Morris to C.W. Baty (no day given)/7/64.
15. Ibid./Letter from R.A. Becher to C.W. Baty dated 8/9/64.
16. Ibid./New possibilities in the teaching of Classics p. 9.
17. Ibid./Letter from R.A. Becher to C.W. Baty dated 24/9/64.
18. Ibid./Letter from R.A. Becher to C.W. Baty dated 8/9/64.
19. Ibid./New possibilities in the teaching of Classics p. 8.
20. Ibid., p. 9.
21. Ibid.
22. Nuffield Foundation/Minutes of 141st meeting of Nuffield Trustees (January 1965) Ref. V.363.
23. Nuffield Foundation/EDU 121/Letter from R.A. Becher to J.T. Christie dated 20/10/64.
24. JACT/Nuffield File/Letter from C.W. Baty to R.A. Becher dated 23/9/64.

25. Ibid./Letter from R.W. Morris to C.W. Baty (no day given) 7/64.
26. Ibid./Letter from R.W. Morris to C.W. Baty (no day given) 9/64.
27. Nuffield Foundation/Minutes of 141st meeting of Nuffield Trustees (January 1965) Ref. V. 363.
28. JACT/Nuffield File/Handwritten list of possible participants.
29. Ibid./Letter from R.A. Becher to C.W. Baty dated 20/10/64.
30. The chief source for the first conference: Ibid./Summary of Nuffield Lodge discussion 27/11/64. For the second conference: Nuffield Foundation/EDU 121/Draft note on second Classics meeting at Nuffield Lodge 30/12/64.
31. C.W.E. Peckett and A.R. Munday, *Principia: a Beginner's Latin Course* (Shrewsbury: Wilding, 1949) and *Thrasymachus: a New Greek Course* (Shreswbury: Wilding, 1965).
32. JACT/Nuffield File/In a letter from C.W. Baty to R.A. Becher dated 21/10/64 Miss Gough's work is described as 'fantastically interesting'.
33. Ibid./ C.W. Baty to R.A. Becher dated 13/10/64.
34. Ibid./Summary of Nuffield Lodge discussion 27/11/64.
35. Ibid./Letters from C.W. Baty to J.T. Christie dated 31/10/64 and 7/11/64.
36. JACT/Nuffield File/Letter from C.W. Baty to J.T. Christie dated 31/10/64.
37. Ibid.
38. Ibid.
39. JACT/Nuffield File/Letter from C.W. Baty to R.A. Becher dated 7/11/64.
40. Ibid./Letter from K.G. Todd to C.W. Baty dated 28/11/64.
41. Ibid./Letter from C.W. Baty to K.G. Todd dated 30/11/64.
42. Ibid./Summary of Nuffield Lodge discussion 27/11/64.
43. Ibid./Letter from C.W. Baty to K.G. Todd dated 30/11/64.
44. Nuffield/EDU 121/Classics/Draft note on second classics meeting at Nuffield Lodge 30/12/64.
45. JACT/Nuffield File/Summary of Nuffield Lodge discussions 27/11/64.
46. Ibid.,
47. D.J. Morton (ed.) *Secondary Reorganisation and the Classics*, JACT Pamphlet 2 (London: JACT, 1965).
48. See note 32 (above).
49. Nuffield Foundation/EDU 121/Draft note on second classics meeting at Nuffield Lodge 30/12/64.
50. Ibid./Letter from C.W.E. Peckett to B.M.W. Young dated 31/12/64.
51. Ibid./Draft note on second classics meeting at Nuffield Lodge 30/12/64.
52. Ibid.
53. Nuffield Foundation/Minutes of the 141st meeting of Nuffield Trustees (January 1965) Ref. V. 363.
54. Ibid.
55. Ibid.
56. JACT/Nuffield File/Letter from J.C. Dancy to C.W. Baty dated 20/1/65.
57. Ibid.
58. Ibid./Letter from Professor D.M. Balme to C.W. Baty dated 31/10/64.
59. Ibid.
60. Nuffield Foundation/EDU 121/Letter from J.E. Sharwood Smith to R.A. Becher dated 1/12/64.
61. JACT/Nuffield File/Letter from C.W. Baty to R.A. Becher dated 3/11/64.
62. Nuffield Foundation/EDU 121/Letter from J.E. Sharwood Smith to R.A. Becher dated 1/12/64.
63. Ibid. Ironically, the named contact at Longman, Miss Rosemary Davidson, was, in the years ahead, to play a leading role in publishing the CSCP's materials on behalf of the Cambridge University Press.

64. Nuffield Foundation/EDU 121/Letter from Professor D.M. Balme to R.A. Becher dated 31/10/64.
65. Ibid./Letter from R.A. Becher to Professor D.M. Balme dated 1/1/65.
66. Correspondence between R.A. Becher and the author dated 30/4/90.
67. JACT/Nuffield File/Letter from R.A. Becher to C.W. Baty dated 15/2/65.
68. JACT/Gulbenkian File/Letter from C.W. Baty to J. Thornton dated 19/1/65.
69. JACT/Nuffield File/Letter from R.A. Becher to C.W. Baty dated 20/1/65.
70. Ibid./A Cambridge school Classics programme—very rough draft.
71. Ibid./A new school Classics programme.
72. Ibid.
73. Ibid.
74. Ibid./Letter from R.A. Becher to C.W. Baty dated 11/2/65.
75. Ibid./Letter from R.G. Coleman to R.A. Becher dated 11/2/65.
76. Ibid.
77. Ibid./Letter from R.A. Becher to C.W. Baty dated 15/2/65.
78. Ibid./Letter from R.A. Becher to R.G. Coleman dated 12/2/65.
79. Ibid./Letter from A.G. Hunt to C.W. Baty dated 16/2/65.
80. Ibid./Letter from C.W. Baty to A.G. Hunt dated 13/2/65.
81. Ibid./Letter from R.G. Coleman to R.A. Becher dated 4/3/65.
82. Ibid./Letter from R.A. Becher to C.W. Baty dated 11/3/65. The reasons for this decision to exclude the Kennedy Professor of Latin from membership of the Committee has been the subject of much discussion. Brink played a controversial role within the Classics Faculty at Cambridge and it was suggested at the time that his active participation in the early stages of the scheme would have been fatal to its acceptance. By this date, Brink had also been involved in other contentious debates with colleagues including the moves to reform Part I of the Tripos of which he was a proponent. For this information, I am endebted to Professor H.D. Jocelyn of the University of Manchester, who has recently been working on an account of Charles Brink for the British Academy.
83. Ibid./Letter from R.A. Becher to C.W. Baty dated 11/3/65. JACT/Nuffield file/Letter from W.A. Lloyd to the Secretary, Nuffield Foundation dated 8/3/65. JACT/Gulbenkian File/Letter from C.W. Baty to J. Thornton dated 22/3/65.
84. JACT/Nuffield File/R.A. Becher to C.W. Baty dated 22/3/65.
85. Ibid./Press statement 29/4/65.
86. Ibid./C.W. Baty to K.G. Todd dated 14/3/65.
87. Ibid.
88. Ibid./Letter from R.G. Coleman to R.A. Becher dated 4/3/65. Ibid./Letter from A.G. Hunt to C.W. Baty dated 16/2/65.
89. Ibid./Letter from C.W. Baty to A.G. Hunt dated 19/2/65.
90. Ibid./Letter from C.W. Baty to A.G. Hunt dated 13/2/65.
91. Ibid. Baty's intentions are confirmed in a letter from the same file which he wrote to Becher on 13/2/65.
92. JACT/Nuffield File/Letter from R.A. Becher to C.W. Baty dated 1/2/65.
93. Ibid./Letter from Professor D.M. Balme to C.W. Baty dated 19/2/65.
94. Ibid./CSCP Appointment of Director and Assistant Director, (text of advertisement).
95. Ibid./Press notice issued by the Nuffield Foundation 29/4/65.
96. *Times Educational Supplement* 30/4/65, p. 1281.
97. Nuffield Foundation/EDU 121/Classics/Letter from D.J. Morton to R.A. Becher dated 23/10/64.
98. Ibid./Note on the teaching of Classics in schools dated 6/1/65.

NOTES

Chapter Four

1. Public Schools Commission, *Second Report Vol. I Report on Independent Day and Direct Grant Schools* (London: HMSO, 1970), p. vii.
2. *Times Educational Supplement* 25/3/66, p. 912.
3. The Times, *House of Commons 1966* (London: Times Newspapers, 1966), p. 16.
4. Interview with R.W. Morris 16/12/86. Morton himself recalls that he was 'tipped the wink' by Becher at a conference held in April at Coventry. Interview with D.J. Morton 20/2/87.
5. JACT/Nuffield File/Appointment of Director and Assistant Director (text of advertisement).
6. CSCP Committee Minutes 19/5/65.
7. Ibid.
8. Ibid.
9. JACT/Nuffield File/Letter from D.J. Morton to C.W. Baty dated 25/5/65.
10. Ibid.
11. Ibid./Letter from C.W. Baty to R.A. Becher dated 5/2/65 and letters from D.M. Balme to C.W. Baty dated 20/5/65 and from C.W. Baty to D.M. Balme dated 22/5/65.
12. Although Baty was at pains to say to Balme that he had 'no authorization to speak for anyone', it is clear from his correspondence with Becher that Baty was sounding out the feasibility of such a link.
13. JACT/Nuffield File/Letter from C.W. Baty to R.A. Becher dated 22/5/65.
14. CSCP Committee Minutes 28/5/65.
15. Ibid.
16. JACT/Nuffield File/Letter from R.A. Becher to C.W. Baty dated 1/6/65.
17. CSCP/W.A. Lloyd Papers/Memorandum prepared for the CSCP Committee by A.G. Hunt dated on the meeting held at Queen Mary College dated 8/6/65.
18. Ibid.
19. Ibid.
20. CSCP/W.A. Lloyd Papers/Letter from D.J. Morton to A.G. Hunt dated 9/6/65.
21. Ibid.
22. Ibid.
23. CSCP Committee Minutes 2/7/65.
24. CSCP/W.A. Lloyd Papers/Letters from D.M. Balme to A.G. Hunt dated 10/6/65.
25. CSCP Committee Minutes 10/8/65.
26. Ibid., 4/10/65.
27. The one exception to this arrangement was Miss E.P. Story who was appointed from 1/9/67 as Evaluation Officer.
28. Mrs J.A. Notley became the first full–time Project Secretary.
29. Mr R.F. Farrington was appointed cleaner.
30. CSCP/W.A. Lloyd Papers/A new School Classics programme.
31. CSCP/Advisory Panel Minutes 4/12/65.
32. Ibid.
33. Ibid.
34. Ibid.
35. Ibid.
36. Refers to W.B. Thompson, an early advocate of Classics taught through the medium of English (see p. 10), who was one of the contributors to D.J. Morton (ed.) *Secondary Reorganisation and the Classics*, JACT Pamphlet 2 (London: JACT, 1965).
37. E.O. Furber was author of *Vivus per ora* (published by Centaur Books; C.H. Craddock was joint author with G.S. Thompson of *Latin Books 1 to 4* (published by Blackie; M.G. Balme was joint author with M.S. Warman of *Aestimanda* (published by Oxford University Press).

38. *JACT Bulletin* 6, October 1964, p. 5.
39. Cambridge School Classics Project, *Preliminary School Trial: Teachers' Notes*, Mimeo. (Cambridge: CSCP, 1966).
40. Ibid., p. 8.
41. Ibid., p. 9.
42. CSCP Advisory Panel Minutes 4/12/65.
43. Ibid.
44. CSCP/Bristol Collection/Programme and staffing document.
45. The programme was subdivided into phases of nine months. Each phase identified stages of development to be reached in relation to the Project's twin tasks and the staffing that would be required in order to achieve these goals. See also C.Greig and W.A. Reid, 'Proposals and possibilities in curriculum development: a study of the Cambridge School Classics Project' *Journal of Curriculum Studies* 10 (4) (1978) pp. 332–33.
46. CSCP Advisory Panel Minutes 4/12/65.
47. CSCP Advisory Panel Minutes 22/10/66. The problems were said to be associated with an 'inductive methodology', the 'linguistic analysis' and 'manipulative reinforcement'.
48. CSCP Advisory Panel Minutes 22/10/66.
49. CSCP Committee Minutes 13/7/66.
50. Ibid.
51. CSCP/W.A. Lloyd Papers/Letter from J.B. Wilkins to D.J. Morton dated 10/5/68.
52. CSCP Committee Minutes 21/3/66.
53. After 1 September when a second Assistant to the Director was expected to join the team.
54. CSCP Advisory Panel Minutes 21/5/66.
55. M.D. Shipman commenting on his own involvement with the Keele-based Integrated Humanities Project states: 'The production of materials for publication came to dominate the life of the project in a way that excluded other developments' (M.D. Shipman, D. Bolam and D. Jenkins *Inside a Curriculum Project* (London: Methuen, 1974) p. 153.
56. CSCP/D.J. Morton/In-service courses file 1966–7.
57. Ibid./Letter from E.P. Story to D.J. Morton dated 15/10/65.
58. Ibid./Letter from L.W. Warren to D.J. Morton dated 14/1/66 and list of conference members.
59. Ibid./Papers pertaining to the conference held at Bristol 30/4/66.
60. Ibid./Classical studies in CSE: list of conference members.
61. The East Midlands Regional Examinations Board was the only one of the original boards to establish a Classics panel from the outset and to offer a Mode I syllabus, which did not require candidates to have a knowledge of Latin or Greek.
62. Interim bulletins on both the Latin course and non–linguistic developments were eventually published for general purchase in 1967.
63. JACT Research Panel Minutes 26/2/66.
64. *CA Proceedings* (1966) pps. 19–21.
65. Ibid.,
66. *Latin Teaching* XXXII (3) (1966) pp. 165–66.
67. The author recalls attending a conference held at Nottingham University 10/12/66 at which teachers listened in awe and in some cases in a state of apparent consternation at what was proposed. Robin Griffin, another former Assistant to the Director who also heard Morton speaking in 1966, recalls listening spellbound as David Morton expounded the Project's early thinking to the ARLT Summer School.
68. CSCP Advisory Panel Minutes 4/12/65.

69. Thompson Collection/University of Leeds Institute of Education; course publicity leaflet for January 1965.
70. Interview with W.B. Thompson 17/2/86.
71. Thompson Collection/Course publicity leaflet for April 1966.
72. CSCP/Bristol Collection/Letter from B.J. Trollope to D.J. Morton dated 23/5/66.
73. CSCP Advisory Panel Minutes 4/12/65.
74. Ibid.
75. Ibid., 22/10/66.
76. Ibid.
77. Ibid.
78. CSCP Committee Minutes 25/10/66. The final agreement of the Schools Council had not been given by the date of the interviews. The job was therefore offered on the understanding that the post would begin on 1 January (as advertised) or at a later date or not at all!
79. CSCP/Bristol Collection/Non–linguistic post job description.
80. T.W. Melluish, 'A presidential Address', *Latin Teaching* XXXII (3), pp. 92.
81. T.W. Melluish, 'Latin Prose Composition', *Latin Teaching* XXXII (2), pp. 50–51.

Chapter Five

1. Cambridge School Classics Project, *Bulletin No 1: Towards a New Latin Reading Course* (Cambridge: CSCP, 1967), p. 26.
2. Ibid., pp. 13–16.
3. Ibid., p. 18.
4. Ibid., p. 2.
5. CSCP Advisory Panel Minutes 29/4/67.
6. The third and fourth points had already been discussed at the previous meeting held on 22/10/66. Concern had been expressed concerning the 'frequency loading of a number of morphological and lexical features' which was felt to be too low. The need for a close definition and analysis of the proposed 'O' level corpus had also been urged.
7. CSCP Advisory Panel Minutes 21/5/66.
8. CSCP Committee Minutes 13/7/66.
9. CSCP Advisory Panel Minutes 22/10/66.
10. CSCP Advisory Panel Minutes 30/9/67. Difficulties arose once again from the in–built contradictions in the Project structure. The Linguistic Consultant needed time to develop his proposals for step by step implementation, but the Project had now acquired large–scale commitments to schools which it was duty bound to honour.
11. CSCP Advisory Panel Minutes 10/3/68.
12. CSCP/Bristol Collection/Re–appraisal of the programme, memorandum to the Project Committee by the Assistants to the Director.
13. CSCP/W.A. Lloyd Papers/Letter from W.A. Lloyd to D.J. Morton dated 25/1/68.
14. Ibid./Letter from D.J. Morton to W.A. Lloyd dated 21/3/68.
15. In the letter to Lloyd dated 21/3/68, Morton had in fact asked the Committee to accept his resignation as from 31/8/68 and sooner if possible. This offer had been refused, but its effect was to secure support for the strong line which Morton wished to take with his colleagues.
16. CSCP/W.A. Lloyd Papers/Letter from D.J. Morton to W.A. Lloyd dated 19/5/68.
17. These sentiments were originally expressed in a letter sent by the Director to the Committee Chairman: Ibid./Letter from D.J. Morton to W.A. Lloyd dated 18/7/66. The renegotiated arrangement with Wilkins, referred to above, recognised the in-creased amount of time that the Linguistic Consultant was now spending on the Project working as an integral member of the team.

18. Ibid./Memorandum sent by D.J. Morton to his fellow team members dated 1/4/68.
19. Ibid. The imposition of a guillotine which effectively curtailed the design process for each stage again points back to the in–built contradiction of linguistic research versus curriculum development. Such a move was bound to bring matters to a head sooner rather than later.
20. CSCP Committee Minutes 26/4/68.
21. CSCP/W.A. Lloyd Papers/Revised schedule.
22. CSCP Committee Minutes 26/4/68.
23. CSCP/W.A. Lloyd Papers/Letter from D.J. Morton to C. Greig and J.A. Jones dated 30/4/68.
24. Ibid./Letter from C. Greig and J.A. Jones to W.A. Lloyd dated 1/5/68.
25. Ibid.
26. CSCP Committee Minutes 2/10/68. Such an agreement could only go a small way towards recognising the increased amount of time that Wilkins was now spending in Cambridge.
27. Ibid.
28. CSCP/W.A. Lloyd Papers/Letter from C. Greig and J.A. Jones to W.A. Lloyd dated 1/5/68.
29. Ibid./Letter from J.B. Wilkins to W.A. Lloyd dated 15/5/68.
30. Information from E.P. Story. Si and Sii sentences represent the two basic sentence patterns which are identified: *Caecilius est in horto* (Si) and *Caecilius in horto dormit* (Sii).
31. These letters and associated correspondence are to be found in CSCP/W.A. Lloyd Papers.
32. Ibid./Letter from J.B. Wilkins to W.A. Lloyd dated 31/12/68.
33. Ibid./Letter from D.J. Morton to W. A. Lloyd dated 11/1/69.
34. Ibid.
35. Ibid.
36. Ibid./Letter from C. Greig and J.A. Jones to W.A. Lloyd dated 12/1/69.
37. Ibid.
38. Ibid./Letter from W.A. Lloyd to D.J. Merton dated 17/1/69.
39. Ibid./Letter from D.J. Morton to W.A. Lloyd dated 17/1/69.
40. Ibid./Letter from D.J. Morton to W.A. Lloyd dated 26/5/69.
41. Ibid./Letter from D.J. Morton to J.A. Jones dated 26/5/69.
42. Ibid./Letter from C.W.E. Peckett to W.A. Lloyd dated 25/3/69.
43. Ibid.
44. Ibid.
45. Ibid./Letter from C.W. Baty to W.A. Lloyd date 2/4/69.
46. Ibid.
47. Ibid.
48. Ibid./Letters from W.A. Lloyd to C.W.E. Peckett and C.W. Baty both dated 23/5/69.
49. Ibid./Letter from C.W.E. Peckett to W.A. Lloyd dated 25/3/69.
50. Ibid./Letter from W.A. Lloyd to C.W.E. Peckett dated 23/5/69.
51. Ibid./Letter from W.A. Lloyd to D.M. Balme dated 23/5/69.
52. Ibid./Letter from D.J. Morton to W.A. Lloyd dated 23/5/69.
53. Ibid./Letter from C.W.E. Peckett to W.A. Lloyd dated 3/6/69.
54. Ibid./Letter from C.W. Baty to W.A. Lloyd dated 27/5/69.
55. CSCP Advisory Panel Minutes 31/5/69 to 1/6/69.
56. Ibid. With hindsight it is worth emphasising that what Peckett had in mind was way beyond the capacity of available machines at that time.
57. Ibid.
58. CSCP Advisory Panel Minutes 31/5/69 to 1/6/69.

59. Ibid.
60. Ibid.
61. Ibid.
62. *Latin Teaching* XXXII (5) (1967) pp. 239–40.
63. Ibid., p. 240.
64. *Latin Teaching* XXXII (6) (1968) p. 306.
65. G.G.L. Brooks, 'The 45th Summer School, Durham: A Canadian at the ARLT Summer School' *Latin Teaching* XXXIII (1) (1968) p. 36.
66. *Latin Teaching* XXXIII (2) (1969) p. 76.
67. *Latin Teaching* XXXIII (4) (1970) p. 148.

Chapter Six

1. CSCP/Bristol Collection/Letter from R.C. Frost to C. Greig dated 22/9/66.
2. Ibid./Letter from R.C. Frost to M.St.J. Forrest dated 19/4/67.
3. Ibid./Letter from J. Wood to M.St. J. Forrest dated 5/2/67.
4. Ibid./Letter from J. Murrell to D.J. Morton dated 27/2/66.
5. Ibid./Letter from N. Slater to D.J. Morton dated 20/3/67.
6. The first port of call was the publisher Jonathan Cape, whose resource packs on a whole range of historical topics, entitled *Jackdaws*, were widely popular with teachers, though they were not originally designed with school use in mind. Initial discussions were cordial but unproductive.
7. Cambridge School Classics Project, *Foundation Course Folders I–V Teacher's Handbook* (Cambridge: Cambridge University Press, 1972) p. 95.
8. CSCP/Bristol Collection/Memorandum to the Schools Council dated January 1968 and Nuffield Foundation/Letter from D.J. Morton to B.M.W. Young dated 15/1/68.
9. CSCP Committee Minutes 2/10/68.
10. CSCP/Bristol Collection/In-service File 1968–70.
11. LACT, 1970, Appendix pp. 44–49.
12. *Latin Teaching* XXXIII (2) 1969, p. 76 and XXXIII (3) (1969), p. 113.
13. The broadcasts were supported by a teacher's booklet, which drew heavily on the Project's trial materials and approaches . The series was repeated two years later.

Chapter Seven

1. Lloyd–Jones' letter in the *Times Educational Supplement* 27/2/69, p. 9, complaining of the damage done to Latin and Greek by comprehensive reorganisation followed a headline news story in which the Head of Classics in a Northamptonshire grammar school resigned in protest against local reorganisation plans. JACT, as on other occasions was anxious that its earlier public neutrality towards comprehensive schools should be maintained.
2. JACT/Schools reorganised: Classics/Correspondence between C.W. Baty and a number of teachers undergoing reorganisation *passim*.
3. B. Young, 'Address to the Joint Association of Classical Teachers', *Latin Teaching* XXXII (4) (1967) pp. 195–207.
4. The Project's initial plans were to construct a three-year course to 'O' level which could be started by pupils at the age of 13+ in comprehensive schools, where it was believed that an earlier start would have been impossible. It was expected that many pupils in state schools would begin their Latin not earlier than the age of 13. In practice there were still many secondary schools offering Latin earlier than 13+ and the Project's trial schools included only a handful which did not introduce Latin at 11+ or 12+!
5. *JACT Bulletin* 20 June 1969.

Chapter Eight

1. *Report of the 64th Annual Conference* (London: Labour Party, 1965) p. 210.
2. *The 68th Annual Conference* (London: Labour Party, 1969) pp. 336, 343.
3. Ibid., p. 342.
4. Ibid., p. 343.
5. *Times Educational Supplement* 27/3/70, p. 6.
6. C. Benn and B. Simon, *Halfway There* (London: McGraw-Hill, 1970) pp. 348–49.
7. *Times Guide to the House of Commons, 1970* (London: Times Newspapers, 1970) p. 30.
8. *The 88th Annual Conference* (London: Conservative and Unionist Association 1970) p. 19.
9. Ibid., p. 20.
10. The large number of reorganisation plans approved during Margaret Thatcher's period of office was due to the fact that local plans set in motion under the Labour government had, by now, passed through the appropriate period of consultation. Margaret Thatcher's 'achievement' was, of course, due more to the length of her time in post and to the particular moment at which she held it, rather than to any affection for comprehensive schooling.
11. *Times Educational Supplement* 26/6/70, p. 1.
12. The Classics Committee was one of ten subject committees set up as part of the executive organisation of the Schools Council after October 1964. The Committee's twin tasks were to keep Classics under review in relation to curricula and examinations and to undertake tasks allocated to it by the Governing Council (Schools Council for Curriculum and Examinations Constitution dated 12 December 1968.)
13. JACT Committee Minutes 1/3/69.
14. *Times Educational Supplement* 17/10/69, p. 3.
15. Schools Council Classics Committee Minutes, Memorandum dated 26/9/69.
16. J. Simpson, 'Teaching the Cambridge School Classics Project Latin Course' *Dialogue* 13 (1973) pp. 3–5 and M. Forrest, 'Teaching the Cambridge School Classics Project Foundation course' *Dialogue* 13 (1973) pp. 6–7.
17. D.J. Morton, '*Tempora Mutantur*' *Dialogue* 3 (1969) pp. 10–11.
18. The working paper (Number 55) was published in 1975.
19. *CA Proceedings* (1971) p. 36.
20. M. Ricketts, 'The Cambridge Latin Course: An appraisal' *Didaskalos* 4 (1) (1972) pp. 173.
21. *CA Proceedings* (1971) p. 35.
22. Ricketts op. cit., p. 166.
23. Ibid., p. 165.
24. *CA Proceedings* (1971) p. 35.
25. J. Pinkess, A. Spratling and G. Harries, 'The ARLT and Classical Association Weekend Refresher Course held on March 13th 1971 at the French Institute and Lycee, Kensington' *Latin Teaching* XXXIII (6) (1971) p. 237.
26. Ibid., p. 238. The issue of transition to 'A' level Latin was the subject discussed at a conference of Classics teachers held during 1971 at Queen Mary College, London. Professor David Balme later unsuccessfully petitioned the Schools Council Classics Committee in the hope of establishing an agreed core of syntactical structures and even specified areas of literature.
27. A.C.F. Verity, 'Review of School Books', *Greece and Rome* XXI (2) (1974) p. 218.
28. A.C.F. Verity, 'Review of School Books', *Greece and Rome* XIX (2) (1972) pp. 226.
29. Ricketts, op. cit., p. 168.
30. Ibid., pp. 169–70.
31. D.G. Bentliff, 'The 47th Summer School, Shrewsbury' *Latin Teaching* XXXIII (5) (1970) p. 186.

32. C. Greig, 'The Approach to Latin, first and second parts: A review' *Didaskalos* 3 (2) (1970) pp. 358–59. A reply was given to this article by E.G. Macnaughton in the same volume of *Didaskalos*, pp. 360–64.
33. N. Critchley, 'Some thoughts on proposals to reform the O level syllabus' *Latin Teaching* XXXIII (4) (1970) p. 131.
34. Ibid., pp. 131–32.
35. N.C. Dexter, 'Changing Patterns of Examinations', *Latin Teaching* XXXV (1) (1973) p. 8.
36. Ibid., p. 9.
37. Ibid., p. 10.
38. London Association of Classical Teachers (LACT), *Results of Questionnaire on Classics in London Schools*, Mimeo (London: LACT, 1971).
39. Department of Education and Science (DES), Classics in Comprehensive Schools: A Discussion Paper by Some Members of HM Inspectorate of Schools, Matters for Discussion 2 (London: HMSO, 1977, p. 8).
40. Ibid., p. 11.
41. Ibid., p. 14.
42. The first batch of pupil's materials and teacher's handbooks were published in autumn 1972.
43. C. Greig, 'Classics and the Certificate of Secondary Education' *Didaskalos* 4 (1) (1972) p. 90.
44. S. Sharp, 'Classical Studies: The Medium not the Message' *Didaskalos* 4 (2) (1973) p. 276.
45. Ibid., p. 279.
46. Ibid., p. 278.
47. Ibid., p. 277 fn.
48. J.E. Sharwood Smith, *On Teaching Classics* (London: Routledge, 1977) p. 9.
49. H. Hollinghurst, 'Classics for All (I)', *Latin Teaching* XXXIII (6) (1971) pp. 218–23 and 'Classics for All (II)', *Latin Teaching* XXXIV (1) (1971) pp. 269–74.
50. Hollinghurst *Latin Teaching* XXXIV (1) p. 274.
51. *Didaskalos* 3 (3) (1971) Editorial p. 427.
52. JACT Council Minutes 7/11/70.
53. Miss Telford's address was pubished as a supplement to *JACT Bulletin* 27, November 71.
54. *CSCP Newsletter* 4, 4/4/73.
55. Ibid.
56. CSCP/Bristol Collection/Classical Studies in the middle years: course programme 29/8/72 to 2/9/72.
57. J. Graham, 'Classics without the languages?' *Trends in Education* 25 (1972) pp. 6–10.
58. DES 1977 op. cit., Preface.
59. Ibid., pp. 58–59.
60. The first materials were published by Oliver and Boyd, 1971.
61. Verity 1972, op. cit. p. 226.
62. J.R.C. Richards, 'Book Reviews' *Latin Teaching* XXXIII (6) (1971) p. 225.
63. DES 1977, op. cit. p. 9.
64. These Classics teachers had already been involved in teaching on the St Matthias Course, Classical Studies in the middle years.
65. See p. 73.
66. G.R. Lambert, 'The Cambridge School Classics Project' *Echos du Monde Classique/Classical News and Views* XIV (3) (1970) pp. 65–75.
67. These events took place at Frankfurt 2–4 January 1969 and at Canterbury 5–8 April 1971. Papers contributed to the *Colloquia Didactica* have been published in *Didactica Classica Gandensia* (University of Gent, Belgium).

MODERNISING THE CLASSICS

68. A summary of these meetings is contained in P. Wülfing and G. Binder, *Zwischenbericht über ein colloquium 'Die Altertumswissenschaft im Schulunterricht'* (Köln: Institut für Altertumskunde der Universität zu Köln, 1972).
69. *JACT Bulletin* 33 (1973) p. 7.
70. F.W. Walbank, *The Decline of the Roman Empire in the West* (London: Cobbett Press, 1946) p. 7.
71. Ibid., p. 21.

Chapter Nine

1. A. Sked and C. Cook, *Post–war Britain: A Political History*, fourth edition (Harmondsworth: Penguin, 1993) p. 292.
2. Ibid., p. 293.
3. *Education Authorities Directory and Annual* 1975, pp. lxv–lxvi.
4. Sked and Cook, op. cit., p. 298.
5. *Education Authorities Directory and Annual* 1976, p. lx.
6. *Education Authorities Directory and Annual* 1977, pp. 561–606 *passim*.
7. CSCP Cambridge/Evaluation Report (draft and typescript).
8. Cambridge School Classics Project, *Supplementary Handbook* (Cambridge: Cambridge University Press, 1980) Appendix A: The evaluation of the course pp. 54–59.
9. See Appendix 1 of this book for a full list of the published materials.
10. Project evaluation data, include four data sources related to this evaluation study. These comprise preliminary enquiry postcards, school information questionnaires, evaluation questionnaires and punched cards from the computer analysis. All the documentation generated by this evaluation study has been retained in the Project's archive at Cambridge.
11. CSCP Cambridge/Evaluation Report (draft and typescript) pp. 3–4.
12. The percentage of teachers claiming to use the handbooks 'rarely' or 'never' is shown in CSCP 1980, pp. 56–57, as '70%'. This appears to be a misprint for '20%'.
13. CSCP Cambridge/Evaluation Report (draft and typescript), p. 11.
14. Ibid.
15. Ibid., pp. 11–12.
16. Ibid., p. 58.
17. T.R.A. Reader, 'The Cambridge School Classics Project: linguistic principles and course design', *Hesperiam* 1 (1978) pp. 56–73.
18. Ibid., p. 72. Part of Reader's critique is, at this point, a quotation from J.P.B. Allen and P. van Buren (eds) *Chomsky: Selected Readings*. (London: OUP, 1971).
19. R. Griffin 'Future developments in the teaching of the Cambridge Latin Course,' *Hesperiam* 2 (1979) pp. 41–57.
20. Ibid., p. 42.
21. Ibid.
22. Ibid., p. 43.
23. Ibid., pp. 47–49.
24. Ibid., p. 52.
25. Interview with Miss E.P. Story, now Director of the Cambridge Project 19/12/88.
26. Cambridge School Classics Project, 1980, op. cit., p. 3.
27. J.B. Wilkins, 'Teaching the classical languages: towards a theory I' *Didaskalos* 3 (1) (1969) pp. 168–97 and 'Teaching the classical languages: towards a theory II' *Didaskalos* 3 (2) (1970) pp. 365–409. Interview with Dr J.B. Wilkins, 15/12/88.

178

NOTES

NOTES

Chapter Ten

1. CSCP Bristol Collection/Schools Council SC 72/424.
2. CSCP Committee Minutes 2/10/73.
3. Cambridge School Classics Project, *The Roman World: An Experimental Handbook.* Mimeo (Bristol: CSCP, 1974).
4. Ibid., p. 3.
5. Ibid., pp. 4–5.
6. Cambridge School Classics Project, *The Roman World Teacher's Handbook 1* (Cambridge: CUP, 1978) p. 4.
7. Ibid., p. 5.
8. Department of Education and Science, *A Language for Life: Report of the Committee of Inquiry Appointed by the Secretary of State for Education and Science, under the Chairmanship of Sir Alan Bullock* (London: HMSO, 1975). C. Walker, *Reading Development and Extension* (London: Ward Lock, 1974).
9. CSCP Committee Minutes 27/3/74.
10. CSCP Bristol Collection/Schools Council SC 74/394.
11. CSCP Committee Minutes 2/4/75.
12. For the CSCP 13–16 publications, see Appendix 1.
13. Like its sister developments on the linguistic side, the Project's foundation course materials also generated interest in Holland (see p. 114). A parallel development which also made use of translated epigraphic sources was that sponsored by the *Stichting voor de Leerplanontwikkeling* (SLO), a body equivalent to the Schools Council. The Dutch Classical Project team was led by Frans Tielens.

Chapter Eleven

1. Schools Council 1980 *Impact and Take–up Project: a Condensed Interim Report— Secondary Schools*, p. 8.
2. S.D. Steadman, C. Parsons and B.G. Salter, *Impact and Take–up Project: An Enquiry into the Impact and Take–up of Schools Council Funded Activities*, draft version for limited circulation only (London: Schools Council, 1980), A 58, The Cambridge Schools [sic] Classics Project.
3. Impact and Take–up Project's CSCP database (A 58).
4. Cambridge School Classics Project, *Supplementary Handbook* (Cambridge University Press, 1980), p. 58.
5. Impact and Take–up Project's CSCP database (Appendix A58).
6. Letter written by J.E. Sharwood Smith to *JACT Bulletin* 33 (1973) pp. 6–7.
7. With regard to the Project's teachers, at least, there are special reasons for this. The trial school teachers, by their very nature, were volunteers and they were keen to see a successful outcome to their participation in the trial programme. The 'Hawthorne effect' (initial improvement in performance following an innovation) must also be taken into account.
8. DES, *Classics in Comprehensive Schools: a Survey by HMI*, Matters for Discussion 2 (London: HMSO, 1977) p. 11.
9. Ibid., p. 8.
10. Ibid., Appendix B (1).
11. E.C. Milleounis, 'The status of the Classics in the secondary school curriculum today' (unpublished doctoral thesis, University of Leeds, 1976) p. 552.
12. LACT, *Results of Questionnaire on Classics in Schools*, Mimeo (London: LACT, 1971).
13. Milleounis, op. cit., p. 551.
14. *CA Proceedings* (1975) p. 19.

15. C.A. Stray, 'Classics in crisis: the changing forms and current decline of Classics as exemplary knowledge, with reference to the experience of Classics teachers in South Wales' (unpublished master's thesis, University of Wales, 1977).
16. Ibid., pp. 191–207.
17. Ibid., p. 206.
18. Ibid., p. 207.
19. Ibid., p. 199.
20. Ibid., p. 237.
21. CSCP/Evaluation Data Base.
22. DES 1977, op. cit., p. 50.
23. Some of the teachers by this time had taught the CLC right through two or three times. They were thus in a position to see the course in perspective and to evaluate its strengths and weaknesses.
24. The first Black Paper had been published early in 1969 (C.B. Cox and A.E. Dyson (eds), *Fight for Education: A Black Paper* (London: Critical Society Quarterly, 1969) with a second hard on its heels (C.B. Cox and A.E. Dyson (eds), *The Crisis in Education* (London: Critical Quarterly Society, 1969). These publications drew attention to a range of concerns across the education system. Whilst they were dismissed by the Labour Secretary of State, Edward Short, as an assault on the comprehensive system and upon liberal ideas in education (*Times Educational Supplement* 11/4/69, p. 1168), they nonetheless touched a nerve with many people in the community and provided meat and drink for education correspondents in the British media.

Chapter Twelve

1. Department of Education and Science, *Classics in Independent Schools: a Survey by HMI* (London: HMSO, 1984) p. 37.
2. Ibid.
3. Ibid., p. 2.
4. North American Second Edition, Preface.
5. Ibid.
6. Ibid.

Chapter Thirteen

1. *Hansard, House of Commons* 2/11/87, Col. 763.
2. Details of the survey undertaken by Jeannie Cohen, Executive Secretary of JACT for selective publication in the *JACT Bulletin* were supplied to the author during 1993.
3. Schools Council History 13–16 Project, *A New Look at History* (Edinburgh: Holmes McDougall, 1976).
4. J. Farrall and M. Forrest, *Classics in the Primary School: A Pilot Study during 1986–7* (Cambridge: CSCP, 1989).
5. R. Cowen, A Study of the *Ancient Greeks with Upper Juniors* (Cambridge: CSCP, 1992).
6. Six booklets entitled *Themes: The Use of the Classical World in the National Curriculum for Primary Schools*. Five were published as a set in 1989; the sixth was added in 1991.
7. *Learning about Ancient Greece, the Language and Customs* (1994), published as part of the Open School's Greek and Latin programme.
8. JACT members were urged to respond to SCAA in late 1993, during the period of the Dearing Review.
9. Department for Education, *History in the National Curriculum* (London: HMSO, 1995).
10. *Times Educational Supplement* 5/5/95, p. 1.

Select Bibliography

Below are the sources cited in the notes to each chapter. These include major sources of archival data which have been generated by the Cambridge School Classics Project during more than a quarter of a century, collections of papers belonging to the Project's two sponsoring bodies, the Nuffield Foundation and the former Schools Council for Curriculum and Examinations, and private collections of papers.

Cambridge School Classics Project Archives

All documentation, unless otherwise stated, is held at the Project's Cambridge Office, 17, Panton Street, Cambridge.

CSCP/Committee Minutes: Minute Book covering the period 17/5/65 to 2/10/68. Project files include duplicated minutes of all later meetings.
CSCP/Advisory Panel Minutes: Minute Book covering the period 4/12/65 to 15/6/68. Project files include duplicated minutes of all later meetings.
CSCP/Evaluation Report (draft and typescript): a summary of findings of the 1976 evaluation. This report has never been published in full.
CSCP/Evaluation Data: preliminary enquiry post cards, school information questionnaires, evaluation questionnaires (twenty-two pages in length) and punched cards for computer analysis.
CSCP/W.A. Lloyd Papers: files of correspondence between the former Chairman of the Project Committee and others associated with the Project during its full–time existence.
CSCP/Bristol Collection: archival material pertaining to the Project's non–linguistic developments at Cambridge, and later at Bristol. The Collection comprises administrative files, examples of all classical civilisation trial materials at various stages of development. The Collection also includes duplicate copies of some Schools Council papers including Minutes of the Schools Council Classics Committee (see below). The Collection is currently in the possession of Dr Martin Forrest, Faculty of Education, University of the West of England, Bristol.
CSCP/D.J. Morton: files currently held by Mr D.J. Morton at Nottingham.

The Project Office at Cambridge also holds copies of all trial materials prepared and disseminated by the Project as well as copies of Bulletins and newsletters issued by the Project to trial schools and to other interested parties.

Nuffield Foundation

All the documentation was studied at Nuffield Lodge, Regent's Park, London, before the papers were transferred to new premises at Bedford Square, London. Papers relevant to the Cambridge School Classics Project include:

Nuffield Foundation/Minutes of the Trustees: abstracts relating to the Cambridge School Classics Project from January 1965.
Nuffield Foundation EDU 121 or CLASSICS: files of correspondence and associated documentation.

The Schools Council for the Curriculum and Examinations

Documentation was studied at Newcombe House, Nottinghill Gate, before the papers were transferred to the Public Record Office. Other collections of Schools Council papers exist in private hands.

Schools Council/Classics Committee Minutes: a record of termly meetings of the specialist committee together with minutes of working parties and other related documents.
Impact and Take–up Project: CSCP database comprising answers completed by 100 teachers with reference to the Cambridge Project's materials.

The Classical Association

The main collection of archival material resides with the Honorary Secretary of the Association. Council and Sub–committee Minutes together with selected correspondence covering the period 1939 to 1968 were studied at University College, Cardiff. Duplicate copies of Council and Sub–committee minutes also exist in private collections (see below).

CA Council Minutes: a record of Council and Schools Sub–Committee deliberations.

Joint Association of Classical Teachers

A full set of JACT Committee/Council and Research Panel minutes is held at the JACT office in the Institute of Classical Studies, Gordon Square, London. Duplicate copies of minutes exist also in private collections (see below). Files relating to various aspects of JACT administration during the early years of the Association were studied at the JACT Office during the 1980s.

JACT Committee Minutes: a record of the deliberations of the Committee which from its 14th meeting held in October 1968 was known as the Council.
JACT Research Panel Minutes: a record of the deliberations of the JACT Committee constituted as a 'research panel' on the mornings of JACT Committee days from 1964.
JACT papers: miscellaneous files relevant to the early history of the Cambridge School Classics Project.

SELECT BIBLIOGRAPHY

Private Collections of Papers

Thompson Collection: the collection of school classics text books, personal files and miscellaneous archival material relevant to the teaching of classics was accumulated by W.B. Thompson during his time at the University of Leeds. Much of this material is now housed in the Brotherton Library, University of Leeds. Some minutes of CA Council and Education Sub–committee meetings are to be found in this collection as are some early minutes of the JACT Committee.

Sharwood Smith Papers: a collection of files relevant to the founding of JACT accumulated by J.E. Sharwood Smith. The collection includes a set of minutes of the JACT Committee/Council from the Association's inauguration to 1973.

Dora Pym Papers: a collection of papers accumulated by the late Mrs Dora Pym during her time at the University of Bristol. This collection is now in the possession of Dora Pym's daughter, Mrs Nancy Silver.

B.A. Knott Papers: a collection of miscellaneous papers belonging to Mr Bev. Knott, who trained as a teacher under David Morton at the University of Nottingham and who later spent a large part of his teaching career in a Bristol Secondary School, participating in most of the Project's trial programmes and contributing to the revision of Project materials.

Vyvyan Jones Papers: a collection of papers accumulated by the late Rev. Canon F.C. Vyvyan Jones, a former Chairman of Bristol City Council's Education Committee, which are now in the possession of his family.

Unauthored citations in serial publications to which reference has been made in the text

The Classical Association Proceedings
Latin Teaching
JACT Bulletin
Didaskalos
Hesperiam

Interviews

Interviews referred to in the text took place as follows:

R.W. Morris	16/12/86
W.B. Thompson	17/2/86
E.P. Story	19/12/88
Dr J.B. Wilkins	15/12/88
D.J. Morton	20/2/87
K. Todd	12/8/86

Authored works

Baty, C.W., 'Classics in the schools' in T.W. Melluish (ed.) *Reappraisal*. Supplement to *Greece and Rome* IX (1) (1962) pp. 10–14.

Benn, C. and Simon, B., *Halfway There* (London: McGraw-Hill, 1970).

Bentliff, D.G., 'Why no more Latin?' *Greece and Rome* XV (45) (1946) pp. 114–18.

Bentliff, D.G., 'The 47th Summer School, Shrewsbury' *Latin Teaching* XXXIII (5) (1970) pp. 183–89.

Board of Education, *Report of the Consultative Committee on Secondary Education with Special Reference to Grammar Schools and Technical High Schools*, The Spens Report (London: HMSO, 1938).

Board of Education, *Curricula and Examinations in Secondary Schools, Secondary Schools Examination Council chaired by Sir C. Norwood* (London: HMSO, 1943).

Bolgar, R.R. (ed.) *Classical influences on Western Thought AD 1650–1870: Proceedings of an International Conference held at King's College, Cambridge, March 1977* (Cambridge: CUP, 1977).

Brink, C.O., 'Small Latin and the University' *Latin Teaching* XXX (7) (1960) pp. 194–201.

Brink, C.O., 'Small Latin and the Classics' in T.W. Melluish (ed.) *Reappraisal*, Supplement to *Greece and Rome* IX (1) (1962) pp. 6–9.

Brooks, G.G.L., 'The 45th Summer School, Durham: a Canadian at the A.R.L.T. Summer School' *Latin Teaching* XXXIII (1) (1968) pp. 35–39.

Cambridge School Classics Project, *Preliminary School Trial Teacher's Notes.* Mimeo (Cambridge: CSCP, 1966).

Cambridge School Classics Project, *Bulletin No1: Towards a New Latin Reading Course*, Mimeo (Cambridge: CSCP, 1967).

Cambridge School Classics Project, *Foundation Course Folders I–V Teacher's Handbook* (Cambridge: CUP, 1972).

Cambridge School Classics Project, *The Roman World—An Experimental Handbook.* Mimeo (Bristol: CSCP, 1974).

Cambridge School Classics Project, *The Roman World Teacher's Handbook 1* (Cambridge: CUP for the Schools Council, 1978).

Cambridge School Classics Project *Cambridge Latin Course Supplementary Handbook* (Cambridge: CUP, 1980).

Clarke, M.L., *Classical Education in Britain 1500 –1900* (Cambridge: CUP, 1959).

Cox, C.B. and Dyson, A.E. (eds) *Fight for Education: a Black Paper*, Black Paper One (London: Critical Society Quarterly, 1969).

Cox, C.B. and Dyson, A.E. (eds) *The Crisis in Education*, Black Paper Two (London: Critical Quarterly Society, 1969).

Critchley, N., 'Some thoughts on proposals to reform the O level syllabus' *Latin Teaching* XXXIII (4) (1970) pp. 131–37.

DES (Department of Education and Science), *A Language for Life. Report of the Committee of Inquiry Appointed by the Secretary of State for Education and Science, under the Chairmanship of Sir Alan Bullock* (London: HMSO, 1975).

DES (Department of Education and Science), *Classics in Comprehensive Schools: a Discussion Paper by some members of HM Inspectorate of Schools*, Matters for Discussion 2 (London: HMSO, 1977).

DES (Department of Education and Science), *Classics in Independent Schools: a Survey by HMI* (London: HMSO, 1984).

Dexter, N.C., 'Changing patterns of examinations' *Latin Teaching* XXXV (1) (1973) pp. 8–16.

Extispex, 'The first decade: a scrutiny of JACT' *Didaskalos* 4 (2) (1973) pp. 259–75.

Fairbairn, A.N. (ed.) *The Leicestershire Plan* (London: Heinemann Educational, 1980).

Forrest, M., 'Teaching the Cambridge School Classics Project Foundation Course' *Dialogue* 13 (1973) pp. 6–7.

Forrest, M.St.J., 'Classics teachers, comprehensive reorganisation and curriculum change' (unpublished doctoral thesis, University of Exeter, 1989).

Fowler, W.S., 'Common core classics' *Latin Teaching* XXX (4) (1958) pp. 121–25 .

Graham, J., 'Classics without the languages?' *Trends in Education* 25 (1972) pp. 6 –10.

Greig, C., 'The approach to Latin, first and second parts: a review' *Didaskalos* 3 (2) (1970) pp. 358–59.

Greig, C., 'Classics and the Certificate of Secondary Education' *Didaskalos* 4 (1) (1972) pp. 89–105.

Greig, C. and Reid, W.A., 'Proposals and possibilities in curriculum development: a study of the Cambridge School Classics Project' *Journal of Curriculum Studies* 10 (4) (1978) pp. 329–48.

Griffin, R., 'Future developments in the teaching of the Cambridge Latin Course' *Hesperiam* 2 (1979) pp. 41–57.

Havelock, R.G., *The change Agent's Guide to Innovation in Education* (Englewood Cliffs, NJ, USA: Educational Technology Publications, 1973).

Hollinghurst, H., 'Classics for all (I)' *Latin Teaching* XXXIII (6) (1971) pp. 218–23.

Hollinghurst, H., 'Classics for all (II)' *Latin Teaching* XXXIV (1) (1971) pp. 269–74.

IAAM (Incorporated Association of Assistant Masters in Secondary Schools), *The Teaching of Classics* (Cambridge: CUP, 1954).

JACT (Joint Association of Classical Teachers), *Report of the JACT Conference held at Hughes Hall, Cambridge on 27–28 June 1964, on the 'Leicestershire Plan' and its Effect on Classics teaching*, Mimeo (London: JACT, 1964).

LACT (London Association of Classical Teachers), *Roman Home Life*, revised edition (London: LACT, 1970).

LACT (London Association of Classical Teachers), *Results of Questionnaire on Classics in London Schools*, Mimeo (London: LACT, 1971).

Lambert, G., 'The Cambridge School Classics Project', *Echos du Monde Classique/ Classical News and Views* XIV (3) (1970) pp. 65–75.

MacNaughton, E.G., 'Reply (to C. Greig)' *Didaskalos* 3 (2) (1970) pp. 360–64.

Mason, S.C., *The Leicestershire Experiment and Plan*, revised edition (London: Councils and Education Press, 1963).

Melluish, T.W., 'Why Latin?' *Greece and Rome* XIII (38–9) (1944) pp. 59–67.

Melluish, T.W. (ed.) *Reappraisal*, Supplement to *Greece and Rome* IX (1) (London: Classical Association, 1962).

Melluish, T.W., 'Latin Prose Composition' *Latin Teaching* XXXII (2) (1966) pp. 50–54.

Melluish, T.W., 'A presidential address' *Latin Teaching* XXXII (3) (1966) pp. 87–98.

Milleounis, E.C., 'The status of the Classics in the Secondary School Curriculum Today' (unpublished doctoral thesis, University of Leeds, 1976).

Morton, D.J. (ed.) *Secondary Reorganisation and the Classics*, JACT Pamphlet 2 (London: JACT, 1965).

Morton, D.J., 'Tempora Mutantur' *Dialogue* 3 (1969) pp. 10–11.

Morton, D.J., 'Linguistic aspects of the course', in Cambridge School Classics Project *Cambridge Latin Course Supplementary Handbook* (Cambridge: CUP, 1980 pp. 1–7).

Peckett, C.W.E. and Munday, A.R., *Principia: a Beginner's Latin Course* (Shrewsbury: Wilding, 1949).

Peckett, C.W.E., 'The role of Classics in modern education' *Latin Teaching* XXX (5) (1959) pp. 144.

Pedley, R., *The Comprehensive School* (Harmondsworth: Penguin, 1963).

Peterson, A.D.C., 'The examination syllabus' *Latin Teaching* XXX (4) (1958) pp. 116–18.

Pinkess, J., Spratling, A. and Harries, G., 'The ARLT and Classical Association Weekend Refresher Course held on March 13th 1971 at the French Institute and Lycee, Kensington' *Latin Teaching* XXXIII (6) (1971) pp. 235–39.

Public Schools Commission, *Second Report Vol. I Report on Independent Day and Direct Grant Grammar Schools* (London: HMSO, 1970).

Reader, T.R.A., 'The Cambridge Latin Course: linguistic principles and course design' *Hesperiam* 1 (1978) pp. 56–73.

Richards, J.R.C., 'Book Reviews' *Latin Teaching* XXXIII (6) (1971) pp. 224–26.

Ricketts, M., 'The Cambridge Latin Course: an appraisal' *Didaskalos* 4 (1) (1972) pp. 165–73.

Schools Council, *An Approach Through Classics*, Humanities for the young school leaver series (London: HMSO, 1967).

Schools Council, *Teaching Classics today: a Progress Report*, Working Paper 23 (London: HMSO, 1969).

Sharp, S., 'Classical Studies: the medium not the message' *Didaskalos* 4 (2) (1973) pp. 276–89.

Sharwood Smith, J.E., *On Teaching Classics* (London: Routledge, 1977).

Shipman, M.D., Bolam D. and Jenkins, D., *Inside a Curriculum Project* (London: Methuen, 1974).

Simpson, J., 'Teaching the Cambridge School Classics Project Latin Course' *Dialogue* 13 (1973) pp. 3–5.

Sked, A. and Cook, C., *Post–war Britain: a Political History*, fourth edition. (Harmondsworth: Penguin, 1984).

Steadman, S.D., Parsons, C. and Salter, B.G., *Impact and Take–up Project: an Enquiry into the Impact and Take–up of Schools Council funded Activities*, draft version for limited circulation only (London: Schools Council, 1980).

Stray, C.A., 'Classics in crisis: The changing forms and current decline of Classics as exemplary curricular knowledge, with reference to the experience of Classics teachers in South Wales' (unpublished master's thesis: University of Wales, 1977).

Telford, M., 'Presidential Address' published as a supplement to *JACT Bulletin*, 27 November 1971.

Times (The), *House of Commons 1966* (London: Times Newspapers, 1966).

Times (The), *Guide to the House of Commons 1970* (London: Times Newspapers, 1970).

Verity, A.C.F., 'Review of school books' *Greece and Rome* XIX (2) (1972) pp. 225–26.

Verity, A.C.F., 'Review of school books' *Greece and Rome* XXI (2) (1974) pp. 217–18.

Walbank, F.W., *The Decline of the Roman Empire in the West* (London: Cobbett Press, 1946).

Walker, C., *Reading Development and Extension* (London: Ward Lock, 1974).

Wilamowitz (von Wilamowitz–Moellendorff), U., *Geschichte der Philologie* [1921] published in 1982 as *History of Classical Scholarship*, translated by A. Harris (London: Duckworth, 1982).

Wilkins, J.B., 'Teaching the classical languages: towards a theory I' *Didaskalos* 3 (1) (1969) pp. 168–97.

Wilkins, J.B., 'Teaching the classical languages: towards a theory II' *Didaskalos* 3 (2) (1970) pp. 365–409.

Wülfing, p. and Binder, G., *Zwischenbericht über ein colloquium 'Die Altertumswissenschaft im Schulunterricht'* (Köln: Institut für Altertumskunde der Universität zu Köln, 1972).

Young, B., 'Address to the Joint Association of Classical Teachers' *Latin Teaching* XXXII (4) (1967) pp. 195–207.

Index

187